T0090304

Fighting the Good Fight

Thomas D. Logie

Order this book online at www.trafford.com
or email orders@trafford.com

Most Trafford titles are also available at major online book retailers.

© Copyright 2011 Thomas D. Logie.
All rights reserved. No part of this publication may be reproduced, stored in a retrieval
system, or transmitted, in any form or by any means, electronic, mechanical, photocopying,
recording, or otherwise, without the written prior permission of the author.

Printed in the United States of America.

ISBN: 978-1-4269-5092-6 (sc)
ISBN: 978-1-4269-5093-3 (e)

Trafford rev. 01/25/2011

 www.trafford.com

North America & international
toll-free: 1 888 232 4444 (USA & Canada)
phone: 250 383 6864 ◆ fax: 812 355 4082

— PART ONE —
Spiritual Sketches from Scriptures of History

GENERAL INTRODUCTION

Human nature remains essentially the same from generation to generation. Because humanity improves in learning and technology but not does not improve morally, history is a generally reliable guide to the course of future events even though cultures and technologies change. Even Solomon about 3000 years ago wrote that *"There is nothing new under the sun."* Ecclesiastes 1:9. We do not at this point have any contemporary written records that survived the Flood, although we do have Moses' account revealed by the Holy Spirit to Moses many years after the Flood. Archeologists have discovered writings from post-Flood ancient civilizations at least as far back as Mari, estimated at 2700 BC. So writing in some form predates even Solomon by about 1800 years at least. These discoveries are fascinating but are fundamentally inferior to the Scriptures themselves, which are transmitted from God to humanity by the Holy Spirit using multiple authors. Therefore, I am concentrating on the Scriptures rather than secular writings outside the Scriptures. In quoting Scriptures, I usually use the Modern King James version with occasional variations.

The consistency of human nature gives wisdom to the saying "back to the future." We can learn much about our future by studying the Biblical past. But such study is rare. So many Christians think of the historical books of 1 & 2 Samuel, 1 & 2 Kings and 1 & 2 Chronicles as dry and dusty tomes that are dead today. I have revisited them periodically for nearly 40 years and am drawn back to them again and again for fresh instruction from God. I was at first preparing to serve God and have sought to serve Him in law and politics throughout my adult life, but one does not need a specialized calling of God for law and politics to profit from these books. I am seeking to help the newcomer to these Scriptures get started and at the same time trying to help the experienced reader dig deeper.

The same is essentially true of the Shorter Prophets. These are often called the Minor Prophets, but I dislike the name because it implies that these Scriptures are unimportant. It is rare today to hear in churches systematic teaching from these Scriptures. I trust and pray that this book will help Christians to fill in the gaps for themselves with respect to both history and prophecy. No church is perfect and no pastor or set of pastors can teach everything at once. The individual adult believer is responsible to study the Scriptures for himself or herself. For those with families, responsibility rests especially on the spiritual leader of the family to teach the entire family at a level of instruction that each member of the family can understand and to stretch each family member for improvement.

The historical books and the Shorter Prophets contain critical teaching concerning human nature, politics and the coming climax of human history when the conflict between God and Satan bursts out into spiritual and physical warfare without restraint as described in Revelation and elsewhere in the Bible. If knowledge is power, then the books that I seek to introduce are some of the most powerful in the world.

The largest portion of this book is composed of 3 mini-books dealing with David and Solomon, then selected Kings of Judah and Israel and then the Shorter Prophets. The overall purpose is to give the reader a springboard into vital portions of Scripture that are virtually unknown to most believers. Most of the focus is on the years from the rise of David to the fall of Jerusalem to Babylon in about 586 BC. I am estimating David's birth at about 1030 BC with the establishment of his kingdom at Hebron at about 1000 BC. We take brief glances backward as far as Joshua's conquest and forward to the restored province (not kingdom) under the Persians and indeed look forward on occasion to both comings of the Lord Jesus Christ. This volume is by no means a comprehensive history. I would pray that it would help you to start or to restart your study of some of the most neglected portions of the Bible.

The first section focuses on David and Solomon, when Israel rose from a precarious existence beset by enemies to a first-rank power in political terms. More important than the geo-political gains were the spiritual progress made by Israel during these comparatively golden years and the unfolding of God's historical plan toward the coming of His Son in human flesh. David himself wrote about half the Psalms, and others were written by Levites under David's patronage. Solomon wrote Proverbs, Psalm 72, the Song of Solomon and Ecclesiastes. The Ark of the Covenant had a permanent home in the Temple for the first time in history. Israel had a permanent capital and had much greater unity than at any time since Joshua's generation.

With the division of Israel into two kingdoms, more and more of the geo-political progress was lost. There are still many spiritual lessons to be learned from studying the history of both kingdoms from the death of Solomon to Nebuchadnezzar's conquest. For the sake of historical flow and brevity, I am leaving to you considerable detail to study for yourself, although I am taking a quick survey of major points after Solomon's death.

Most of the Shorter Prophets were written either during the time of the divided kingdoms or after the Northern Kingdom had been destroyed by Assyria at approximately 722 or 721 BC. To compare this with the longest prophets, Isaiah's prophetic service started when the Northern

Kingdom was still clinging to political existence but extended long past its final downfall. Jeremiah was written during the last days of the Southern Kingdom under the godly Josiah and his feckless successors. Ezekiel and Daniel were written during the Exile; Haggai, Zechariah and Malachi were written after the return to Judea of the first new settlers from Babylon. So the first two portions of this book lay a brief historical setting for a first glance at the Shorter Prophets, which are probably the least known of all the Scriptures. By God's grace I want to change that or at least decrease our ignorance of these important Scriptures.

INTRODUCTION TO PART 1 —
DAVID & SOLOMON

My method to try to bring King David and King Solomon alive to 21st-century readers will be to imagine that we have modern news commentators like those featured in the opinion section of a major newspaper or on a cable TV network such as Fox News, MSNBC or CNN. I am imagining various newspaper or community TV commentaries or in some cases battlefield dispatches. Technologically speaking, this is an obvious anachronism. But human nature has not changed in the approximately 3000 years since David and Solomon lived. I am sure that rumors and arguments swirled around Israel using the slower technology of the day. Once King Saul had created a central government, jockeying for position and popularity started, according to the accounts of 1 Samuel. With different columnists I will try to recreate different viewpoints as the conflicts are recorded in Holy Scripture. At times, I may be portraying a mistaken or even an evil viewpoint, giving its strongest arguments in order to test that viewpoint against the Scriptures. As in any debate, one has to state a viewpoint accurately before one can assess it. Perhaps we may better learn how ancients erred --in some cases, starting with good intentions or at least good camouflage for evil intentions-- so that we can avoid those errors in our lives.

I am not going to give a verse-by-verse exposition in this volume. That would be a good project, but my concern is that the history from Joshua's conquest to the prophets is so little known that a contemporary-style presentation will be more helpful to many readers as a springboard to stimulate careful study of the historical and prophetic Scriptures. I hope and pray to treat all the Scriptures with utmost reverence. In composing my imaginary columns, I have made an effort to be faithful to the Scriptures as the fully inspired and infallible Word of God, even if I am portraying an enemy viewpoint. My intent is to present a modernized study that will help readers get started in these rich Scriptures and to study them in order to test the accuracy of my presentation and to improve it.

When I give references to Scriptures, I am again using an anachronism because verse divisions were not introduced into the Scriptures until several centuries after the New Testament had been written. We should also recall that in the time of David and Solomon only that portion of the Bible up through Ruth (and even Judges and Ruth may not yet have been in final written form) plus Job would have been widely available. Psalm 90, Moses' psalm, would have been known. 1 and 2 Samuel might have been freshly written but the technology of the day would have meant that these books would not have been in common written circulation. In fact, written copies of the Scriptures would have been rare, and Biblical knowledge for most people would have depended on trained memory and oral transmission of memorized Scripture. At the time of my first imaginary column only the Law and Job would have been composed.

Santayana was basically right when he said, "Those who do not know history are doomed to repeat it." This is one reason why God included so much history in the Scriptures. In the New Testament the Book of Acts is history, and the Gospels certainly contain history. In the Old Testament the entire section starting with Joshua through Esther is history. This volume is an attempt to start with David and Solomon using the literary device of fictitious commentary (but with lessons based on the Scriptures!). The next segment will survey the most prominent of the kings of Judah and of Israel, and then we will move on to the Shorter Prophets who were called to speak and write portions of God's Word after the death of Solomon. At least this will give some introduction to portions of Scripture that represent a "black hole" in the knowledge of most believers today. This should not be! *"For whatever things were written before were written for our learning, that we through the patience and comfort of the Scriptures might have hope."* Romans 15:4. Speaking of the history of Israel during Moses' time, Paul wrote, *"Now all these things happened to them as examples, and they were written for our admonition, upon whom the ends of the ages have come."* 1 Corinthians 10:11.

THE ORIGINS OF DAVID

The origins of David are rooted in the times of the judges who led Israel (or parts of Israel in some cases) after Joshua's generation up to the time of Samuel, the priest who anointed both Saul and David at the command of God in each case. A summary verse to sum up those centuries is repeated in Judges 17:6 and in Judges 21:25, *"In those days there was no king in Israel; everyone did what was right in his own eyes."* If unrestrained by precepts of Scripture, this would lead to disaster. From time to time Israel became unfaithful and foreign oppression would follow. Then came a disaster in which the tribe of Benjamin refused to permit divine justice to be meted out to sexually perverted people who were lustful to rape people of either sex. The resulting disaster as recorded in Judges 19-20 nearly wiped out the whole tribe of Benjamin. As a whole, the closing portion of Judges shows the perverting of divine liberty into lustful license. Samson too was guilty. Samuel's sons disrespected the sacrifices of the Lord. 1 Samuel 8:3-9. Without self-restraint, liberty will become untenable. This was one pressure behind the elders' request for a king. But Samuel was wise enough to know that a kingship is not a real solution to the problem of disorder. One takes two major risks with monarchy: (1) That one will elevate a lawless person to absolute power, so that the last evil becomes worse than the first (see Proverbs 28:15-16); and (2) That the temptations of monarchy will make the monarch lawless even if he starts as a restrained and apparently humble man. In the history that we scan, both of these risks will prove to be all too true. King Saul is one example, and King David behaved similarly concerning Bath-sheba.

While a plausible case can be made that a monarchy was becoming more necessary because of the mounting internal disorder and the growth of Israel's external enemies (which indeed was beginning to require some way for a more unified response more like the military unity under Joshua), God's diagnosis was that the request for a king implied that the nation was rejecting God as King (1 Samuel 8:7) just as the leadership was to do more directly over 1000 years later. Pilate asked them, *"Shall I crucify your King?"* The tragic final answer for that generation was, *"We have no king but Caesar."* (See John 19:14-15 for the complete exchange.) By this answer the elders directly rejected not only Jesus but His Father as king, with horrible consequences recorded by Josephus and mirrored in Titus' triumphal arch in Rome. These consequences were prophesied by Jesus Christ in Matthew 24, Mark 13 and most of Luke 21.

What might have been best politically would have been more judges like Gideon (Judges 8:22-23) who recognized only God as king and refused to be made king themselves but exercised inspired leadership. (Gideon's action in Judges 8:24-27 in taking personal reward was wrong and clearly has multiple counterparts today in the multinational spate of officials using their positions to become wealthy.) Perhaps a structure of tribal leaders more like Moses' methods in the Wilderness might have been workable if combined with a system of signal fires or couriers to spread news throughout the land of an attack from any quarter. But the people wanted to be like the surrounding nations instead of being a *"peculiar people"* or *"people for His own possession"* (varied translations of part of 1 Peter 2:9), so they asked for a king. God gave them one, although with certain restraints including a separation of the crown from the priesthood.

When King Uzziah tried to breach this separation after a generally good record, he was immediately struck with leprosy by God and had to live in isolation for the rest of his life. (2 Kings 15:5 identified as Azariah; 2 Chronicles 26:16-21). Even with those restraints, God warned of the flaws of monarchy through Samuel that deserve close study in political science classes even today:

> And he said, "This will be the behavior of the king who will reign over you. He will take your sons and appoint them for his own chariots and to be his horsemen, and some will run before his chariots. He will appoint captains over his thousands and captains over his fifties, will set some to plow his ground and reap his harvest, and some to make his weapons of war and equipment for his chariots. He will take your daughters to be perfumers, cooks, and bakers. And he will take the best of your fields, your vineyards, and your olive groves, and give them to his servants. He will take a tenth of your grain and your vintage, and give it to his officers and servants. And he will take your male servants, your female servants, your finest young men, and your donkeys, and put them to his work. He will take a tenth of your sheep, and you will be his servants. And you will cry out in that day because of your king whom you have chosen for yourselves, and the Lord will not hear you in that day." 1 Samuel 8:11-18

One should note that in taking a tenth the king was taking a share equal to God's tithe, which in itself would warn of an overreach of power. There is no question that the king or any government would need resources for national defense in Samuel's time, but the growth of government would be alarming and eventually crushing. As we scan the history ahead, consider just how true Samuel's warning became even under relatively great kings like David and especially Solomon. Even the best kings had serious and even critical failures.

Although a monarchy is not the best form of government when sinful people are in charge, one can perceive that God had a long-run purpose that transcends politics in permitting a monarchy to be formed. By reason of the monarchy David and Solomon were permitted to foreshadow the King of Kings, the Lord Jesus. As in the comparison of Adam to Christ in Romans 5:12-21 and 1 Corinthians 15:45-49, the first dynasty of Saul was swept away and the second dynasty started by David lasts forever. The theme of the Book of Hebrews is the removal of the first covenant of the Law for the second covenant of Christ Himself. *He takes away the first that He may establish the second.* Hebrews 10:9. Similarly, our first personality must die when our new personality is brought to birth when we are converted. Our first body must die (or be raptured) to make way for the spiritual body to come. Even this first creation will be rolled up like a scroll to make way for the second to come. 2 Peter 3:10-13. God has painted illustrations and foreshadows of His ultimate plan using the history of Israel as His canvas and stage.

With this brief survey, let us begin to explore the origins of David.

THE BETHLEHEM BANNER, about 1400 BC.-- A wedding was conducted last Friday in which Salmon, a fighter of the tribe of Judah in the Army of Israel, was married to a bride named Rahab. This wedding has been challenged for at least two reasons:

(1) Rahab in the past was a prostitute, a madam, or both who once lived in Jericho and is a woman of evil and corrupt character; and

(2) Rahab is a Canaanite and has no ancestry among any of the tribes of Israel. In fact Canaanites were to be wiped out.

The challengers point out that Moses commanded this army that prostitution is strictly forbidden (Leviticus 19:29, various verses in Leviticus 20, Deuteronomy 22:13-21 and 23:17-18 for example). Why of all people was Rahab not destroyed with the rest of the people of Jericho? And why

Thomas D. Logie

should a Canaanite woman be permitted to marry a soldier of Israel? Abraham our forefather forbade Isaac to take a Canaanite wife (Genesis 24:3, 7); Esau was disobedient in taking two Hittite women as wives and they made the lives of Isaac and Rebekah miserable! (Genesis 26:34-35) The children of Judah by his Canaanite wife, Er and Onan, were bad seed too (Genesis 38). Rahab will be a source of corruption too because she is a Canaanite! Moses ordered our army to destroy the Canaanites (Deuteronomy 20:16-18). Is there not one Israelite woman good enough for Salmon?

The marriage nevertheless has the approval of Joshua, the army commander, and for this reason has been permitted to go forward. Rahab was indeed either a prostitute or a madam and may have been both. But she sheltered the brave spies of the Israelite Army when they first besieged and attacked Jericho about 10 years ago and was rewarded with her life and the life of her family. She was the only one in Jericho who feared God enough to serve Him over the objection of her own Jericho government. (Joshua 2)

In response to an argument that Rahab as a Canaanite should at least be deported if not killed, Joshua pointed out that the spies had made her a promise to *"deal truly and kindly"* with her (Joshua 2:14) in exchange for her help and we must keep that promise. That certainly excludes deportation as well as execution. Moses did also command (Leviticus 19:33-34) that:

> And if a stranger dwells with you in your land, you shall not mistreat him. The stranger who dwells among you shall be to you as one born among you, and you shall love him as yourself; for you were strangers in the land of Egypt: I am the Lord your God.

So the marriage has gone forward in the face of the controversy. Some predict future trouble, while others say Mazeltov! Time will tell.

MY COMMENTS BASED ON FULLER BIBLICAL REVELATION: We are not actually told of misgivings about the marriage in the Scriptures, but I would be surprised if there were none given the arguments available to those who support rigid application of the Law with no possibility of exception or mercy. I have tried to state them at full strength in my imaginary article. We know the qualms that many parents have concerning interracial marriages today just because of racial or cultural differences. Yet Joshua's hypothetical response based on the Law shows that once Rahab's life was spared that she was to be treated fully and equally as an Israelite. Israel struggles with echoes of this debate concerning the Arab residents within the land of Israel. In the United States the immigration debate centers on a somewhat similar clash of ideas. *Romeo and Juliet* and *West Side Story* in English are echoes of the same types of questions that are implied although not discussed expressly in the Biblical accounts.

In the case of Salmon and Rahab Jesus Christ has settled the argument for all time in expressly approving the marriage. When He came to earth, He deliberately chose Salmon and Rahab as ancestors (Matthew 1:5).

One great lesson from this is that God has the power to set aside His own Law in favor of mercy when He chooses to do so. He did that in laying the guilt of every believer on Jesus Christ, the perfect Passover Lamb. If He did not retain the power to set aside His own Law, we would all be damned forever for our sin. A second lesson is that neither Rahab's admittedly wicked past nor her cursed race disqualified her from be delivered through faith in the true God. As a transformed woman she was a suitable wife for Salmon. As we will see, this marriage set a precedent for generations of boldness climaxing in David and Solomon. A third lesson is that we must have a single set of laws that apply impartially to all, whether of ancient stock or of recent immigrants. That third lesson will be highlighted in the story of Boaz and Ruth.

THE BETHLEHEM BANNER, ca. 1350 BC.-- A BANNER DAY FOR BOAZ!

Boaz for years has been one of the wealthier farmers in Bethlehem and also one of the most eligible bachelors in town, but he is getting a bit old to start a family and contribute to the future welfare of Israel. He has worked so hard at his successful farming that he seems to have no time for women or any eye for them.

Elimelech and Naomi years before took their two children Mahlon and Chilion to Moab to escape the famine here. Their lives were not blessed in Moab. Both Mahlon and Chilion married women of Moab but died young without children. Elimelech also died, leaving Naomi and their two wives with no prospects. So Naomi has recently returned to her ancestral home, bringing a Moabite daughter-in-law named Ruth with her.

Since neither Naomi nor Ruth own any land, Ruth has been gleaning grain for the two of them as provided by the Law as provision for the poor. Leviticus 19:9-10, 23:22; Deuteronomy 24:19-21. Boaz's workers had noticed that Ruth has been taking very few rests under the hot sun. The gleanings at Boaz's barley harvest have seemed to be more generous than usual.

Last week Boaz after his usual hard day's work fell asleep on his threshing floor after dark. In harvest time there is no time to waste going back and forth to one's abode. Around midnight, Ruth went to the threshing floor and slept. Before dawn she asked Boaz to play the part of the redeemer of her deceased father-in-law's lands, which included not only buying out the remaining years before the Jubilee but in this case raising up a child for the deceased Elimelech since Elimelech had no posterity. Boaz was not obligated but was willing, but first had to find the one male closer in blood relationship to the deceased Elimelech than himself. So the man was found and the opportunity was offered before 10 elders of Bethlehem. He apparently was at first willing to buy the land but shrank from the portion of the transaction that involved marrying Ruth and raising up a child for Elimelech. He therefore declined the opportunity and assigned his rights to Boaz, who swiftly exercised them.

The wedding was a joyful affair. Boaz was thankful that Ruth was interested in him instead of a younger man; Ruth was thankful that Boaz would pay attention to her plight instead of looking for a younger woman. Perhaps the family history of Salmon's marriage to a Canaanite woman quieted the issue of Ruth being a foreigner from Moab, a daughter of Lot instead of Abraham. Ruth is apparently a worshipper of the God of Israel. The whole village is celebrating -- Boaz has finally met his match.

POSTSCRIPT: Boaz and Ruth indeed had a son, Obed. Obed in turn became the forefather of Jesse, who in turn had 8 sons, including David, his youngest.

MY COMMENTS BASED ON FULLER BIBLICAL REVELATION: Ruth showed great faith and boldness in this entire situation. At first she left her homeland to stay with Naomi. Ruth's declaration recorded in Ruth 1:16 took real faith:

> But Ruth said: "Entreat me not to leave you, or to turn back from following after you; For wherever you go, I will go; and wherever you lodge, I will lodge. Your people shall be my people, and your God, my God."

She had no idea what her reception might be, but she went in faith. Beyond loyalty to Naomi, she trusted in God even with the lack of material prosperity in Moab. There are times and places where God demands boldness -- even to the point of "going for broke" -- without favorable providences to encourage us first.

Ruth was beginning to build a favorable reputation in Bethlehem, but she put everything on the line with her bold approach to Boaz. She went to the threshing floor and in effect presented herself for marriage. A rejection would have been crushing and might even have jeopardized her slender lifeline of gleanings from Boaz's fields. This is the same quality of faith that drove Elijah forward to prepare for God's fire from heaven on his sacrifice on Mt. Carmel. Caution is usually a virtue, but when God is leading us forward He may tell us to cast caution aside for vigorous action based on faith.

Boaz gave Ruth the rights of the poor under Moses' Law to glean grain even though she was not of the children of Israel by birth.

Boaz also acted boldly and decisively. He quickly exchanged his singleness -- which meant that he could concentrate fully on his farming -- for marriage to someone whom he barely knew, although he did have clues as to Ruth's character. His workers knew that Ruth worked hard; Boaz also knew that she was loyal to Naomi and may have known that she worshiped the living God. But that was about all. Boaz did not let a day pass until the issue was settled. This kind of decisive man can supply leadership in many contexts -- in a home, in business, in politics the military or in church. Ruth had no trouble following Boaz's decisive leadership.

There are few things worse than a leader of great responsibility who becomes indecisive in a crisis. Belshazzar in Daniel 5 would be a vivid example. As a contrary example, consider David's faith when he saw the challenge of Goliath in 1 Samuel 17. Elijah's challenge of 1 Kings 18:21 rings true today: *"How long will you vacillate [my word] between two opinions? If the Lord is God, follow Him; but if Baal, follow him."* Make up your mind and then follow Christ Jesus!

A third set of lessons comes from the meanings of the names themselves. Naomi's name meant "pleasant," but her given name had become a reproach because her life was anything but pleasant. Thus she asked others to call her "bitter," not knowing that this was about to change and that she was near to having a "grandson" in her life. Elimelech means that "God is my King," which is indeed true. Mahlon's and Chilion's names both indicated sickness and weakness. Boaz redeemed and married Ruth as a picture of Jesus Christ redeeming and marrying His Bride, the Church. He had both the power and the love to redeem; Ruth was powerless to redeem herself or even to support herself but had to trust God and secondarily trust Boaz.

Both Salmon and Boaz were willing to act unconventionally. This is a trait that appears again in David, one of the boldest of men in both war and worship. In this David was a good example for us today. See for example Acts 4:13, 29, 31; 9:27-29; 14:3, 19:8; Ephesians 3:12, 6:19-20; Philippians 1:14, 20; 1 Thessalonians 2:2; 1 Timothy 3:13; Hebrews 4:16, 10:19, 13:6; 1 John 4:17.

SKETCHES FROM THE LIFE OF DAVID BEFORE HE BECAME KING
(Drawn from 1 Samuel 10-31)

BETHLEHEM BANNER ca. 1015 BC -- ANXIOUS PARENTS WAITING FOR SON TO RETURN FROM SUPPLY MISSION

Obed and his wife, descendants of Salmon and of Boaz, are still waiting with no word about their son David. David's three oldest brothers are with King Saul's army at the battlefront near Azekah on the edge of the Valley of Elah. David, the youngest of 8 children and the family shepherd, departed recently for the front carrying food supplies for his brothers. David is overdue to return. The speculation is that David is simply delayed with his brothers, although some fear that he has either been captured by the Philistines or killed by a wild animal. David has learned as a shepherd to be a slingshot sharpshooter, but he is too young to be involved in any normal military fighting. For now, his parents must wait for word concerning each of their four children at the front.

For a modern comparison, think of the Sullivan family where all five brothers served in the United States Navy on the same ship in 1942. That ship was sunk in the Solomon Islands battle and all five brothers were lost at sea.

One is hard put to think of a simple supply mission that had greater consequences than David's trip to the battlefront described in 1 Samuel 17:14-23. Not even Confederate General Heth's movement toward Gettysburg in 1863 to obtain shoes had consequences as great as David's trip to the front.

David had already been anointed by Samuel as Saul's replacement as related in 1 Samuel 16, but this was yet concealed from Saul and others in authority. But the effect of the anointing -- the presence of the Spirit of God -- was evident when David spent intervals at Saul's headquarters at the end of his supply missions. But 1 Samuel 17 records a single combat that changed the course of all Western civilization. Goliath represents the idea that "might makes right." He projected brute force by his size. Goliath had no trust at all in the living God and in fact cursed Him. In Biblical terms, Goliath represents "the flesh" and self-aggrandizement. David represents submitting to and serving God ahead of self. God defines right regardless of human strength. David represents faith in the living God and not in his own powers. It was the Spirit of God that empowered David. Going into the battle, neither Saul nor Goliath gave David a chance. I might have as much chance at beating LeBron James at one-on-one basketball as David appeared to have against Goliath -- and I am 5'7" at most with little spring in my legs.

But why would God command Samuel to anoint David if David was to die at the hands of Goliath? David had faith in God from that anointing forward. That faith liberated David from conventional thinking, because David was not depending on military strength. But a military mind would perceive that God had given David two advantages over Goliath, although

David probably did not analyze it in these terms. One was mobility: David was not weighed down by heavy armor and therefore could dodge a spear or javelin thrown by Goliath and stay out of Goliath's reach. The other was range: Goliath's ability to kill was limited to the distance he could throw his spear or javelin and thereafter by his arm's reach with his sword. David's slingshot could throw at a greater distance more accurately. He picked out smooth stones to keep his throws straight -- irregular stones would have created a curve and therefore inaccuracy for the same reason that baseball stitches permit a pitcher to throw a curve deliberately. David had no intention of getting close enough to Goliath to be hacked by a sword and he intended to strike first with his primitive slingshot artillery. David's victory was rooted in faith, but God did not create a miracle by suspending the laws of physics. Instead God permitted David to use aspects of His Creation laws that were not understood by the Philistines for victory. On this occasion the Philistine superiority in iron technology did Goliath no good. 1 Samuel 13:19-22. David does turn out to be a military genius, but it was the Lord of Hosts whose Spirit rested upon David Who gave David such power.

But genius alone is not enough. It took courage for David to undertake the challenge of fighting Goliath in the first place, and more courage for David to maintain a steady aim as the huge Goliath was bearing down on him. David's shepherd training helped. Goliath was terrifying in appearance, but he had nowhere near the speed, mobility and raw power of either a bear or a lion. From where did David's courage come? Psalm 121 gives the answer:

I will lift up my eyes to the hills -- from whence comes my help?

My help comes from the Lord, Who made heaven and earth.

He will not allow your foot to be moved; He who keeps you will not slumber.

Behold, He who keeps Israel shall neither slumber nor sleep.

The Lord is your keeper; The Lord is your shade at your right hand.

The sun shall not strike you by day, nor the moon by night.

The Lord shall preserve you from all evil; He shall preserve your soul.

The Lord shall preserve your going out and your coming in from this time forth, and even forevermore.

So courage, too, is rooted in faith in God and in the assurance of His protection, whatever happens on earth and even whatever happens to our bodies. The promise is clear: the Lord will preserve our souls not only for our time on earth but especially forever after.

The Gaza strip today (2010) is a territory wedged between Israel and Egypt populated by Palestinian Arabs. Most of this population wants to dismantle Israel. The <u>de facto</u> government there is controlled by Hamas, a political party that combines a welfare mini-state like the old Tammany machine in Manhattan with the objective of overthrowing the government of Israel and substituting a dictatorial Sunni Islamic government. In the past few years Hamas won in the Gaza Strip a civil war against Fatah, Yassir Arafat's older revolutionary faction.

So thing have nearly come full circle. At the time of the combat between David and Goliath, Gaza was one of the five principal cities of the Philistines near the Mediterranean Sea. The Philistines were a seafaring people (probably originating in Cyprus) who worshiped a fish-god Dagon. The Philistines had at times waged war with both Egypt and with the Israelite tribes after the Israelites had conquered the hill country in the Holy Land promised to Jacob and his descendants. Then as now, Gaza and the surrounding area was a source of recurring trouble for Israel, although today's Gaza Strip is geographically smaller than the old

Philistine territory. The next imaginary Philistine columnist writes just after David's victory over Goliath.

THE GAZA GAZETTE -- CA 1015 BC -- GOLIATH DEAD; ARMY ROUTED

The expedition against the Hebrews which began with such promise has come to disaster. The commander of the expedition permitted the giant Goliath to challenge any Israelite soldier to single combat. The Israelites found a new young champion David, about whom nothing has been known previously. He accepted Goliath's challenge as Israel's champion and at the start of the combat hit Goliath in the forehead with a stone from a slingshot at long range. Goliath fell dead; to make sure and to prove Goliath's death, David hacked off Goliath's head with Goliath's own sword. Panic seized our Philistine army and the Hebrews pursued hard.

There needs to be a major investigation into this failure. Why did the commander permit Goliath to challenge Israel to single combat when we should have the advantage because of our superior armament and discipline? Why did we stay in the same place for so long instead of exposing the Israelites' lack of experience through assault or maneuver? Did the long period of inactivity rot Army morale?

Some people perceive a deeper problem than military strategy or tactics. Why has Dagon been relatively ineffective against the God of the Hebrews when we have the foundations of military superiority on our side? We have guarded our superior iron technology jealously. These Israelites are landlubbers -- surely Dagon as a sea-god has no affection for them. Is there something wrong with our worship of Dagon that he refuses to fight for us?

A few people are discussing a more radical conclusion -- that Dagon is inferior to the God of the Hebrews at all times or that Dagon is not really a god at all. The Israelites certainly gave us trouble with Samson. After

Delilah subdued him, he still managed to kill so many of us even after his eyes were gouged out. By what power? Certainly not of his blinded and beaten body! After that, we did capture the Ark of the Covenant and put it in Ashdod. But then the image of Dagon fell twice before the Ark with no apparent explanation and the second time was broken for good. (1 Samuel 4) The people of Ashdod got a disease so painful that they had to send the Ark away. (1 Samuel 5) One can at least understand why some skirmishes would be lost with Samson fighting for Israel, but we have lost this campaign even though Goliath was fighting for us without a comparable soldier on the side of Israel.

The God of the Hebrews is a morally demanding God who forbids all images connected with religious worship. He commands that every seventh day be a day of rest. He forbids all sex outside of marriage; accepting His worship would eliminate all fertility rites and all human sacrifice. There would be no priestesses. All idol-worship is forbidden. Philistine society would have to change its ways if it ever accepts the God of the Hebrews.

MY COMMENTS BASED ON FULLER BIBLICAL REVELATION: A few Philistines did later come over to David and worshiped the God of Israel. A unit of 600 commanded by Ittai the Gittite (of Gath) remained loyal during Absalom's rebellion. 2 Samuel 15:18-21. Probably these men had had contact with David when he fled from Saul to Gath. 1 Samuel 27-29.

Unfortunately, most of the Philistines remained idolaters and enemies of Israel. David all but obliterated them before he was done many years later, and the Philistines remained as a minor power until the Assyrians wiped them out at about the same time that Assyria wiped out the Northern Kingdom.

There is a pattern in Scripture of Satan acting through false gods trying to imitate the power of the true God. As the Philistines tried to treat the Ark as a powerless captured relic, the Egyptian magicians tried to imitate Moses' miracles. The Baalist priests tried to pray down fire from heaven for several hours before Elijah actually did so. The seven sons of Sceva tried to invoke the power of "Jesus Whom Paul preaches." Acts 19:13-20. God sometimes permits limited false miracles to test our faith. For example, see Matthew 24:23-26; Revelation 13-14. But there is not even a question of whether any false god can ever genuinely threaten the True and Living God. That is impossible, although Revelation does teach that the AntiChrist must run his course. When one looks at Revelation 11-13, it may appear to unaided human sight for a short time as if God might be overthrown on earth and maybe even in heaven. (Compare 2 Kings 6-7 for extended examples of the difference between physical and spiritual sight.) But you can bank of God's overwhelming triumph when He exercises His full power.

The triumph over Goliath catapulted David from obscurity to fame in both Israel and Philistia. This was a significant test of the quality of David's soul. Consider the changes that David faced as you read and study 1 Samuel 18:

1   He lived in Saul's court instead of at home in Bethlehem;

2) He became a son-in-law to King Saul, marrying his daughter Michal;

3) He became more popular than the King himself, at least in the hit song of the day. "Saul has killed his thousands, and David his tens of thousands."

4) As Saul's armor bearer and then as a unit commander, he held a responsible military position;

5) He began to rise in the musical world as the one artist who could soothe Saul's moods.

6   David's brothers had looked down on him as the upstart youngest son, but Prince Jonathan was a genuine friend.

All of this could easily have given David a swelled head. As Solomon later wrote, *"As the fining pot for silver, and the furnace for gold; so is a man to his praise."* (Proverbs 27:21 KJV) David was tested by his skyrocketing popularity and status as other men may be tested by hardship.

The Scriptures make it clear that David was able to keep his bearings and behave prudently. 1 Samuel 18:14, 30. He still trusted God more than himself. Perhaps David's head would have burst if King Saul had not turned on David and tried to kill him. But before David fled the court, David did receive valuable training in both military and administrative matters, preparing David for the day when God would make Samuel's anointing a reality. This time of advancement in the royal court, like the next period of hiding from Saul in the wilderness, was part of God's training to prepare David for the throne of Israel. David's place at court also sharpened his musical skills, which were to serve God later when David wrote about half the Psalms.

BETHLEHEM BANNER-- ca 1010 BC -- CIVIL WAR ERUPTS BETWEEN DAVID AND SAUL

From various leaks at court, it is apparent that the tension between King Saul and his son-in-law David has grown to the point where the two men cannot endure one another. Samuel had publicly rejected Saul as King, and Saul now fears that David will be his successor and therefore seeks to kill David. [Compare this to Herod's reaction of killing the Bethlehem babies when he learned that the King of the Jews had been born in Bethlehem a bit more than 1000 years later. In fact Saul's fears were correct.] Saul set an unusual dowry for Michal -- killing 100 male Philistines. Sources comment that Saul hoped that the Philistines would kill David and solve his problem. David and his battalion actually killed 200. Reports indicate that David has twice evaded spears thrown at him by Saul and that David fled to avoid arrest. Saul has also quarreled with his son Jonathan and with his daughter Michal, David's wife. Apparently both of them assisted David's escape.

Saul wants to see his son Jonathan succeed him. Jonathan is content to be David's lieutenant, to his father's great displeasure. Saul has the natural desire to prepare for this posterity to succeed him. Jonathan apparently thinks that God has tapped David for kingship and is content with his military responsibilities. Michal chose loyalty to her husband over her father's wishes. Except for other members of his family, King Saul is increasingly isolated. Samuel no longer pays attention and some of Saul's officers believe that David may be the more able man.

Now Saul is preparing a military force to hunt David to his death. Saul still has overwhelming military superiority if he can track David down in the open. In the meantime David is heading for remote, defensible areas and drawing on the enormous respect that the people have for his achievements. David's strategy is to avoid battle and to wear Saul down. How Saul will pressure David and still maintain Israel's security against the Philistines and other potential enemies is hard to see. As Saul tries to do both, he will have the difficult problem of avoiding damage to his own subjects. Saul may have to choose between pursuing David and his normal duties of the defense of Israel.

MY COMMENTS BASED ON FULLER SCRIPTURAL REVELATION:

In actual practice Saul became more and more obsessed with David as opposed to his other responsibilities, even though Saul did at least once break off his pursuit of David to defend against the Philistines. 1 Samuel 23:27-28. In 1 Samuel 22:6-23, we have the terrible story of how one of Saul's Edomite officials at Saul's command slaughtered the priests and their families because they fed David and some of his men. (R.C. Sproul in the notes to the *Reformation Study Bible* observes that Saul here behaved towards God's people most unjustly after he had refused to carry out God's command to exterminate the Amalekites, who were indeed God's enemies and enemies of Israel as well. This certainly helped tip public opinion toward David from Saul.) This lack of regard for the fact that the priests were anointed by God stands in stark contrast to David's unwillingness to kill Saul because Saul was the Lord's anointed when David had two opportunities to do it. If this precedent of the killing the priests had stood, the crown would have had nearly absolute power. David gradually built up from men with questionable pasts a small, mobile and disciplined military force that Saul had to take into account.

THE CARMEL CLARION ca 1008 BC -- NABAL, THE SHEEP MAGNATE, DIES

A prominent and wealthy descendent of the faithful Caleb died recently in Carmel. Nabal apparently "had it all." He was wealthy and was married to a beautiful and understanding wife. Yet he was known as one of the most sour and hardhearted men in the district, even though he had good business sense. He hated David and refused him supplies. Nabal had no regard for runaway servants or slaves even though the Scriptures commanded that runaway slaves were not to be compelled to return to their masters. Deuteronomy 23:15. Further, Nabal drank too much wine, and this clouded his judgment and undermined his health. Nabal came near disaster when he curtly refused David any help at all. Only the quick thinking of his wife Abigail in sending supplies to David saved Nabal from a devastating military raid from an angered David.

Nabal had no good reason to be angry with David. Everyone agrees that David's troops were on their best behavior. Contrary to the history of most armies, they took nothing belonging to Nabal even though David's men clearly have a continuing need for supplies. But Nabal by nature is an angry man and he behaved according to his nature toward David.

But Nabal was so hardhearted that he was blind to deliverance when it was under his nose. When his wife Abigail told him what she had done, he became overcome with anger to the point that he had a heart attack. At this point his physical condition mirrored his hardhearted spiritual condition. Nabal died of the heart attack about 10 days later.

To complete the irony, David was so impressed with Abigail's wisdom that he married her right after Nabal died. So Abigail went from the wife of a nasty husband to a wife of the anointed king, though that king was still on the run from Saul.

MY COMMENTS FROM FULLER REVELATION OF SCRIPTURE:

Nabal is the epitome of the able and hard-charging man of business and money who has no concern for his own soul. Nabal provoked God to anger. The Scriptures say that "his heart became as a stone" and that God struck Nabal dead. Meshing these together, it seems clear that Nabal at the appointment of God died of a heart attack that was triggered by his huge anger.

Moses through the Holy Spirit had commanded that kings should not multiply wives to themselves. Deuteronomy 17:17. Although David was married to a king's daughter, he showed a weakness concerning women early in life. While he was dodging Saul, David met and ultimately married Abigail, a wise and generous woman who seemed more mature than Michal and was certainly far wiser than her first husband. In mitigation of David taking a second wife, it is true that Saul had given Michal to another man after David fled for his life. 1 Samuel 25:44. But David in this respect did not know when to stop. David took still another wife at this time. The records of 1 Chronicles 3:1-9 show that by the time David had been established in Hebron as king (during the civil war against Saul's son Ishbosheth) that he had at least 6 wives besides Michal, his original wife. The first seeds of the later tragic family conflicts involving Amnon, Tamar, Absalom and Adonijah were sown during this period when David kept adding wives in the manner of an Oriental king, contrary to God's Word even at that time before there was an absolute bar to polygamy itself. Deuteronomy 17:17. Solomon to his sorrow went further into this same essential sin and ended up with 700 wives and 300 concubines. As he summed up his bitter lessons about multiple wives in Proverbs 5:14, *"I was almost in all evil in the midst of the assembly and congregation."* In David's case, this same weakness appears in more tragic form later in the affair of Uriah and Bathsheba. If it were today, we might call the affair "Uriahgate."

SHILOH SENTINEL -- CA 1005 BC -- JONATHAN: TRAPPED IN THE MIDDLE

Insiders in Saul's court point to a further fragmentation in King Saul's regime now that David has hidden in the Judean wilderness. Now Jonathan and his father are at odds persistently. Saul wants Jonathan to be his successor, and few doubt Jonathan's ability to be a good king. Saul is desperate to establish his posterity on Israel's throne even though the prophet Samuel has informed Saul that he has been rejected by God. But Jonathan thinks that God has designated David as King and therefore defers to his friend and above all defers to God Himself. As Jonathan is now Saul's deputy, he professes that he would be content to play the same role for David. But this makes Saul furious.

Jonathan is naturally torn between love for his father and love for his best friend. He apparently left the court temporarily and visited David in a wilderness stronghold, encouraging him. Perhaps the slaughter of the priests stirred Jonathan to this step of open defiance of his father. Jonathan did return to his father's headquarters. It appears that King Saul too is torn between his ambition for his son and his knowledge that Samuel the Prophet has anointed David as King already.

Saul is clinging to power in the face of his estrangement from God as well as the concerns of Jonathan his son. Saul is an unhappy man but cannot find a way to let go of his power. So he continues to pursue David in a potentially deadly game of hide-'n'-seek.

By contrast, David seems in no hurry to take power even when he has had two opportunities. Twice during Saul's pursuits David was in a position to kill Saul when Saul had camped during the pursuit, but David refused to even wound Saul on either occasion. He contented himself with embarrassing Saul to prove that the opportunity to kill Saul was there. While Saul seeks to kill David, David regards Saul as God's anointed and therefore refuses to strike at his person. Saul would kill David if he could even though David was anointed by Samuel; David has refused to kill Saul when he could because Saul was once anointed by Samuel. Saul has verbally admitted that David is more righteous than he himself, but yet Saul cannot bring himself to yield power or permanently end his attempts to kill David. So the strange twilight war continues and David continues to wander the wild regions of southern Judah.

In the meantime Jonathan is trapped between his loyalty to his father and his loyalty to David. Jonathan would prefer that his father abdicate, but like David Jonathan is not prepared to shove his father off the throne. So Jonathan bears up under disagreeable life with his irritable father when Jonathan would prefer the spiritual fellowship of David.

MY COMMENTS BASED ON THE FULLER REVELATION OF SCRIPTURE:

The fellowship between David and Jonathan is an example of what fellowship in the Christian church should be like, though it often is not. Fellowship of this depth requires two spiritual people who are committed to God first and friendship next before their own interests. Contrast Philippians 2:21. But there is great reward for such fellowship when it can be found.

Jonathan is also a great example of setting aside his own claims when God has spoken. His obedience is a tremendous example. Saul is likewise a poster child of clinging to the trappings of power in defiance of the verdict of God. Saul disobeyed God in the matter of sacrifice and then in sparing the Amalekites (1 Samuel 13 & 15). So God disowned Saul. 1 Samuel 15:35, 16:1. We must take warning from Saul's end: apostasy in consulting a medium and then suicide near the end of a lost battle. (1 Samuel 28 & 31) If we have done or omitted something to cause God to remove His blessing, then we must submit and repent. Saul did not repent and never heard from God again. But Samson's ability to pray (Judges 16:28-30) was restored after great misery, so for any who will repent and submit to God there is hope.

Taking Jonathan's attitude one step further, it is a lesser reflection of the later attitude of Jesus Christ as expressed in Philippians 2:5-11. Jonathan was willing to set aside his right to the throne in David's favor. Jesus Christ, though equal with God, was willing to take the form of a servant and sacrifice His equality with His Father in order to die on the Cross as a human being. Of course Christ made the far larger sacrifice in exchanging heaven for earth and being killed as a sacrifice by His inferiors, but Jonathan's smaller sacrifice may help us understand the infinite sacrifice of Jesus Christ in terms of rank and right.

David was faithful to his friendship with Jonathan even after Jonathan died in battle against the Philistines. When David was established as King of all Israel, he sought out a surviving son of Jonathan to show kindness. 2 Samuel 9:1-13. There was one, Mephibosheth, who had permanent defects in both feet. Surely he was a "useless mouth" with no potential as a soldier. But that is not how King David saw him. Though physically helpless, he was a human being whom David determined to treat with grace. Spiritually, we were helpless like Mephibosheth until Jesus Christ paid for our sins and set us free. A secondary lesson for us is that even "useless mouths" should be loved and supported. A human being is more than economic production. Contrast Adolf Hitler's orders to kill the insane with former Governor Palin's care for her Down's Syndrome child.

David's restraint and humility reflected his deep love for God and fear of Him. Sparing Saul's life twice took self-control that few people possess, especially when Saul had admitted that his pursuit of David was unjust and resumed it later. Like Jonathan, David did not view the kingdom as something for him to seize but rather as something that God would give in His good time. In this respect David surpassed Abraham and Sarah in faith. They had decided to exercise self-help to have a child by introducing Hagar into the picture. (Genesis 16) Thus Ishmael was born. Ishmael became the father of a great nation but was not the son of promise. David waited for God to kill Saul; God used the Philistines to do this (1 Samuel 31).

But David's faith sagged when he decided to enter Philistine territory (1 Samuel 27:1). He now feared death at Saul's hand after years of hiding, even though his anointing from Samuel was as valid as ever. One infers that David and his men and their families were simply tired of the constant running through the Judean wilderness. David's motives appear to have been wrong, but several good results did come from David's Philistine sojourn.

1. The families of David and of his men got to stay at a home in Ziklag;

2. David's supply problem was essentially solved;

3. David was able to carry forward the extermination of the Amalekites which God had commanded Saul to carry out. They had been military enemies of Israel since the time of Moses and had tried to help corrupt

the children of Israel before they entered the Promised Land. David's raids helped secure Israel's southern border. God apparently treated them as the equivalent of the Canaanites who lived corruptly in the time of Joshua;

4. Saul indeed stopped chasing David;

5. David was able to better organize and discipline his little army;

6. David and his men got some rest which was badly needed;

7. Some Philistine soldiers joined David and worshiped the true and living God;

8. David was plainly innocent of any complicity in the death of Saul and his 3 children and the slaughter of Saul's army. While Achish of Gath wanted David's forces to fight with them, he was providentially overruled by the other Philistine leaders. As a result, David was instead rescuing his families many miles away while King Saul and his forces were being destroyed. This absence helped David unify the country later;

9. David probably was able to secure some iron weapons or at least iron technology. In later battles the armies of Israel appear to have been better armed than before.

10. David avoided any life-or-death situation with Saul or his forces that would have involved David or his men shedding blood of his fellow Israelites.

David deceived Achish during his stay in Ziklag. Within the setting of the long-running war between the Philistines and Israel, this was probably morally permissible as a war measure to deceive an enemy. David was careful to do no direct damage to his host even though his host was in the long run an enemy. David did not abuse Achish's hospitality or commit treachery by attacking the Philistines during this time. But David did lie to Achish about where he was actually conducting military raids. David told Achish a series of lies when he said he was attacking Judah or tribes allied to Judah when in truth he was attacking Judah's enemies other than the Philistines. Achish was hoping that David would permanently sever his allegiance to Israel and become a clan chief beholden to Achish. But David had not forgotten that the Philistines were enemies of God and of Israel. David submerged his enmity for the Philistines for the time being in the interest of fulfilling his call from God to become King of Israel under conditions in which all of the tribes could be unified. He would deal with the Philistines later. During World War 2 we allied with Soviet Russia despite the despotic nature of Stalin's Russia. David's conduct is not a model for general life, although it may be instructive to a military leader or a spy. Churchill said in context of the D-Day invasion plans of 1944 that "The truth is so precious that it must be guarded by a bodyguard of lies." Such measures may for now be necessary, but not when Jesus Christ reigns universally in heaven and earth.

We have seen the gradual disintegration of King Saul's regime. There followed the disintegration of King Saul himself. Years earlier, he had already been subject to fits of madness which David had been able to soothe with his music. King Saul had acted self-destructively in driving away the very person who had been able to help. His massacre of the priests turned the remaining Levites against him. Earlier in his life Saul had had regular contact with Samuel and then with both Jonathan and David, all godly men. Later Samuel and David had withdrawn completely before Samuel's death and Saul was in fundamental disagreement with his own son Jonathan. Now the silence from God toward Saul was deafening. 1 Samuel 28:6.

Saul became so desperate that he consulted a medium or witch, even though Saul well knew that such was *verboten*. Deuteronomy 18:9-14. Saul himself had initially obeyed the Law and forbidden witchcraft in its various forms as commanded by Moses. But then Saul himself committed what he himself had forbidden. 1 Samuel 28:7-25.

One of the consequences of the internal disintegration of the Israel's commander was the destruction of the Israeli Army on Mount Gilboa the next day. Three of Saul's sons were killed in battle; Saul himself committed suicide. His work of keeping Israel free from Philistine domination was in ruins and many Israelis fled their homes and farms in the western part of Israel for the hills which were easier to defend. For the moment, Israel's oppression at the hands of the Philistines was probably as bad as it had been when Samson first started to free Israel. The long-term prospects for freedom again looked bleak.

A RETROSPECT ON SAUL AND HIS LIFE

To try to learn spiritual lessons from Saul's life, one should first consider the general trend of his life. When Samuel first found Saul, Saul was humble and astonished that he should be anointed as king. 1 Samuel 9:21. But this humility did not last. Saul began to make excuses when God's prophet rebuked him. 1 Samuel 13:7-24 (offering sacrifice himself instead of waiting for Samuel the priest, whose job it was); 1 Samuel 15:13-35 (sparing Agag). Yet Saul ordered the slaughter of the priests of God when Saul had no command from God for any such act. 1 Samuel 22:9-20. Saul admitted that he had no justification to seek David's life (for example 1 Samuel 24:16-22; 26:21-25) and but sought to capture and kill him anyway, from the time he first threw a spear at David and missed. (1 Samuel 18:6-12) For a long time Saul did pay attention to his kingly duties of keeping the Philistines at bay. But finally Saul descended to consulting a medium and then suicide.

Was Saul a saved man? I am not Saul's judge, but for purpose of spiritual instruction my answer would be "probably not." Saul never got over his jealousy toward David. From this bitter root sprang many sinful acts, even against the priests of the Lord. The general moral course of Saul's life was downward: from humility to pride; from apparent faith to fear and unbelief; from respect for the Law to wholesale violation. Saul saved his worst for last, as did Ahithophel (2 Samuel 15-17, especially 17:23) and Judas. He left Israel with a shattered army and partly under Philistine occupation again. The fruits of the victory over Goliath and even the efforts of Samson had been wasted.

There are also Biblical clues. When God made His covenant with David in 2 Samuel 7, God said of Solomon that *"I will not take my mercy from him as I took it from Saul"* (v. 15). Further, both Samuel and David are mentioned as heroes of faith in Hebrews 11:32, but Saul is not. Saul did not show the spiritual endurance that is a consequence of saving faith. (My previous book Endurance: How Faith Helps You Win the Race, published by Trafford Publishing Company, goes into detail on this topic.) To keep to our primary subject I would refer the reader to this book and to Matthew 7, 13 and 24 as primary sources for the doctrine that with saving faith comes endurance.) It is probable that our Lord Jesus will tell Saul to *"depart ... into the everlasting fire prepared for the Devil and his angels."* Matthew 25:41

SKETCHES FROM THE REIGN OF DAVID (Drawn from 2 Samuel & 1 Kings 1-2)

The death of Saul did not lead immediately to an uncontested reign for David. There was a 2-year civil war between David's forces and Benjamites loyal to Saul's surviving son Ish-bosheth. These forces were led by Abner, Saul's uncle (1 Samuel 14:50, 2 Samuel 2:8-10). Abner was the mainspring of the struggles of the House of Saul to retain the throne. Abner was a much stronger personality than Ish-bosheth, as is apparent in 2 Samuel 3 and 4. The Scriptures are silent as to whether Ish-bosheth was present at Mount Gilboa when his father and brothers were killed, but it is clear that he could not control his military leaders and that this failing eventually contributed to his death. But in the meantime the civil war that had started with Saul chasing David continued between David and Ish-bosheth. David reigned in Hebron because his own tribe of Judah was loyal, and Hebron was a relatively secure base. This represented military progress from either being chased by Saul or isolation in Ziklag and was accomplished after David's prayer and God's answer. 2 Samuel 2:1.

HEBRON HERALD CA 998 BC -- BENJAMITES COLLAPSE; DAVID RULES UNCONTESTED

The long civil war between the House of Saul and the House of David is now over, and David has triumphed. National authority has passed to the youth years ago anointed by Samuel as king over Israel while Saul yet lived. David's capital at Hebron has now become the temporary seat of the national government. Now the responsibility to beat back Israel's numerous enemies, especially the Philistines, rests on David -- David would add as he said before his combat with Goliath that he can succeed because he reigns and fights in the name of God, not because of his own strength. Abiathar, who survived Saul's massacre of the priests through Doeg and then joined with David, now becomes the high priest of the entire nation.

The collapse of Saul's dynasty appears complete. Of Saul's four sons, three died in the awful debacle on Mt. Gilboa attempting to hold back the Philistines. Ish-bosheth, the survivor, had the least military and leadership qualities. During the latest phase of the civil war, it was apparent to his own military that Ish-bosheth was ill-suited to be a wartime king. Ish-bosheth might be able to preside over a royal court but he lacked the drive necessary to defend Israel's borders.

A series of events which David did not orchestrate has combined to wipe out the leadership of the holdouts against David. Ish-bosheth and his military commander Abner quarreled over one of Saul's concubines which

Abner had enjoyed. Apart from the immorality of this, Abner's gesture was an expression of his claim to leadership of the Benjamite faction despite Ish-bosheth's titular kingship. Because Abner was in fact the leader, he decided to dump Ish-bosheth in favor of David. Two other military officers, hoping to curry favor with David, assassinated Ish-bosheth and brought proof to David. David had them executed summarily as murderers just as he had executed one who falsely claimed to have killed Saul.

So Abner arranged for the elders of Israel to swear loyalty to David. Having done that, he was a threat to Joab, David's incumbent army commander. Abner had both the skill and the connections to continue to unite all of Israel under David. But Joab had an old score to settle because Abner had killed Joab's brother Asahel in battle. So at a meeting between the two when David was absent, Joab killed Abner without David's approval. David made a major point to mourn Abner's passing even though until recently Abner had commanded the enemy army. People on both sides of the civil war were persuaded that David had not ordered the killing of Abner. This got David over the worst of the problem, but he still has the awkward problem of having Joab as his army commander when Joab lured Abner to his death. Joab is the most skilled for the job and has great influence in David's army and in Judah generally, but Joab has been tainted in Abner's death. Joab has been loyal through David's darkest days. It remains to be seen how David will cope with this issue from here.

David faces another delicate issue over the location of the permanent national capital. Hebron is closely associated with Judah. David may be reluctant to establish his capital among one of the northern tribes lest he be cut off during a revolt from his bases in Judah, but David desires to make a move to conciliate his former foes within Israel.

David has also moved to reclaim his wife Michal. When David's separation from Saul's court became permanent, Saul gave Michal to another man even though she was married to David. As sovereign, David felt empowered and perhaps required to reclaim his first wife. He does not want to appear to completely devalue the House of Saul. Yet there is genuine misery for the second husband, and Michal herself faces a completely different domestic situation from the time that she was David's only wife living in her father's court. Many observers expect future friction.

But domestic concerns will take second place with this warrior-king to Israel's national security. The Philistines to the west and southwest are David's most immediate threat, but David faces potential threat from the Midianites and Amalekites from the south, from the Edomites, Moabites and Ammonites from the southeast and east and from various Aramaean kings from the northeast. His first job will be to unify the army to utilize his remaining interior lines of communications to fight each of these enemies separately before they have any chance to unite against Israel.

MY COMMENTS BASED ON THE FULLER REVELATION OF SCRIPTURE:

In a long series of campaigns, David did succeed in keeping his enemies divided and beating them one by one. In fact, David had subjugated most of them before he died, and passed to Solomon a greatly augmented Israel that approximated the expanded borders that were mentioned in the covenants of God with Abraham and Moses. In modern terms, David had established overlordship over most of Jordan and Syria and had a military boundary on the right bank of the upper Euphrates. The Philistine state in the southwest was reduced to a rump, larger but roughly similar to the Gaza Strip today. David had a secure defensive alliance with Hiram, King of Lebanon. Modern Israel probably sought a similar situation in Lebanon in the 1980s, but Syria and Hezbollah have prevented that so far (2010) although they have not been able to restore the ability to bombard northern

Israel that existed before the 1967 war when Syria held the Golan Heights. In fact, one might consider how various later campaigns (especially the Sennacherib campaign about 701 BC against Hezekiah) might compare with the prophecies of the last great Middle Eastern war prophesied in Ezekiel 38, portions of Zechariah 9-14 and various other Scriptures.

But none of these later prophecies nor the history would make any sense unless Jerusalem had become the capital of Israel. When all of the tribes accepted David as king, Jerusalem was still in the hands of the Jebusites who had held it before Joshua led the Israelites into the Promised Land. Their ancestors had deceived Joshua into making a treaty with them (Joshua 9). Their descendants made the mistake of mocking David (2 Samuel 5:6). So David's army climbed through the water shaft and took the city, which became Jerusalem. It had an ideal location for a capital of Israel. There was a good water supply and steep slopes for easy defense. It was on the border between Judah and Benjamin, so that all of Israel could view Jerusalem as national instead of tribal territory. Yet Judah alone could reach and defend it if necessary. There were good communications to all parts of Israel. Most of all, the place where Abraham had sacrificed the ram in the place of Isaac was on Mount Moriah, one of the hills in the vicinity of the city. It was on this hilltop that God commanded the Temple to be built. The site was confirmed in 2 Samuel 24. So David established Jerusalem as the capital of Israel, and Israel so considers it today even if some government offices are in Tel Aviv. The issue of Jerusalem as capital of Israel when the Palestinians want East Jerusalem as the capital for a Palestinian state is a major bone of contention today. Today's issue is somewhat similar in this respect to the situation at the start of David's reign over all the tribes of Israel.

David probably made one indirect effort to replace Joab as commander recorded in 1 Chronicles 11:6, by opening up the post to the first to take Jerusalem. Joab's attack succeeded. He took the point position himself. In a military sense, Joab again proved his worth. He was a thorough military professional, perhaps like Patton or Rommel in the 20th century. With this, David apparently dropped the issue of the death of Abner until the end of his life when he was instructing Solomon about unfinished business. Most of the nation also let the matter drop.

Another unsolved problem at the start of David's reign over all of Israel was the Ark of the Covenant. It had been captured by the Philistines and then sent away because of the plague that afflicted the Philistines when the Ark were in their territory. The image of their false god Dagon had been destroyed without human action. David determined to bring the Ark to the new capital. After a false start because it was not carried in the Scriptural way leading to the death of one man (2 Samuel 6), David succeeded in bringing the Ark to Jerusalem amidst great celebration and worship. So David was establishing new ways of worship, such as psalms. Before David was done, he had organized the Levites into choirs praising God around the clock and had written extensive music for them to sing. (1 Chronicles 24-25)

Indeed David and Michael did not last as husband and wife. Certainly their time apart and Michal's time with another man did not help. The final straw was that Michal was offended by the exuberance that David showed when he moved the Ark to Jerusalem and was thereafter cloistered. (2 Samuel 6:20-23)

GOD'S COVENANT WITH DAVID -- 2 SAMUEL 7

It is a rare honor granted by God that He would make a covenant with a sinful man. When we really think about it, it is astounding that God would even hear our prayers because His power is more than sufficient to do what He wills without our cooperation. God promised Noah that He would not again flood the entire earth. God made a covenant with Abraham (and confirmed it with Isaac and with Jacob) that his descendants through the son of promise would settle in the Promised Land, now known as Israel. A second and ultimately greater prong of that covenant is that all nations would be blessed through Abraham, which has come true through Jesus Christ, with more yet to come. Moses mediated the covenant of the Law with Israel. Joshua began the initial fulfillment of the promises concerning the Land of Israel; the people began in part to live according to the outward commandments of the Law, although inward compliance was often missing even within the majority in the nation of Israel. Now God made another covenant with a descendent of Abraham, specifically from the tribe of Judah as predicted in Genesis 49:10.

When one thinks of Abraham, Moses and David, they all were men of prayer. Abraham pleaded with God for Sodom. Even though Abraham's prayers were ultimately answered "no," his pleading with God in Genesis 18 (especially vv. 22-33) shows a man intimate with God. Moses on several occasions pleaded with God to spare his generation of Israel. God granted Moses' requests for the time being to permit the rise of a replacement generation of Israel, although only Joshua and Caleb of the original Exodus adult generation entered the Promised Land. A survey of David's psalms will likewise show that David was on intimate terms with God, faults and all. If you desire covenant blessings from God, then be a man or woman of prayer as Abraham, Moses and David were.

With that background, we should examine 2 Samuel 7:12-16 more closely:

> *When your days are fulfilled and you rest with your fathers, I will set up your seed after you, who will come from your body, and I will establish his kingdom. He shall build a house for My name, and I will establish the throne of his kingdom forever. I will be his Father, and he shall be My son. If he commits iniquity, I will chasten him with the rod of men and with the blows of the sons of men. But My mercy shall not depart from him, as I took it from Saul, whom I removed from*

before you. And your house and your kingdom shall be established forever before you. Your throne shall be established forever.

Initially, the initial "seed" turned out to be Solomon, even though both Absalom and Adonijah tried to set themselves up as kings before Solomon was established. Indeed Solomon's kingdom was established as a great power of its time, both militarily and economically. Silver was not even valuable in Solomon's kingdom. 1 Kings 10:21. Solomon's Temple as originally constructed and ornamented would have been one of the architectural wonders of any age. Indeed Solomon did "build a house" for God's name. The Spirit was behind the veil in the Holy of Holies and departed roughly 350 years later as Ezekiel 8-11 makes clear. Solomon was indeed chastened when he sinned. The Book of Ecclesiastes gives some of the wisdom learned through chastening and the first 10 chapters of Proverbs gives more. But did Solomon's kingdom with its capital at Jerusalem last forever? No! It fell to Nebuchadnezzar starting about 605 BC through 586 BC and never recovered full sovereignty with any descendent of Solomon upon an earthly throne.

So how was the portion of David's covenant fulfilled which promised an everlasting kingdom? The genealogies of Matthew (starting with Matthew 1:1, who immediately identifies Jesus as the Son of David and of Abraham) and of Luke (starting at 3:23) make it clear that Jesus was the King of Israel. Nathaniel, one of the disciples, immediately recognized Jesus as such. John 1:49. So did Pilate, who executed Jesus despite qualms of conscience precisely because He was the King of the Jews (John 19:12-22) and therefore a potential rival to the Emperor in Rome. Hebrews 1:8-9 quotes from Psalm 45:6-7. Psalm 45 is a psalm of David about the Messiah-King and His kingdom promised by God to be fulfilled. Because the risen Christ (the same word in Greek for the Hebrew Messiah) has a throne, He must be a King. Jesus is identified as King of Kings in 1 Timothy 6:15, Revelation 17:14 and Revelation 19:16. For a psalm with still more detail concerning this same covenant, consider Psalm 89, which closely tracks the promises of God given in 2 Samuel 7. Psalm 89 speaks of the everlasting nature of the covenant even as it acknowledges that the King would be struck dead and Israel scattered (vv. 38-48), but then ends in praise. Why? The King rises from the dead (Psalm 16) and Israel is redeemed finally (Romans 9-11, Ezekiel 36-39 and Zechariah 9-14).

Many of the portions of the covenant that Solomon fulfilled initially had a greater fulfillment through Jesus Christ. Jesus Himself proclaimed Himself to be *"greater than Solomon."* Matthew 12:42. He also built a spiritual temple or house for His Father. 2 Corinthians 6:16; Ephesians 2:19-22; Hebrews 3:1-6. We as individuals are also called temples of the Holy Spirit. 1 Corinthians 3:16-17; 6:19. Likewise, our Lord Jesus spoke of His own body as a temple. John 2:19-21. While Solomon's building was beautiful and was a home for the Holy Spirit for over 300 years, its greatest significance is that it was a precursor to the indwelling of the Holy Spirit in all believers and a precursor to the modern living Body of Christ, His true worldwide Church. Long after its destruction its meaning remains true. All of this was part of God's covenant with David, which Christian believers enjoy around the world.

DAVID'S GRACE TO MEPHIBOSHETH -- 2 Samuel 9

With David now having moved the Ark successfully to his new capital and now in the joy of God's everlasting covenant, David reflected God's grace to him by showing favor to the helpless Mephibosheth, the grandson of Saul and the lame son of Jonathan. Mephibosheth was trying to live "under the radar" in Lo-Debar, meaning a place of "no pasture." I would infer that this was a place of semi-desert. This was on the edge of the kingdom. Mephibosheth was probably afraid that David would take revenge for his grandfather's wrongs committed to David and wanted to blend quietly into the scenery. But David, having received kindness from God, showed kindness to Mephibosheth in memory of Jonathan's friendship rather than remembering Saul's wrongs. This can be good advice -- to remember the good rather than the evil. In 1 Corinthians 13:5 as translated literally in the Greek-English New Testament of Berry, love "does not reckon evil." I have heard this paraphrased that love does not keep score or count of evil. This idea is similar to the passages (Job 14:17; Psalm 103:12; Micah 7:18-19) when God separated us forever from our transgressions. So David invited Mephibosheth permanently to his meals, as once long ago David had regularly eaten with Saul and Jonathan. This was true even though Mephibosheth had nothing to bring to the table in either a military or political sense, whereas David had great military skill to bring to Saul's table. David gave us a miniature example of God's grace. We were *"dead in trespasses and sins"* (Ephesians 2:1) and were as spiritually helpless as Mephibosheth was in body. God had every reason to deal with us as the enemies we once were (Romans 5:8-10), just as David had reason to finish off Mephibosheth to remove any possible rival to the throne. Humanly speaking, it was certainly within David's reach to do that; many other kings and rulers have responded that way. In the case of King Ahab's house in the Northern Kingdom about 200 years later, God Himself commanded Jehu to do just that. (2 Kings 9:7-10) This was probably because of the especially gross evil of Ahab and Jezebel which would have been reflected in their children and to give the Northern Kingdom some temporary stability. But David instead acted from undeserved love, as God has acted toward His Church with similar unmerited favor where we deserve His wrath instead. So Mephibosheth, who could not maintain himself, was maintained by his King, though from a rival house. So we, enemies of God by nature, are maintained by God and eat at His table by His overwhelming grace.

DAVID'S GREATEST SIN -- "URIAHGATE" -- 2 Samuel 10-12

David was apparently at his zenith after God entered into the covenant with him. This was true militarily and diplomatically. David's wars had been successful and profitable. David had an alliance with Lebanon, securing his north and northwest boundary. He had good relations with King Nahash to the east, the king who had originally attacked Israel when Saul first was king. Now Nahash had just died and David had sent diplomats to express condolence and to continue the friendship with Nahash's son, the new King of Moab. In our times it is customary that the Vice-President of the United States lead a similar delegation when a major national leader has died. But the new King of Moab was stupid enough to insult the diplomats, cut up their clothes and shave half their beards! Naturally David decided to teach the Moabites a lesson that they would never forget and sent Joab on an invasion. Where David started to go wrong was that he did not go on the expedition personally as he had in the past.

When David was looking over Jerusalem from his rooftop at the highest point of the city, he saw a beautiful woman bathing on her roof, where she probably supposed she had privacy. But David was high enough to spy on her over her roof parapet. *"Lust, when it has conceived, brings forth sin. Sin, when it is finished, brings forth death."* James 1:15 (I have modernized the language.) David sent an aide to find out who the woman was. What he learned should have stopped him in his tracks. The woman was married to Uriah the Hittite.

Uriah was no ordinary man. He was one of David's top soldiers -- probably the equivalent of a brigadier or major general today. He is listed among the greatest soldiers in David's army. 1 Chronicles 11:41. For David to take a general's wife while the army was fighting a war for the nation risked the loyalty of the entire army. Yet David plunged on and summoned Bath-sheba to the palace for a tryst. There is no indication that she was unwilling, but surely both knew it was wrong. Reality set in when Bath-sheba realized she was pregnant and told David.

At this point David did not have murder on his mind. He summoned Uriah home to Jerusalem so that he would cohabit with his wife. In that way the people would assume that the child was Uriah's child when born, and David's responsibility for the pregnancy would go undetected. But Uriah identified so strongly with his unit that he refused to enter his house and enjoy his wife, preferring to sleep outside his house as his men were fighting at the front. The whole city knew that Uriah had not touched his wife. So David's plan of concealment failed and David remained desperate to cover up his sin. So what he did was to write a sealed order that Uriah be left dangling in battle so that he would be killed, and had Uriah carry it unopened to Joab. Joab carried out David's order (a dirty secret that probably made Joab almost impossible for David to remove as commander) and Uriah died. Then David added Bath-sheba to his wives, providing a plausible innocent explanation for her coming childbirth. *"But the thing that David had done had displeased the Lord."* 2 Samuel 11:27.

David had not fooled God. David became severely ill in the aftermath of Uriahgate by the chastening hand of God. While not all illness is caused by a particular sin that has displeased God, in this particular instance that is what happened. Psalm 38 describes David's illnesses and their divine origin. Psalm 32:4 makes clear that the very part of the body with which David had sinned was dried up as part of God's chastening. After David had begun to feel God's chastening for his disobedience, he finally resumed praying, as Jonah was to do about 2 centuries later. Psalms 38, 51 and 32 are the main psalms coming from this terrible time, although there are references peppered though David's later psalms. In gracious and undeserved answer to those prayers, God send Nathan the Prophet with His verdict (2 Samuel 12).

Nathan did not confront David directly at first but told the King a parable about a man who stole and killed his neighbor's lamb for a guest's meal when he had several lambs of his own. David in part pronounced his own sentence, applying the Mosaic Law of fourfold restoration and declaring Nathan's imaginary offender worthy of death. 2 Samuel 12:5-6. David lost 4 children through the consequences of his sin: his firstborn son by Bath-sheba (2 Samuel 12:14-23); his daughter Tamar as a rape victim (2 Samuel 13); Amnon the rapist, struck down by Absalom (2 Samuel 13) in revenge for the rape; and Absalom, probably the most energetic and able of David's earlier children, because of his rebellion against David (2 Samuel 15-18). David probably saw some of his own decisiveness in Absalom and could not bring himself to want Absalom dead or even disciplined no matter what Absalom did. This blind spot of David for his children was nearly fatal for the entire kingdom. Consider that David did nothing to Amnon and he wanted to spare Absalom. After David's death Adonijah too was executed as a rebel against Solomon. (1 Kings 2:13-25).

David also said that the man who took his neighbor's lamb should die. This applied to himself, as he already had several wives whereas Uriah apparently had but one. Under Moses' Law David's capital sentence, which would have rebounded on himself, was legally correct. He had broken the Sixth and Seventh Commandments against adultery and murder, each independently a capital offense. But God in His infinite mercy said no. After David had confessed his sin. Nathan put God's verdict this way, *"The Lord also has put away your sin; you shall not die."* 2 Samuel 12:13. This raises two questions for us to consider:

(1) Why did God permit all this terrible sin and its tragic consequences in the first place?

(2) Why did God forgive David when David had in effect spat in God's face after all His blessings on David?

I will not give complete answers to either, but they are so important that we must wrestle with them because they go to the very heart of God's dealings with fallen humanity.

Paul wrote concerning the entire Old Testament that *"For whatever things were written before were written for our learning, that we through the patience and comfort of the Scriptures might have hope."* Romans 15:4. So David's history was preserved for our sake. I hope that none of my readers have ever physically committed adultery or murder, but realism tells me that someone reading this will have actually done one or even both of these things. But spiritually in the mind virtually every reader of mine -- including myself -- is guilty of both crimes. Concerning adultery, our Lord Jesus said, *You have heard that it was said to those of old, "You shall not commit adultery." But I say to you that whoever looks at a woman to lust for her has already committed adultery with her in his heart.* Matthew 5:27-28. There are very few mature men who can claim innocence with a straight face. And concerning murder our Lord said, *You have heard that it was said to those of old, "You shall not murder, and whoever murders will be in danger of the judgment." But I say to you that whoever is angry with his brother without a cause shall be in danger of the judgment. And whoever says to his brother, 'Raca!' [meaning something like "Blockhead!"] shall be in danger of the council. But whoever says, 'You fool!' shall be in danger of hell fire.* Matthew 5:21-22. Have you ever been angry with someone -- perhaps a parent, a child, a boss or a spouse -- without cause? Have we ever called someone a nasty name? Then we too have violated the Seventh Commandment and face the same death sentence that David faced. We need forgiveness as David needed forgiveness.

Without this terrible sin David would not have understood forgiveness in the way he did. He never would have written Psalms 38, 51 and 32 from his own soul. The Holy Spirit used the chastening and restoration of David to teach His people through the ages of His steadfast love for us even in the face of our wavering love for Him. Portions of other psalms (for example, Psalm 31:9-10) also show the mark of David's sin, chastening and restoration. In turn, the Apostle Paul bases his teaching of the righteousness of God in Romans 4 on Psalm 32. The New Testament truth that Christ died in my place and paid my penalty is the logical culmination of David's teaching after his spiritual recovery from Uriahgate. The Cross is the method that God used to *put away my sin.* This truth recurs in various other Scriptures:

Bless the Lord, O my soul; and all that is within me, bless His holy name! Bless the Lord, O my soul, and forget not all His benefits: Who forgives all your iniquities, Who heals all your diseases, Who redeems your life from destruction, Who crowns you with lovingkindness and tender mercies ... Psalm 103:1-4

As far as the east is from the west, so far has He removed our transgressions from us. Psalm 103:12

My transgression is sealed up in a bag, and You cover my iniquity. Job 14:17

Who is a God like You, pardoning iniquity and passing over the transgression of the remnant of His heritage? He does not retain His anger forever, because He delights in mercy. He will again have compassion on us, and will subdue our iniquities. You will cast all our sins into the depths of the sea. Micah 7:18-19

In Him [Jesus Christ] we have redemption through His blood, the forgiveness of sins, according to the riches of His grace ... Ephesians 1:7

This is the most essential teaching to come out this terrible conduct on the part of David, but there is much more to be learned.

If there were a Hall of Fame for worshipers of the true and living God, David would be a first-round, unanimous choice. He walked in covenant with God. He added greatly to worship with his Psalms. David was also a prophet who foretold the coming of our Lord Jesus Christ and therefore had the indwelling Holy Spirit even before Pentecost. (1 Peter 1:11) He subdued kingdoms (Hebrews 11:33) and obtained the throne of Israel through faith. He worshiped God only and avoided idolatry, which Aaron permitted in Moses' absence. But even the best saint short of Jesus Christ is fully capable of terrible things, such as adultery and murder. If a great saint like David could and did do such things, what does that say about us? *Therefore let him who thinks he stands take heed lest he fall.* 1 Corinthians 10:12.

David's story is a warning to the believer against committing known sin based on the fact that our eternal salvation cannot be lost. Consider the extent of the chastening that David suffered because of his sin. The serious illness of Psalm 38 was only the start. Imagine the loss of his firstborn son by Bathsheba. David fasted the 7 days until the child's death was final. Then imagine the grief he felt when one of his sons raped one of his daughters. Two years later another son, a full brother of the daughter, killed the rapist in revenge and then fled for his life. Then that son returned and rebelled against David. David had to flee for his life with his most loyal troops and then fight an army led by his own son. I have no way to quantify David's pain. So another reason that God permitted these events to unfold is that they are a warning to us to maintain our spiritual guard at all times as a good soldier of Jesus Christ (2 Timothy 2:3-4), lest we fall into a similar trap as David did.

Another set of warnings from these passages for those of us who have children now or may have them in the future is the danger of rose-colored glasses when assessing them. David fell short here. When Amnon raped Tamar, David was very angry, as he should have been. 2 Samuel 13:21. But what did David do about it? Nothing! And there is the problem. Moses' Law would have demanded death for Amnon on grounds of both incest and rape. Leviticus 18:9,29; 20:17; Deuteronomy 27:22. Amnon got away with his crime for 2 years. One probable reason for David's inaction is that David knew that he himself had committed two capital offenses. He reluctant to punish Amnon when he himself was equally guilty. So the administration of justice suffered because of David's own offenses, just as in today's world a judge is suspect in judging a pornographer if the judge has pornography on his own computer. A case of this type has actually happened in Federal court in California.

Absalom, Tamar's brother, bided his time as he saw his father's inaction. Without visible warning, he set a trap for Amnon and sprang it successfully. Although execution was warranted, Absalom was not the person who had the authority to kill. Neither had there been a trial at which the truth was established before two or three witnesses. Numbers 35:30; Deuteronomy 17:6, 19:15. So Absalom too was wrong in being judge, jury and executioner. He knew it and fled.

When Absalom with Joab's assistance was allowed to return from exile by David, Absalom continued to expand his activities into the vacuum left by David in the administration of justice. 2 Samuel 15:2-6. When Absalom thought that he was popular enough to win, he rose in revolt. Note the progression from the original revenge against Amnon to criticism for general inefficiency in the justice system to revolt itself, all of which festered because David did not act decisively. Joab had assisted in Absalom's return, but to his credit he realized that he had helped create a monster.

BAHURIM BULLETIN -- during David's retreat from Jerusalem, ca 980 BC

As David retreated toward the Jordan to gain time to strengthen his meager forces, Shimei of Benjamin loudly cursed David, calling him a man of blood because he caused the downfall of the Benjamite and formerly royal House of Saul. David's forces did nothing, an indication of David's political weakness. {This was also a repeat of David's self-restraint that he showed in sparing Saul twice, but a virulent anti-David columnist would not mention that.} In fact, Shimei did not state the full case against David.

David admittedly was a blessing to Israel when he killed Goliath, but he made too much of himself after that. Saul may have advanced him too rapidly based on one battle {not really true, but a plausible charge that a polemicist would make}. David was not ready for marriage when Saul unwisely gave David his daughter Michal. Neither was he ready to advance from common soldier to a commander. The people were also taken with David's dash and daring without considering his youth and inexperience {again mostly not true but plausible spin}. The popular song said that Saul had killed thousands and David tens of thousands, even though David had truly killed but one and participated in raids that had killed another 200 to marry Michal {but what of the morale effect of David's victory over the enemy's best and of David's declaration of faith in God? half-truth at most} In their infatuation with David, they overlooked the importance of all the planning and administration that Saul did and his role as commander-in-chief.

David got a taste of adulation and power and wanted more, even to be crowned king himself {forgetting Samuel's anointing, but again plausible}. He was insubordinate {forgetting Saul's attempted murders} and went absent without leave without cause. {Of course, Jonathan, who knew the truth, was dead.} Of course Saul suspected him! Then David ran away completely and gathered together malcontents, debtors and runaway slaves {Nabal -- 1 Samuel 25:10} to start his rebellion. This rebellion forced Saul to shuttle back and forth between the Philistines in the west and David in the south and ended up causing the disaster on Mount Gilboa. David shares responsibility for all the suffering even if his soldiers did not fight for the Philistines {not true but plausible}.

Furthermore, David violated the Scriptures by multiplying wives to himself (Deuteronomy 17:17) during the rebellion {true}. He married Abigail before her husband Nabal was cold in the grave and took several other wives in addition to her, when he was already married to Michal {see 1 Chronicles 3 -- there is some truth to some of this, although one can hardly blame Abigail -- there is also the mitigation that Michal had been given to someone else even though she was loyal to David during his escape}.

Worse, David refused to accept Ish-bosheth as Saul's successor and waged open civil war to bring him down, in which he was ultimately successful because Abner gave up the fight {again ignoring the anointing from God through Samuel}.

When David did come to power, he was so undignified in taking off his kingly clothing when he brought the Ark to Jerusalem that he offended even Michal, his wife. When she tried to correct him, he shut her away and refused to bear her children!

David keeps the murderous Joab as commander even though Joab ambushed Abner as a settlement was being finished over the civil war {the best that can be said for this is that Abner died outside the city of refuge when he could have been safe within, but David did recognize the wrong done but felt powerless to remove Joab without a suitable replacement -- compare what happens concerning Amasa later}.

David has been less than careful in selecting high subordinates, sometimes going outside of Israel. Ittai, a Philistine from Gath, marched with him past Bahurim. Uriah, the murdered general, was a Hittite. Yet David treacherously had Uriah killed when he wanted Bath-sheba, his wife and still lives with Bath-sheba now. In total Bath-sheba has borne David four children, one of whom died shortly after birth. So David completely ignores his first wife Michal while continuing his affair with a woman who had taken a foreigner for a husband and then supposedly married David after her husband's murder. Disgusting!

Now David's day of reckoning for all of his crimes has come! Arise, Benjamin and all Israel and finish him off, even though it is David's son instead of Saul's house that is the instrument of divine justice {of course this did not happen}.

MY COMMENTS IN THE LIGHT OF THE FULLER REVELATION OF SCRIPTURE:

1. Look what a spinmeister can do with our sin! Remember that Satan is the past master of spin.

2. We must realize what reproach we bring to the name of Christ with public sin and avoid sin for that reason alone.

3. Consider the depth of the mercy of God to David -- and to ourselves.

4. My imaginary spinmeister naturally leaves out any mention of David's contribution to the worship of God. He also leaves out any mention of Saul's guilty acts and leaves out the call of God to David.

5. David was driven to hiding by Saul's attempted murder, but David never struck against Saul or against Israel when he had the chance. How could David stay when Saul personally tried to kill him?

6. There is truth in the accusations about David's women even though it seems that both Abigail and Bath-sheba were unusually intelligent.

7. There is also truth that David after Uriah did neglect the duties of justice. He failed to discipline his children properly.

8. God sovereignly chose to forgive David's sin instead of exacting punishment. Similarly, God stayed His hand against Israel during the Exodus. Until David was ready, God propped up Saul on Israel's throne even though Saul had forfeited his right to rule.

When David fled, Absalom went to David's concubines. This was more a political statement than an expression of lust, although lust was involved. By gesture Absalom was proclaiming his own sovereignty and also proclaiming total war against his father. In violation of Leviticus 18:8, Absalom violated some of those who had been intimate with his father and so himself committed a capital offense under the Law of Moses. Provoked by David's apparent weakness, Absalom dishonored his father in violation of the Fifth Commandment and swiftly was forced to pay the penalty.

Absalom's rebellion was Joab's finest hour of service to Israel. David was distraught over the rebellion of what was probably his favorite son. Joab kept David's army together. Barzillai of Gilead and Moabites helped keep that army supplied. The measure of David's distress is reflected in his command to his army not to kill Absalom (2 Samuel 18:5) and his mourning when he learned that Absalom was dead (2 Samuel 18:33). In the first portion of 2 Samuel 19, Joab had to admonish King David not to mourn his son so excessively and to comfort his supporters. With the caveat that we are told in the New Testament to love our personal enemies (Matthew 5:43-48), Joab's words are still wise advice for political leaders even today:

> *Today you have disgraced all your servants who today have saved your life, the lives of your sons and daughters, the lives of your wives and the lives of your concubines, in that you love your enemies and hate your friends. For you have declared today that you regard neither princes nor servants; for today I perceive that if Absalom had lived and all of us had died today, then it would have pleased you well. Now therefore, arise, go out and speak comfort to your servants. For I swear by the*

> *Lord, if you do not go out, not one will stay with you this night, and that will be worse for you than all the evil that has befallen you from your youth until now. 2 Samuel 19:5-7.*

If an enemy is persistent and will not be persuaded, one may be compelled to oppose that enemy even to the point of deadly force in order to love our friends or even our fellow-citizens.

Joab was absolutely right to kill Absalom notwithstanding David's command to the contrary. Joab may not have known God's hidden purpose to destroy Absalom (2 Samuel 17:14), but Joab knew now that Absalom was a willful young man who would be a disaster for the country as a ruler. Though Joab's faults were many, he was loyal to David until David was nearly dead. Joab could perceive the rebelliousness of Absalom and that he never could be disciplined at this point. For the sake of the nation having one unquestioned king as opposed to the calamity of civil war, Absalom had to die. Joab's actions founded a precedent in Judah (though not in the breakaway Northern Kingdom nearly a century later) that the genealogical succession was not to be questioned. This principle was observed except for Athaliah until foreign powers dominated Judah after Josiah's death over 350 years later. While monarchy is not the best form of government, civil war between rival kings is tragic even when there is just cause to fight. The Wars of the Roses in England in the second half of the 15th century and the Civil War in the United States are but two examples. Joab, knowing that Absalom was dead, also wisely called his army back from pursuit because he realized that there was no further reason to fight now that Absalom was dead. So Joab nipped this civil war in the bud with minimum casualties and damage. With David emotionally incapacitated, Joab kept his head and acted wisely in this case. Neither did Joab himself attempt to usurp David's place as King, as some men might have done.

It is also true that Joab would stop at nothing -- not even murder -- to keep his place as Army commander. This was illustrated again in 2 Samuel

20:8-10, when Joab murdered Amasa to remove his second military rival as he had previously killed Abner. But this proud and selfish aspect of Joab's character should not blind us to the fact that Joab's clear-headed realism was a divinely appointed corrective for David's rose-colored view of Absalom. Joab had helped to create a monster in bringing Absalom back from exile-- Joab at least put that same monster to rest and kept Israel united for more than a generation. I would not recommend Joab as a good personal example to my child nor to the Christian Church as a whole. His crimes eventually caught up with him. But someone who has military or political responsibility should find Joab in his dealings with Absalom's rebellion (although not with Abner nor Amasa) an excellent instructor in statecraft and military command.

Both Nathan the Prophet and Joab show another positive trait: the willingness to risk the displeasure of King David in order to tell the truth. Nathan introduced his subject with a parable, while Joab spoke the plain, unvarnished truth. Nathan's parable worked. While any such situation may cause us to "hold our breath" as we proceed, we must speak the truth even if it is a friend or loved one who may be displeased. That does not mean that we have to insult our hearer. But the Scriptures do command us to *"speak truth with [our] neighbor."* Ephesians 4:25. Both Nathan and Joab had the courage to warn even the King.

We have already observed how Absalom's sin progressed from murder for revenge to preparing for rebellion to the actual rebellion itself and his sexual acts to burn his bridges to his father. A brief civil war resulted. We should also note how David's sexual sins of multiple wives expanded from two to multiple and finally to his desire for Bath-sheba when she was a soldier's wife, and then murder of Bath-sheba's husband. In the New Testament the Apostle Paul wrote in 2 Timothy 2:16-18 that false doctrine will spread like gangrene (the literal -- the King James version will speak of cancer). So will other forms of sin. As Christians we must be vigilant in our own lives, in our family lives and in our churches to stop open sin before it takes root. Personally we are commanded to *"put to death the deeds of the flesh."* Romans 8:13. This portion of David's life is an illustration of what happens when either inward or outward sin is ignored, whether by us personally or by a church body of believers. *Lust, when it is conceived, brings forth sin; sin when it is finished, brings forth death.* James 1:15.

Yet it is also true that David's life speaks to us of God's constancy in His covenant with His children, even when they fail miserably. In this respect David is representative of all true believers, who are in covenant relationship with God through Jesus Christ even though they are still imperfect. For example, see Hebrews 7:22; 8:6-10. The chastening we receive is a mark of a continuing family relationship. Hebrews 12:7-13. In David's case, God permitted no less than 4 children to be born to David by Bath-sheba (spelled Bath-shua in 1 Chronicles 3:5, but the same woman). Was this to replace the four children who died as a result of David's sin? I cannot say for sure, because I do not know whether the first listed child was the one who died a week after his birth. The Bible does not comment directly on this question of restoration of David's dead children, but this is a reasonable inference. A similar principle is stated in Joel 2:25, *"So I will restore to you the years that the swarming locust has eaten, the crawling locust, the consuming locust and the chewing locust, My great army which I sent among you."* Not only this, but when we look at Luke's genealogy we find that the Messianic line (probably of Mary) passes through Nathan, the third listed child of David and Bath-sheba. Luke 3:31. The royal succession passed through Solomon, the fourth listed son of David and Bath-sheba. Solomon is listed as an ancestor of Joseph, the adoptive and legal father (although not the biological father) of Jesus the Messiah. Matthew 1:6. As with Salmon and the former prostitute Rahab and again with Boaz and the Moabitess Ruth (a foreigner), it is apparent that God once again used an improbable marriage (and in this case one with grossly sinful origins, to boot!) to bring His Son Jesus into the world. I do not know all the reasons why, but I would suggest some:

1) To show His power of sovereign choice;

2) To show His power to overcome human sin;

3) To show His mercy to His chosen people;

4) To show that no human lineage is pure;

5) To show His grace even in the depth of our sin, as with Samson when he was grinding corn;

6) To show His constancy contrasted with our inconsistency; and

7) To show our utter dependence on Him.

God is never taken by surprise nor has any of His plans destroyed by human action or sin. He is the past master of making lemonade from lemons as He is equally masterful in making a beautiful Bride from human rejects. 1 Corinthians 1:26.

We have already noted that Bath-sheba had 4 children with David listed in 1 Chronicles 3:5. That is a clue that even with their horrible start she was able to forge a relationship with him that was deeper than his previous relationships. Most of the other wives that David had taken had one or two children listed at most. Further, Bath-sheba apparently had an unusually strong relationship with her son Solomon. This show up when Solomon's rival approaches Bath-sheba rather than Solomon directly (1 Kings 2:13-25). Solomon would not normally have refused his mother, but he perceived the threat behind Adonijah's request for King David's last companion and ordered Adonijah's execution. But this was not because Solomon lacked respect for his mother -- to the contrary he was greatly attached to her. In Proverbs we read twice, " ... *do not forsake the law of your mother.*" Proverbs 1:8, 6:20. So Bath-sheba taught Solomon well concerning the Word of God, which was highly unusual in that day and time. Bath-sheba's combination of qualities was another reason why God, who sees inside all of us, permitted David's terrible plan to go forward. This is not the only time that God has used women of questionable reputation for His purposes. Mary Magdalene certainly had a questionable past. So did the woman at the well in John 4. The woman who wiped Jesus' feet with her hair had not been a holy woman. Luke 7:36-50.

Still another reason why God permitted David's plan with Bath-sheba to proceed was to highlight the importance of and benefits of repentance from sin. David's sin was deep and his psalms of repentance were heartfelt (especially Psalms 51 and 32). David's grievous sin and recovery was a backdrop for the preaching of both Peter and Paul, who called on their listeners to repent. (Acts 2:38 is an example from Peter; Acts 17:30 is an example from Paul.) John the Baptist demanded repentance (Matthew 3:2) and so did the Lord Jesus Christ (Luke 13:1-5). These are only samples of the call to repentance, but plainly the example and history of David would help many people to understand repentance by example.

Our Lord Jesus posed a question to a Pharisee before dinner in Luke 7:36-50. A woman of immoral history had come to the Lord Jesus and anointed Him, kissed his feet and wiped them with her tears and hair. Those at the table did not understand, so the Lord Jesus asked a question which highlights the connection between divine forgiveness and our love for God. In response to Jesus' question the Pharisee answered correctly that a person will love more if he or she has been forgiven more. The woman at the house had been forgiven much, so she loved much. Perhaps God permitted David to sin with Bath-sheba so that David would understand deep forgiveness and in turn could instruct all succeeding generations, including our own. God is never the author of sin and never commands it. James 1:13-15. However, He permits our sinful wills to express themselves to a certain point for His purposes and then restrains sin as He knows best. Psalm 76:10.

Literally, repentance means a change of mind which creates a change of behavior. In simple matters, repentance can be represented by two simple commands: (1) About face!; and then (2) Forward, march! Of course, David was in too deep with Bath-sheba to resolve things so simply, but certainly there was a change in attitude and behavior after Nathan the Prophet induced David to admit that he had *"sinned against the Lord."* 2 Samuel 12:13. This is reflected in David's psalms from later in his life and in his enduring attachment to Bath-sheba, which lasted even to Solomon's coronation in the last year of David's life. 1 Kings 1:28-31. Bath-sheba was the first person called in when David faced his final crisis of Adonijah attempting to seize the throne as David was nearing death. David did not become sinless after Absolom's rebellion was crushed, but he clearly had a change of direction back toward the purer faith of his youth coupled with the lessons of his experience, which ultimately made David the strongest spiritually that he had ever been. For example, consider Psalm 18 (repeated in 2 Samuel 22) and Psalms 69-72, although Psalm 72 was apparently composed by Solomon.

Psalm 69 illustrates still another reason why God permitted David to stumble temporarily into the grip of sin. David experienced the deep loneliness of God hiding His face and even the enmity of those who had been his friends. This gave David the experience from which to have some understanding of the Messiah being forsaken and alone, which in turn was the base from which David drew under the inspiration of the Holy Spirit as David wrote Psalms 22, 41 and 69. All of these psalms prophesy of the forsaking of Jesus the Messiah by all. In the case of Psalm 22 the Messiah was even forsaken by His Father; this is quoted by Jesus Himself on the Cross. Our Lord Jesus was treated as a sinner for our sakes; He Himself was sinless. But David had some understanding of what was to come by his experience of being God-forsaken for a time as a consequence of Uriahgate.

So God permitted David to plunge ahead and turned David's sin to the benefit of countless people who would live later.

There is still our second question to try to answer: why did God choose to have mercy on David rather than exercise his power of judgment without mercy? Again I cannot give a complete answer, but I can make one attempt. First, except for Jesus Christ there is not a human being ever born who deserves the favor of God or any mercy from Him. But God graciously has told us certain reasons why He may withhold judgment. One character trait about David is quite unusual for an ancient king: his patience and readiness to show mercy. David overdid this with Absalom, but David also showed mercy to King Saul and to Mephibosheth. David even declined to put to death a Benjamite who cursed him. 2 Samuel 16:5-13. Our Lord Jesus said in the Sermon on the Mount, *"Blessed are the merciful, for they shall obtain mercy."* Matthew 5:7. Once again He stated, *For with what judgment you judge, you will be judged; and with the measure you use, it will be measured back to you.* Matthew 7:2. So God may have chosen to show David mercy because David had shown mercy to his enemies in the past. Contrast David to the unmerciful man in Matthew 18:23-35, who wound up in torment from God for his lack of mercy. God was under no obligation to show David mercy, but these Scriptures give a clue as to why He chose to show David mercy.

David in the last portion of his reign laid important spiritual and civil foundations for the future of Israel after his death. The details are found mainly in 1 Chronicles 22-29. David planned for the construction of the Temple and had considerable preliminary work started before his death, although he did not live to see the Temple actually started. David organized the priesthood and the singers. Some of the singers composed psalms as did David himself. Asaph and Heman are mentioned, for example. The priesthood was organized in preparation for centralizing the great sacrifices such as the Passover at the Temple and for the musical praise of God. David also left to Solomon a thoroughly organized army and an alliance with the Lebanese, which gave Solomon access to seafaring expertise which Solomon used to economic advantage. (See 1 Kings 5, which also mentions materials for Temple construction.) The Egyptians and Philistines were quiet and Israel had military control over the remaining nations bordering Israel. At the start of Solomon's reign Israel's security situation was the best in its history through the mercy of God. But an internal crisis had to be surmounted first.

THE SUCCESSION CRISIS -- 1 Kings 1-3

After Absalom's rebellion was crushed, there were no further challenges to David's reign while he remained healthy. David did order a census at Satan's instigation (1 Chronicles 21:1), which God permitted because He Himself was angry with Israel. (2 Samuel 24:1). In the resulting plague 70,000 people died. David did repent for ordering the census (probably out of pride in how far he had come) and bought Araunah's threshing floor, which became the Temple site. However, none of this resulted in a renewed challenge to David's authority. But as David's health declined, there was a dispute over the succession. In other countries such a dispute has frequently caused civil war. For another generation Israel's unity and prosperity hung in the balance.

In any disputed succession the temptation is strong to try to move first to establish authority before rivals have an opportunity to act. So it was with Adonijah. But if one strikes too soon, the existing ruler may remain strong enough to quell the revolt. Striking too late may mean that the opportunity is gone. This line of thinking weighs human psychology but does not consider the sovereignty of God. An example from American history was the rush to establish a Confederate government after the 1860 election before Abraham Lincoln took office on March 4, 1861.

Adonijah moved first and was able to persuade both Joab, the Army commander, and Abiathar, the priest, to support him. But the old lion David had one more roar in him. He assembled most of the government to support the accession of Solomon to the exclusion of Adonijah. When the sound of this celebration was heard, Adonijah's party melted away and Solomon was able to take the throne with his father's support without fighting, in contrast to the American Civil War. This was a vital step to the unprecedented prosperity of Israel during Solomon's reign.

One further probable reason why God allowed David and Bath-sheba to go forward can be perceived as one considers 1 Kings 1-2. When Adonijah had proclaimed himself king, it was Bath-sheba and Nathan that moved David to act in Solomon's behalf (1 Kings 1:11-30). Nathan had been the faithful prophet who had rebuked David and pronounced the sentence that David and Bath-sheba's first son would die when David had murdered Uriah to clear his path to marry Bath-sheba. Yet years later Bath-sheba and Nathan are close allies, not mortal enemies as one might expect. Bath-sheba had obviously learned from her previous sin and its chastening. David and Bath-sheba are still close as well, so close that Nathan sends Bath-sheba to David first to prepare the way for his advice. And David responded to them both. As a result the throne of Israel was deflected from the fleshly Adonijah (who wanted David's last bedroom companion, who slept in his bed although David was no longer virile -- see 1 Kings 1:1-4 and 1 Kings 2:13-23) to the infinitely more spiritual and wiser (though imperfect) Solomon. At stake was a whole spiritual heritage represented in part by Proverbs, Ecclesiastes and Song of Solomon. There was the fantastic growth of Israel with an economy that was unprecedented for its time under Solomon. The Hebrew Scriptures spread through the Middle East. It is probable that God chose to permit the sin of David and Bath-sheba at the beginning of their relationship as an improbable foundation for mercy to Israel at the end of David's life. There is an element of mystery here that only Jesus Christ can fully penetrate.

Adonijah afterward admitted that it was the Lord that had given the kingdom to Solomon. 1 Kings 2:15. He had professed allegiance to Solomon by bowing down before him (1 Kings 1:53) but belied that profession by asking for King David's last companion as his wife. His request for such a wife indicated that he still coveted the crown himself. This request was similar to the act of Absalom in going in with David's concubines. Solomon viewed Adonijah as a dangerous hypocrite and therefore ordered him executed. Apparently few people regretted this.

When David knew he was nearing physical death, he warned Solomon of certain leftover rebels from his reign. One of these was Joab, who had defected from David to support Adonijah. David reminded Solomon of Joab's killings of Abner and Amasa, two rivals for command of the Army. David therefore recommended that Joab be executed. It is interesting to note that David no longer blamed Joab for killing Absalom. David probably realized that in Absalom's case Joab had been right.

Joab was intelligent enough to realize that he had passed the point of no return with Solomon and therefore fled to the horns of the altar, claiming refuge. He may have been expressing his faith in the God of Israel also. In clinging to the altar, Joab may have been casting himself on the mercy of God, seeing that there was no human mercy left for him. Of course Joab had shown no mercy to his rivals and expected none for himself from Solomon. He was getting back the measure he himself had given. If Joab was truly symbolizing faith in God, then better late than never! Our Lord Jesus hired laborers even at the 11th hour and saved one of the robbers after he had already been nailed to his cross. Matthew 20:1-9; Luke 23:39-43. Some eleventh hour conversions are real! The Lord Jesus will judge whether Joab's was genuine or not.

Another leftover rebel was Shimei, who had cursed David when he fled before Absalom. 2 Samuel 16:5-8. Shimei was a Benjamite who opposed any ruling house in Judah. Solomon did not strike immediately; he agreed with Shimei that Shimei must live in Jerusalem so that he could be watched closely. When Shimei left Jerusalem to retrieve a runaway slave, he had broken parole. Solomon then executed the suspended death sentence.

In Abiathar's case, Solomon banished him from Jerusalem to his family lands rather than execute him in consideration of Abiathar's long loyalty and service to David. However, Abiathar's priesthood was at an end. Solomon appointed a new priest from the appropriate genealogical lineage and elevated Benaiah to command the Army. Thus the succession was secure.

SKETCHES FROM SOLOMON

King Solomon continued the practice of his father of political marriages. He married a princess from Egypt, surely for the purpose of securing his southwestern border from attack. It is highly unlikely that there was any spiritual connection between Solomon and this wife. David had first married Saul's daughter and later had married a daughter of a kingdom northeast of Israel (1 Chronicles 3:2) among his wives. Later Solomon abandoned all restraint and accumulated 700 wives and 300 concubines. In the process he nearly ruined himself and did cause serious damage to the Kingdom of Israel, when one considers the enormous taxation necessary to maintain such a royal establishment. Solomon also followed idolatrous practices in violation of the Third Commandment. Where David had failed, Solomon did far worse. The lack of sexual self-control bore bitter fruit in Israel as it has ever since. 1 Kings 11 gives more detail of what happened when Solomon's sin came to full flower.

One of the consequences of Solomon's sexual sins spelled out in 1 Kings 11 was that any political benefit that came from his original

Egyptian marriage was lost because he obviously mistreated his first wife by taking these other wives. So the ruler of Egypt gave shelter to refugee exiles from Moab who opposed Israeli rule and also sheltered Jeroboam, who later displaced David's dynasty over the Northern Kingdom. But we have jumped ahead of ourselves chronologically in order to follow a thread of consequences across of Solomon's reign of 40 years. Before these consequences really began to be felt there was an era of great blessing and prosperity from God.

Women apart, Solomon started off well in asking for wisdom to rule properly instead of selfishly asking for long life, death for his enemies or wealth. (See 1 Kings 3:5-15) So God gave Solomon the wisdom he sought, along with the other blessings for which he had not asked. The wisdom was first apparent when Solomon was able to distinguish the true from the false claim of motherhood where two women claimed to be the mother of the same child. With no DNA testing available to him, Solomon used psychology to bring the truth to light. 1 Kings 3:16-28.

As Solomon superintended the construction of the Temple, his fame grew, reaching all the way to Sheba, about 1200 miles away. The Queen of Sheba decided that the reports were so unbelievable that she would see for herself. So she took her journey across the deserts to Israel. She was unprepared for what she saw and heard. (1 Kings 10) This was probably the spiritual peak of Solomon's reign. The wisdom involved probably included a major portion of the Proverbs starting with Proverbs 10 and containing Solomon's short nuggets of wisdom. The Song of Solomon may have been composed by this time or partly inspired by the Queen of Sheba, although the beloved female in the Song of Solomon is a hardworking vineyard keeper not initially resembling a queen. Since Ecclesiastes and most of the start of Proverbs sounds like the warnings of an experienced old man who had suffered serious damage from sin, I doubt if these had yet been written when the Queen of Sheba came. However, the Temple and its rich decorations were newly built.

The Queen of Sheba was not only impressed with the buildings and the wealth of the country, but especially with God of Israel. Our Lord Jesus made this plain when He said:

> *The queen of the south shall rise up in the judgment with this generation, and shall condemn it: for she came from the uttermost parts of the earth to hear the wisdom of Solomon; and, behold, a greater than Solomon is here. Matthew 12:42*

So she is among those Gentiles who worshiped the God of Israel when the Israelites of Jesus' own times rejected the Son of God sent from heaven. See Luke 4:27 for a reference to Naaman the Syrian as a Gentile leper who was cleansed when lepers in Israel were left in their disease. The men of Nineveh who repented at Jonah's warning of judgment are still another example. Matthew 12:41. So the Queen of Sheba who met Solomon will live forever with the King greater than Solomon Who came to earth to fulfill all the types which the Temple represented.

Of all the women whom we can identify, the Queen of Sheba probably came closest to being a true spiritual match for Solomon. Of course, she could not marry him with her own realm such a great distance away. It is obvious that with 1000 women total that Solomon, as wise as he was, never had a truly satisfying match with any woman. He got off on the wrong foot with a political marriage that had no spiritual unity to support it and never did have an enduring relationship with a woman so far as the Bible reveals. It is clear from the Song of Solomon that he could conceptualize an ideal relationship through the Holy Spirit but never came close to achieving it. Solomon's warnings in the first 9 chapters of Proverbs and parts of Ecclesiastes sprang from Solomon's own family futility. In this respect Solomon learned truth the hard way through bitter experience. With all his wisdom, his relationships with women were Solomon's glaring weakness. But all of us have weaknesses which can be controlled only through the Holy Spirit and must be put to death through the Spirit (Romans 8:13).

For all of Solomon's wealth, Ecclesiastes especially and also portions of Proverbs point out the emptiness of materialism. Possessions by themselves never satisfy, even though they may be useful tools if used rightly. In modern terms, an ax can be used to cut firewood or to kill a human being. But not even a woodsman can have a relationship with an ax. He would need to relate to people and especially to God. Solomon experienced the emptiness of so many modern wealthy people. Most people who get on the treadmill of materialism never get off. Solomon through the grace of God realized his futility before he was dead and was enabled to sound warnings that are still true approximately 3000 years later. As he summarized in Ecclesiastes:

> *Let us hear the conclusion of the whole matter: Fear God, and keep His commandments: for this is the whole duty of man. For God shall bring every work into judgment, with every secret thing, whether it be good, or whether it be evil. Ecclesiastes 12:13-14.*

So far as the Scriptures present Solomon's life, the visit of the Queen of Sheba seems to have been the peak of his reign. The strain of increasing taxation to maintain a huge royal court, the military to hold Israel's territory and a massive and excessive government building program after the Temple was complete (as the late J. Vernon McGee pointed out) began to corrode the unity of the country. Egypt was no longer friendly and harbored various enemies of Solomon, including Jeroboam who had started as one of Solomon's officials. Above all such considerations, God had already given judgment that Israel would be divided after Solomon's death. The pressures were building in the later years of Solomon's reign and exploded shortly after his death.

The eighty years of the combined reigns of David and Solomon were years of historic progress even considering the sins of both kings. When Saul had died, Israel was still internally divided and technologically inferior to the Philistines. The Ark of the Covenant was ignored after the Philistines returned it on a cart. While Psalm 90, the book of Job and the five Books of the Law had been written with perhaps Joshua and Judges, little of the Bible was available in written form to the common people. Israel was on the defensive against most of its enemies even though its internal lines of communication made it difficult for her enemies to coordinate their attacks. Most people were poor.

By the time that Solomon died, the majority of the Book of Psalms had been composed with the Song of Solomon, Ecclesiastes and virtually all of Proverbs. The royal archives which later formed the basis for the books of 1 & 2 Samuel, 1 & 2 Kings and 1 & 2 Chronicles were started. Israel had been free of war for over 40 years. Its trade was widespread and booming to the point that silver was not even considered valuable. Military security was excellent. The Temple had been constructed and the priesthood reorganized for Temple worship and praise. A rough comparison might be the progress in the United States between the ratification of the Constituton in 1789 and the completion of the first transcontinental railroad in 1869, although the United States certainly added more territory during this 80-year period than did Israel under the reign of David and Solomon. There had been as yet nothing comparable to the Civil War in America in Israel by the time of Solomon's death, although the tribe of Benjamin had been almost wiped out during the times of the Judges centuries before. (Judges 19-21) Although few would have expected it, much of this progress was to be swiftly undone by human folly -- although this folly and its consequences were permitted to operate through divine sovereign appointment.

THE TAX REVOLT -- CA 920 BC -- 1 Kings 11-12

Initially, the entire nation was going to accept Rehoboam as King upon Solomon's death. Solomon's older, experienced advisors were aware of troubles that were brewing because of excess taxation. Given what we know about modern politics, Solomon was right when he said that *"there is no new thing under the sun."* Ecclesiastes 1:9. The consequences of excess taxation were known to the experienced government leaders in Solomon's day, nearly 3000 years ago. Solomon's outgoing advisors warned Rehoboam that tax cuts were necessary, with the necessary consequence that reductions in government spending would be necessary. As we have seen, one sensible place to cut would have been the number of wives and concubines supported by the Crown. One wife, the Queen, should have been enough. No doubt that additional government building could have been curtailed and other waste reduced.

But Rehoboam's own contemporaries were arrogant "know-it-alls" who had no time to listen to more experienced advice. They advised Rehoboam to warn that he would increase taxes further and that the people would have to like it. Rehoboam took their foolish advice, with the result that most of Israel revolted and selected Jeroboam -- Solomon's renegade official -- as their king instead of Rehoboam. God was displeased with Israel and permitted this division to take place for His good reasons, including judging the entire nation for its disloyalty to Him. But if we want to learn political right from wrong by the study of Biblical history, we should focus on Rehoboam's tragic errors to learn from them. *"Now all these things happened to them as examples, and they were written for our admonition, upon whom the ends of the ages have come."* 1 Corinthians 10:11.

While we must be critical of Rehoboam's taxation policies and his wives and concubines (2 Chronicles 11:18-21), Rehoboam did one praiseworthy thing -- he stopped his planned campaign to conquer the Northern Kingdom by force when he realized that God was ordering him to let the Northern Kingdom go. 1 Kings 12:23-24. This belated obedience does distinguish Rehoboam from Saul, who kept on chasing David after he twice admitted that David was more righteous that he himself and that David would be his successor. There is no spiritual sense in beating one's head against a wall that God has erected. Even for a determined person, there are times that God insists that we give up an objective that is not His plan.

The raid by Shishak of Egypt (2 Chronicles 12) against Judah was the logical outcome of Egypt's enmity which started when Solomon began to ignore his Egyptian wife. Jeroboam, who had been an exile in Egypt's court, would have expected to have started with more friendly relations with Egypt. The raid was aimed at Judah first, but also at the Northern Kingdom despite the previous friendship between Shishak and Jeroboam. Shishak took the gold shields that Solomon had made and much other wealth. Rehoboam could not replace them with gold, so he replaced them with cheaper bronze instead. They still looked good although they were no match for the originals. However, because Rehoboam humbled himself before God the raid did little long-term damage even though it was shameful at the moment. Egypt was not able to reestablish effective control over either Israeli kingdom even with the division between them, although Egypt did improve its trade position and ease its fears of an invasion from Israel.

Rehoboam's opposite number Jeroboam in the Northern Kingdom showed that he trusted in political policy rather than in God very early in his reign when facing the problem of the required sacrifices at the Temple, which was in territory controlled by Judah. He created a substitute priesthood for the Levites whom God had ordained to be priests. He also raised up two idols similar to those that Aaron had made centuries before in order to dissuade citizens of the Northern Kingdom from going to Jerusalem for the sacrifices. One was at Dan and the other at Bethel. Many Levites fled south to Judah, along with others who feared God and could not stomach idol-worship in violation of the Third Commandment. Thus a sprinkling of the Northern Tribes came to live in the Southern Kingdom. 2 Chronicles 11:13-17.

Jeroboam's creation of a state religion as a substitute to the worship ordained by God through Moses, David and Solomon had enduring consequences which persisted to the days of Jesus Christ in the form of the division between the Jews and the Samaritans. (See John 4 for more detail of the division in Jesus' day.) The Samaritan worship was different from the worship instituted by Jeroboam, but in one form or another there was a religious difference between Jerusalem and much of northern Israel from the time of Jeroboam until the destruction in Israel of all forms of Jewish-derived worship and government during the Jewish War from 66-70 AD. Even today there are less than 1000 people who claim descent from the Samaritans in the north of Israel.

Jeroboam also stands as an example of human ingrates who are raised up by God but do not thank Him for it. Jeroboam was informed of his coming kingship by a prophet of God, so he was aware that he did not earn this position for himself. 1 Kings 11:26-40. Jeroboam knew also that two tribes including Judah would continue to be ruled by the House of David. Yet Jeroboam built idols in direct violation of the Third Commandment. Further, Jeroboam attacked Judah, especially during the brief reign of Abijah. (2 Chronicles 13) Abijah tried to persuade Jeroboam and the Northern Kingdom to live in peace and to return to the faith of the God of all Israel, but Jeroboam would have none of it even though he knew from God's prophet that Kingdom of Judah would remain under David's descendants. The result was a needless slaughter of more than half of the army of the Northern Kingdom. After this, the Northern Kingdom had no humanly realistic hope of conquering the remaining Davidic Kingdom in Judah, with a result that under future kings wars between Judah and the Northern Kingdom were less frequent and there was even a period of alliance. However, the alliance was to cause its own troubles.

King Abijah was not loyal to God as was King David at least at the start of his reign. But he did have his shining moment during his speech recorded in 2 Chronicles 13 in which he proclaimed faith in the God of Israel. When Israel would not heed his call for peace and mutual faith in the God of Israel, God struck the armies of Jeroboam. Abijah is another example of a man who changed course relatively late in life. In later history King Manasseh of Judah is a good though extreme example of a conversion late in life. If you have made a thorough mess of your life but you're still breathing, God still calls on you to repent and salvage spiritually what time you have left on earth.

In contrast to Abijah, we should have no doubt as to the spiritual end of Jeroboam and of his family. Baasha of Issachar raised a military revolt against the Nadab the son of Jeroboam while Nadab was besieging a town held by the Philistines. Baasha struck down Nadab to take the throne of the Northern Kingdom himself. 1 Kings 15:27-29. He also exterminated Jeroboam's family in order to leave no family member who would seek revenge. God allowed this to fulfill the words of His prophet. However, the substitution of Baasha for Nadab did not improve the loyalty of the Northern Kingdom toward God, nor did it result in any immediate improvement of diplomatic relations between Judah and the Northern Kingdom.

Further internal turmoil soon followed in the Northern Kingdom. For more detail, read 1 Kings 16, which pinpoints the fact that Baasha continued with Jeroboam's worship of the calves as the cause. Baasha died and one of his military commanders revolted against Baasha's son two years later. Zimri destroyed the family of Baasha but in turn was destroyed by Omri, who became king after defeating still another rival. Omri was able to form a stable regime and also built Samaria as a capital and fortress. To that extent there was temporary improvement in the Northern Kingdom, but Omri's son Ahab was one of the worst kings any ancient nation ever had even though Ahab had considerable military and diplomatic talent.

As 1 Kings 16:29-34 and chapters 17-19 record, Ahab went back to the ancient practice of a political marriage and married Jezebel of Sidon, who was a worshipper of Baal, an idol. Ahab participated in the expanded idolatry. At this God Himself intervened by raising up Elijah the prophet and also by imposing a drought on the Northern Kingdom for over 3 years. Elijah proclaimed that there would be no rain except at his word and then disappeared to the Brook Cherith, east of the Jordan. Ravens fed Elijah by miracle. As day after cloudless day passed, Ahab sought for Elijah but had no clue where to find him. When the brook dried up, God sent Elijah from the east of Israel to a widow of Zarephath, northwest of Israel and outside of Ahab's jurisdiction. The widow was preparing her last meal for herself and her son when Elijah arrived. When Elijah asked for a share, she consented. While the oil and flour did not rise and fill their containers, they never ran out during the drought. God kept supplying bit by bit. As David said, *I have been young and now am old, yet I have not seen the righteous forsaken nor his descendants begging bread.* Psalm 37:25. In the meantime, even the king had trouble finding water for his livestock.

The evil of the Northern Kingdom as time went on was not confined to worship of idols. It later included human sacrifice of babies (2 Kings 17:13-18), witchcraft and assorted other evils forbidden by the Law of Moses. The major difference between ancient human sacrifice and modern abortion is only one of timing: children today are murdered in the womb while in ancient times they were sacrificed after birth. Today's technology may appear more refined but the murderous result is the same. Athaliah, a daughter of Ahab who eventually was the temporary ruler in Judah, slaughtered all the children descended from David (except one whom she missed) in order to hold power. The one she missed became the rallying point for her overthrow. This is found in 2 Kings 11; we will go into more detail later after we return to Elijah.

Finally the day came when God sent Elijah back to Israel. On the one hand, Ahab hated Elijah and probably wanted to kill him out of hand. On the other, Ahab was finally convinced that somehow Elijah held the key to unlock the drought and that killing Elijah would make matters worse. In any case it was not Elijah's time to die and he knew it, so he had no fear of Ahab. Quickly the antagonists agreed to a trial in the nature of a scientific experiment. Both parties would sacrifice a bull upon a wooden altar but not light a fire. Whoever answered by sending fire from heaven is the true God. There were four logically possible outcomes:

1) The atheist would answer that nobody would answer by fire because no God exists;

2) The polytheist would be prepared to entertain the idea that both Baal and the God of Israel and other gods as well have divine powers, so that both may have been able to answer by fire;

3) The believer in Baal believed that Baal was the only god and that he would answer by fire;

4) Elijah and the faithful of Israel believed in the First Commandment (*"You shall have no other gods before Me."*) and that He is the only real and true God. Isaiah summarized this: *"Thus says the Lord, the King of Israel, and his Redeemer, the Lord of Hosts: 'I am the First and I am the Last; besides Me there is no God.'"* Isaiah 44:6. Moses said in Deuteronomy 4:39, *"The Lord Himself is God in heaven above and on the earth beneath; there is no other."* Thus the God of Israel alone would answer by fire. All of Isaiah 44 is an extended exposition of this idea.

So the experiment was run upon Mount Carmel. The prophets and priests of Baal went first, with no result. Elijah derided them with sarcasm.

To prove their devotion to their imaginary god, the priests of Baal cut themselves to the point of drawing blood and leaped on the altar, offering themselves as a human sacrifice on top of the altar if only Baal would answer by fire.

At the time of the evening sacrifice, Elijah took center stage. He was so full of faith that he ordered the altar and the sacrifice soaked with precious, scarce water three times -- probably to protect the people nearest the altar from being burnt by the fire from heaven that Elijah was sure would come. A trench was dug to contain the water as it drained off the altar. There is a lesson here: if you are praying to God, you need to prepare yourself for His answer. Elijah also reminded the people of the underlying unity of Israel by having 12 stones at the altar, signifying the 12 tribes as one entity even though their political rule was divided. Then Elijah prayed. The God of Israel answered by fire! It was so intense that all of the water that was around the protective trench around the altar was evaporated as the sacrifice and the altar were consumed. The God of Israel was proved to be God alone!

Then Elijah prayed for rain to end the drought. God did not answer instantaneously. Elijah sent a boy to look seven times -- on the seventh look he saw a tiny cloud. That was enough for Elijah to know that the rain was coming. Indeed it did in torrents. Just as prophesied, the drought was broken at the word of Elijah, the prophet of God. The same God Who had answered by fire this time answered by water.

When the people saw God answer by fire from heaven, they took the false prophets of Baal and killed them out of hand.

While Ahab was somewhat moved temporarily by this dramatic demonstration of the power of God, Jezebel did not budge an inch from her worship of Baal and her fleshly ways. The depth of her hatred for the ways of God will be more clearly in focus later in the history, but her reaction to the news of the God of Israel's answering by fire was to threaten Elijah's life. Since I have written in more detail in my previous book of Elijah's spiritual battle (Endurance published by Trafford Press), I will bypass that now in order to keep to the historical flow. Elijah fled to Beersheba, held by Judah instead of the Northern Kingdom.

While Elijah was completing his ministry and laying the foundation for the ministry of his successor Elisha, Jezebel was showing her skill at lying and intrigue. (1 Kings 21) Ahab wanted to buy Naboth's vineyard, but Naboth would not sell because it was agricultural land which could not be sold permanently under the Law of Jubilee given by Moses. Ahab was downcast, but Jezebel ordered local officials to frame Naboth on a charge of blaspheming God. This was done by bribing two false witnesses. Despite the hypocrisy of Jezebel of all people misusing the law against blaspheming the name of God, the officials carried out her plan and had Naboth executed on a trumped-up charge of blasphemy. Jezebel then presented her husband Ahab with the vineyard he wanted. But God was angry. Elijah confronted Ahab and warned that the dogs would lick his blood in that vineyard and that Jezebel's body would be eaten by wild dogs. Ahab temporarily humbled himself, so that God postponed the execution of the extermination of Ahab's family until after his death. Instead He allowed Ahab to die in battle under most unusual circumstances.

No doubt that both the Northern and Southern Kingdoms were sick of the casualties that mounted during their wars against each other. During the lifetimes of Rehoboam and Jeroboam, the Northern Kingdom was stronger, although not decisively so. As time passed, the balance shifted toward the Southern Kingdom, although it continued that neither side had decisive superiority over the other. As one reads on in 1 Kings, one notes that the border tends to shift northward and that Abijah was able to penetrate into the hill country originally allotted to Ephraim in Joshua's time. In the long term, Judah was advancing into Israel's territory. Also, the power of Syria was rising to the northeast of Israel, as reflected in the texts and in the prophecy of Elijah. This trend continues as one reads the first portion of 2 Kings. Ahab missed a chance to destroy the rising power of Syria as recorded in 1 Kings 20, similar to the way in which Saul had failed to carry out God's instructions concerning the Amalekites.

Following Abijam in Judah were Asa and Jehoshaphat, both better kings than normal. Jehoshaphat especially was devout in his worship of the God of Israel. (2 Chronicles 16 & 17) Jehoshapat escaped one political coalition against him by sending the choir to praise God ahead of his army. Jehoshaphat's enemies turned on each other so that Judah did not have to fight a battle at all. (2 Chronicles 20) Jehoshaphat sought a means to end the fighting between Judah and Israel and hit on a marriage of Ahab's daughter Athaliah with his son the Crown Prince Ahaziah. Once again a political marriage without spiritual foundation enters the picture. Geopolitically, Jehoshaphat may have preferred dealing with Israel to facing a powerful Syria. There were sensible reasons for this -- both the Northern and Southern Kingdom spoke the same language and there were prophets of God in both places. Asa his father once used Syria to remove a Northern Kingdom threat to Judah, but in the meantime Syria had become more dangerous and the Northern Kingdom less so. Perhaps Jehoshaphat looked forward to reuniting the kingdoms by means of the arranged marriage. In pursuing this plan, Jehoshaphat allied with Ahab to fight Syria. For more detail, read 2 Chronicles 18-19.

Before the battle, the spiritual differences between Jehoshaphat and Ahab became clear. Jehoshaphat wanted to inquire of the Lord; Ahab knew full well that the Lord was in the process of judging him. (1 Kings 22) At Jehoshaphat's insistence Ahab called for Micaiah, the prophet of the Lord. Micaiah predicted Ahab's death -- Ahab commanded Micaiah to be put in prison on short rations. Moreover, Ahab was scared enough of Micaiah's prediction that he disguised himself while Jehoshaphat was obviously a king during the battle. The Syrian plan was to kill Ahab.

At first they mistook Jehoshaphat for Ahab and attacked Jehoshaphat; when they realized their mistake, they broke off that attack. Like the Norman archer at the Battle of Hastings in 1066 that decided the throne of England, a Syrian fired an arrow without a specific target. The Norman's arrow nailed Harold in his right eye, killing him and raising William the Conqueror to the throne. The Syrian's arrow struck between the joints of Ahab's armor and gave him a fatal chest wound. As Elijah said, Ahab died from his wound and the blood in the chariot was washed out in what had been Naboth's vineyard. The dogs licked the blood.

There is a pointed lesson here. Events that appear random to human eyes remain under God's control and sometimes cause consequences beyond any human expectations. So it was with both the Norman arrow that killed Harold and with the Syrian arrow that killed Ahab. With Ahab's death his son Ahaziah came to rule, although Queen Mother Jezebel still retained considerable power. But he died of an "accidental" fall two years later, and Jehoram -- presumably another son of Ahab -- succeeded him. This Jehoram is not to be confused with King Jehoram of Judah, son and successor of Jehoshaphat. It was Jehoram of Judah who was married to Athaliah -- from this marriage came Ahaziah (not to be confused with the deceased Ahaziah, son of Ahab), the future King of Judah. God wove these strands together to give us an unforgettable picture of His hatred for sin where there is no repentance.

I will jump ahead of strict time sequence to follow through on the consequences of the attempt by Jehoshaphat to rejoin two kingdoms with no underlying spiritual unity. Moral comment on this period can be found in some of the Shorter Prophets, whose work we shall review in greater detail later. One could apply the same lesson to a marriage also

-- there must be spiritual unity for any marriage to work well. With Elijah now having been raptured to God without death, Elisha told one of his assistants to search out Jehu, a chariot commander. Elisha probably could not travel himself both because he was ill and because secrecy was essential. Jehu would be the rough equivalent of a tank battalion commander today. God's commission was to exterminate the family of Ahab, as Elijah had prophesied. Jehu himself would become King of Israel.

Jehu needed no further prompting. He already had a reputation as a hard-driving commander whose approach was recognizable because of the speedy handling of his own chariot. He swiftly dispatched Jehoram (or Joram) of Israel, who had been wounded fighting the Syrians. Ahaziah of Judah was visiting his relative Jehoram and tried to resist Jehu. For that reason Ahaziah and his cousins who had accompanied him died in the skirmish. This left no adult male to rule in Jerusalem, so Athaliah the Queen Mother (but not of the line of David) took power herself and killed all the royal offspring she could find. But she missed one who was hidden in the Temple.

While Athaliah was usurping power in Judah, Jehu turned on the two remaining sources of resistance to his rule in Israel: Queen Mother Jezebel and the other children of Ahab. (2 Kings 9) When he turned on Jezebel, Jezebel tried to deflect him with feminine attractions. She made herself up and looked out the window and challenged Jehu with the memory of Zimri, who overthrew Baasha but then was killed himself. But Jehu was too focused on his mission to be allured by Jezebel's charms. If one is seeking a somewhat comparable modern personality to Jehu, one may try General Sheridan of the Union Army during the Civil War or General Patton during World War 2. There were also two or three castrated servants present who favored the Lord over Baal or at least thought it prudent to say so with Jehu on the scene. Because of the mutilation performed on them as children, they too were immune to Jezebel's charms. They threw

Jezebel out the window. Jehu then drove his horses over Jezebel. As they were accustomed to trampling fallen enemy soldiers, this was routine for the horses. Jezebel, who had been a princess, a queen and then a queen mother, began to feel with the horses' hooves the measure of punishment that will bring her agony forever. Like the rich man in Luke 16:25, the words of our Lord Jesus apply to Jezebel: *"... remember that in your lifetime you received your good things, ... but now ... you are tormented."*

As a further illustration of Jehu's character as an ancient Terminator, Jehu sat down to dinner after dispatching Jezebel. From what the Scriptures say, Jehu felt that he had done a good day's work. He had no sense of mourning for Jezebel. By the time he remembered that Jezebel should be buried as a king's daughter for diplomatic reasons having to do with relations with neighboring Tyre and Sidon, it was too late. The wild dogs had already eaten the body as a further sign to us of the drastic divine punishment inflicted on Jezebel.

Jezebel is an example of wanton women in any time and place. They may often get their way at first with a combination of cleverness and charm. Jezebel tried that same approach to the very end of her life. But in the end such women --and men-- are judged if they do not repent. As confirmation, consider the word of the Lord Jesus in Revelation 2:20-23 concerning a latter-day Jezebel in Thyatira:

> *Nevertheless I have a few things against you, because you allow that woman Jezebel, who calls herself a prophetess, to teach and seduce My servants to commit sexual immorality and eat things sacrificed to idols. And I gave her time to repent of her sexual immorality, and she did not repent. Indeed I will cast her into a sickbed, and those who commit adultery with her into great tribulation, unless they repent of their deeds. I will kill her children with death, and all the churches shall know that I am He who searches the minds and hearts. And I will give to each one of you according to your works.*

Jehu then turned to the city where Ahab's children were housed. The elders of the city, rather than fight, beheaded all of them and sent the heads in baskets to Jehu. (2 Kings 10) With that Jehu was securely in control. To uproot Baal worship, then he pretended to worship Baal and attracted the leading Baal worshipers into a pavilion, which Jehu then burned on top of them. On a larger scale, this would have been like the scene in The Patriot when the fictitious British Colonel Tavington ordered the burning of the church with the villagers locked inside. So Jehu did uproot Baalism. The picture of the burning pavilion with the Baal worshippers inside is a freeze frame foreshadowing the Lake of Fire tormenting both people and angels, including Satan. But Jehu did not remove Jeroboam's idols from Dan and Bethel, so neither he nor Israel followed the Lord faithfully.

Jehu does picture one portion of the coming mission of our Lord Jesus Christ. The picture that Jehu presents is not a full, rounded picture of Christ, but rather a one-dimensional picture of one portion of Jesus' character -- His wrath. Rarely did the world see His wrath when Jesus first came to earth -- His mission was to die in order to pay for the sins of His people and rise from the dead. Jesus did clear the moneychangers from the Temple twice. John 2:14-17; Matthew 21:12-13. Jesus did say that Jewish leaders of his time would *die in [their] sins.* John 8:24. Twice Jesus called religious leaders *"vipers."* Matthew 12:34, 23:33. When His disciples tried to shoo little children away from Jesus, He became very angry. Mark 10:13-14. But the predominant theme of our Lord's life in a human body like ours was love. When Jesus comes to earth the second time, the immediate consequence is the death of the armies confronting Him. The Beast and the False Prophet are thrown alive into the Lake of Fire. Revelation 19:15-21, compare Ezekiel 39. In Matthew 25:41 our Lord Jesus portrayed Himself as commanding human beings to depart from Him into the Lake of Fire. Jehu's burning of the Baal-worshipers in the pavilion is a miniature illustration of the ultimate destiny of unbelievers when the Lord returns to earth. They also will find themselves surrounded and indeed immersed in fire.

When our Lord (Luke 4:16-19) in the synagogue quoted Isaiah 61:1-2, He stopped His reading with *"the acceptable year of our Lord."* When He returns, it will be the next phrase, *"the day of vengeance of our God."* The vengeance of Jehu upon Jezebel, upon the house of Ahab and upon Baal worshippers is a miniature of the vengeance of Jesus Christ upon all unbelievers when He returns to the earth. We cannot worship a distorted, imaginary concept of Christ containing solely His love or solely His wrath. We need to try to embrace both even though we can never fully succeed. Jehu shows nothing of His love but does give a bold, clear image of His wrath. The history of Elijah, Elisha, Ahab, Jezebel and Jehu has been preserved for our instruction.

I remember during my childhood close to 50 years ago the Limelighters in their old phonograph record *Makin' A Joyful Noise* singing an old spiritual:

When Judgment Day is drawin' nigh

Refrain: Where shall I be?

When God the works of man shall try

Refrain: Where shall I be?

When east and west the fires shall roll

Refrain: Where shall I be?

How will it be with my poor soul?

Refrain: Where shall I be?

Chorus: Lord tell me "Where shall I be when that great trumpet sounds?

Where shall I be when it sounds so loud?

It sounds so loud as to wake up the dead!

Where shall I be when it sounds?"

When heaven and earth as one big scroll

Refrain: Where shall I be?

Shall from His earthly presence roll

Refrain: Where shall I be?

When all the saints redeemed shall stand

Refrain: Where shall I be?

Forever blessed at God's right hand

Refrain: Where shall I be?

Through the Lord Jesus you can know the answer -- there is absolutely no need for guesswork. As John wrote in 1 John 5:13: *"These things I have written to you who believe in the name of the Son of God, that you may know that you have eternal life, and that you may continue to believe in the name of the Son of God.."*

Let us now turn back to Judah where Athaliah was in charge. She believed that all of the royal seed of Judah is now dead and claimed to rule in her own right. In truth, although Athaliah may not have known it, this was an attempt by Satan to prevent the coming of the Messiah by killing all of royal line of David, from whom Christ must come by prophecy in 2 Samuel 7. But Athaliah had missed one of the children, who was being raised in hiding in the Temple precincts. The high priest Jehoiada bided his time and then organized his *coup d'etat* carefully. Athaliah sealed her fate when she tried to enter the Temple contrary to the Law -- she was not even Jewish. She was killed out of hand. Then Joash, age 7, took the throne, but Jehoiada was the real power behind the throne. 2 Chronicles 23-24.

This narrow escape for the house of Judah started when Jehoshaphat, in his search for peace, tried to make an alliance without a spiritual basis. It was probably right to seek a way to end the fighting between Judah and Israel, but marrying the two royal families went entirely too far. Because of this marriage Athaliah was in a strategic position to kill so many children in reaction to the death of her own son in battle with Jehu. Choosing evil friends or marriage partners can have severe consequences. Proverbs 21:19, 22:24-25; 1 Corinthians 15:33. But even with this error by Jehoshaphat,

Thomas D. Logie

God preserved the line of David while destroying the lines of all of Israel's kings in due course. The line of David climaxes with Jesus Christ.

Jehu's line ruled Israel to its fourth generation. During this time, Syria and then Assyria were the chief threats to Israel. The growth of Assyrian power was more and more ominous for Israel. In military terms, Israel might be able to match up against Syria, but Assyria was growing too strong for Israel to handle. Israel's kings were not inclined to ask God for help as a rule. An example is found in 2 Kings 6:8-7:20, where Elisha the prophet was trapped inside the capital of the Northern Kingdom by a surrounding Syrian army. At this stage God was still giving Israel some protection, but the text shows that the rulers did not believe in or rely on God. But gradually God withdrew His protection from the Northern Kingdom. The Southern Kingdom of Judah also underwent a supreme trial during the reign of Hezekiah, another great and godly king. When Hezekiah took the throne of Judah, the Northern Kingdom was on its last legs and was finally wiped out by the Assyrians in 722 or 721 BC. Hezekiah was in the sixth year of his reign. Most of the population was deported to other parts of the Assyrian Empire, and most of their descendants have never to this date returned to the Promised Land. There was a minority that either escaped to Judah during the fighting or was able to escape the forced march to exile and slip back into the land. (For a comparable modern event, we know of a few German prisoners at the close of World War 2 who similarly escaped Russian captivity in Eastern Europe and successfully hid when most were marched into the Russian gulag.) The Scriptures do reflect that Hezekiah increased his influence over portions of the Northern Kingdom, especially the central hills, after the fall of Samaria. A summary of the reasons for the collapse of the Northern Kingdom is found in 2 Kings 18:12: *"[T]hey did not obey the voice of the Lord their God, but transgressed His covenant and all that Moses the servant of the Lord had commanded; and they would neither hear nor do them."*

In the meantime, while the Northern Kingdom was gradually falling apart, King Uzziah of Judah had flourished under the protection of God, but like both David and Solomon Uzziah stumbled badly in his prosperity (2 Kings 15 uses his other name Azariah; 2 Chronicles 26). In his case King Uzziah decided that he would participate in the priestly worship that God had committed to the tribe of Levi since Moses' time. For a similar offense God had struck dead by fire from heaven 250 rebels in Numbers 16. In Uzziah's case the punishment was leprosy -- symbolic of persistent sin -- rather than instant death. Not only could Uzziah no longer worship at the Temple at all, he and his retinue had to live isolated from the rest of society from this time until his death. Uzziah's son had to take over the public functions of royalty. *"Let he who thinks he stands take heed lest he fall."* 1 Corinthians 10:12.

Isaiah's call to the ministry came during King Uzziah's reign, and his ministry flourished during the reign of King Hezekiah. Isaiah is best known for his prophesies of the coming of the Messiah, but he was also Hezekiah's advisor when Assyria finally geared up to attack Judah about 20 years after its conquest of the Northern Kingdom. Isaiah 36-37 was his account of the crisis and Isaiah 38-39 was his account of its aftermath.

Hezekiah at first bought time by paying tribute to Assyria, but this was no permanent solution. Assyria, like other tyrants ancient and modern, would be satisfied with nothing less than total domination. Neville Chamberlain and the British of the 1930s had to learn this lesson to their sorrow when he found that they could not appease Hitler; Churchill knew better. A new Assyrian king finally launched its steamroller against a greatly outnumbered Judah. The territory north and west of Jerusalem was ravaged and the Assyrians closed on Jerusalem for the kill. Their spokesman was so insolent toward God that Hezekiah was aroused to pray in the Temple, and God granted Hezekiah's prayer by killing the entire

Assyrian army at one stroke. This was not a matter of military force but was a miracle.

Some effort has been made to explain this as a consequence of Hezekiah's diversion of water into Jerusalem from springs outside the city. The work was done in haste by two teams starting from opposite directions. In the late 1800s, a young Arab boy stumbled upon the tunnel that Hezekiah dug, and Turkish authorities found the inscription and have kept it in Istanbul. This was a prudent measure to take for Jerusalem's defense. There is a lesson to be learned: when we pray to God, we should do what we can to work towards the answer we desire. But we should never delude ourselves into thinking that our effort will ever be enough. In this case God's answer was miraculous. The rediscovery of this tunnel should also reinforce our confidence in the historical truth of God's Word. 2 Kings 20:20; 2 Chronicles 32:30.

Assyria never attacked Judah again with full force because it became embroiled with Babylonian enemies far to the east. This is the background of Hezekiah's imprudent revelations to the Babylonian diplomats. Hezekiah viewed them as friends against his mortal enemy Assyria, little realizing that eventually it would be the Babylonians who would take Judah captive. Perhaps this was the first time that the new Babylonian state realized how rich a target Judah would eventually be for Babylon. The time for the prophecy to be fulfilled about Babylonian domination was almost a century into the future. 2 Kings 20:12-19.

Hezekiah was childless at this point when God extended his life 15 years in response to his prayer. 2 Kings 20:1-11. During this time Hezekiah did have a son, but he grew into the most evil king Judah had ever had. Manasseh, Hezekiah's son, probably was worse than Ahab had been in Israel. His reign is summarized in 2 Chronicles 33 and in 2 Kings 21. Manasseh went to the point of child sacrifice. Like Saul at the end of his life, Manasseh consulted a medium. He worshipped foreign gods even in the Temple area. The Book of Hebrews (11:37) mentions that a prophet was sawed in half -- according to Hebrew tradition this would have been Isaiah suffering martyrdom under Manasseh. Eventually God caused Manasseh to be imprisoned by the Assyrians, and in their jail he repented late in life. God caused Manasseh to be released and restored. As one continues in the history, it is clear that Amon the son of Manasseh was shaped by his father's evil reign, but that Josiah, Amon's son, first came to understanding during Manasseh's late period of repentance and was influenced by that repentance.

Is is really true that Isaiah and Manasseh will co-exist in heaven after Manasseh had Isaiah sawed in half with a bucksaw? Yes! Not only will they co-exist, but they will live together with God in forgiveness and fellowship. At Isaiah's death the demonstration of the forgiveness of God had not yet reached its highest expression of His Son Jesus Christ becoming the permanent Passover atonement for our sins. But both David and Isaiah himself had so prophesied (for example, Psalms 22, 32, 38 and 51 and Isaiah 1:18 and all of Isaiah 53). The forgiveness of God through the blood of Jesus Christ can bridge the widest enmity. Isaiah and Manasseh is one example. Jesus Christ can and does bridge gaps as between the Hatfields and the McCoys, between Argentina and Chile, between Jew and Samaritan in New Testament times, and between Jew and Arab today.

What about you personally? Most likely you do not have innocent blood on your hands as Manasseh did. In fact, Isaiah was only one of many victims of Manasseh who were killed unjustly. In this sense Manasseh might be comparable to Stalin in much of his reign, although Stalin was an atheist where Manasseh worshipped idols. Consider the enormity and variety of Manasseh's sins as expressed in 2 Kings 21:2-9, 16:

> *And he did evil in the sight of the Lord, according to the abominations*
> *of the nations whom the Lord had cast out before the children of*

Israel. For he rebuilt the high places which Hezekiah his father had destroyed; he raised up altars for Baal, and made a wooden image, as Ahab king of Israel had done; and he worshiped all the host of heaven and served them. He also built altars in the house of the Lord, of which the Lord had said, "In Jerusalem I will put My name." And he built altars for all the host of heaven in the two courts of the house of the Lord. Also he made his son pass through the fire, practiced soothsaying, used witchcraft, and consulted spiritists and mediums. He did much evil in the sight of the Lord, to provoke Him to anger. He even set a carved image of Asherah that he had made, in the house of which the Lord had said to David and to Solomon his son, "In this house and in Jerusalem, which I have chosen out of all the tribes of Israel, I will put My name forever; and I will not make the feet of Israel wander anymore from the land which I gave their fathers-only if they are careful to do according to all that I have commanded them, and according to all the law that My servant Moses commanded them." But they paid no attention, and Manasseh seduced them to do more evil than the nations whom the Lord had destroyed before the children of Israel.

Moreover Manasseh shed very much innocent blood, till he had filled Jerusalem from one end to another, besides his sin by which he made Judah sin, in doing evil in the sight of the Lord.

As much as any single man, Manassah was responsible for the apostasy of Judah and the wrath of God that followed with all its human misery. And yet 2 Chronicles 33:11-20 records Manasseh's repentance and God's forgiveness. Do you think that you have done too much evil to be forgiven? Think again! There are very few that have been more evil than Manasseh. The Apostle Paul was an accessory to the murder of Stephen before his salvation. One of the robbers (not just a pickpocket or a thief by stealth, but a violent man who wielded a killing knife) crucified with our Lord Jesus was forgiven. Rahab in Joshua's time was anything but a respectable woman. Our Lord Jesus forgave more than one immoral woman personally. (John 8:1-11, Luke 7:36-50) The very Japanese squadron leader who led the first aerial attack on Pearl Harbor became a well-known Christian after World War 2 was over, testifying to the Gospel to the people of Japan. If you have any concern for your soul, there is hope for you. Humble yourself before the Lord, as Manasseh did, and He can and will forgive you. As James said, *"Humble yourselves in the sight of the Lord, and He will lift you up."* James 4:10.

Perhaps you are not like Manasseh and think that you are more like Isaiah. The rich young ruler claimed that he had kept the Commandments from his youth into his adulthood. Luke 18:21. In truth, he was in trouble with the Tenth Commandment. The Apostle Paul was the same -- he was "blameless" as to the righteousness which is of the Law (Philippians 3:6) but in all kinds of trouble when it came to covetousness. Romans 7:7-10. The Law defines sin but also stirs up our innate desire to sin. *"All have sinned and have come short of the glory of God."* Romans 3:23. Isaiah agrees. He was called initially as a prophet during the reign of Uzziah (Isaiah 1:1) and in the year that King Uzziah died (Isaiah 6:1) he saw his great vision of God and heaven. Though he was a prophet, Isaiah cried out (Isaiah 6:5), *"Woe is me, for I am undone! Because I am a man of unclean lips, and I dwell in the midst of a people of unclean lips; For my eyes have seen the King, the Lord of Hosts."* John the Baptist, the greatest of all men partaking of the nature of Adam, said that he was not worthy even to loose the sandal of Jesus Christ, the Son of God. John 1:27. So whether we have been grossly wicked and have blood on our hands like Manasseh, or whether we think that we have served God, we still must repent and humble ourselves before God. While the differences between men like Manasseh and men like Isaiah are significant in terms of human history, those differences are dwarfed by the immense differences between the greatest sinful human beings and Jesus Christ, Who knew no sin. 2 Corinthians 5:21. The best of us must still repent of our sins and humble ourselves before God as Manasseh did, even if our particular sins are very different from those of King Manasseh.

Manasseh died when Josiah was six years old; Josiah's father Amon died when Josiah was eight. Like Nero of Rome, Amon was killed by his own guard, which suggests to me that Amon would have been awful had he lived a normal life span. But Josiah followed in the direction of Manasseh's late repentance and gave Israel one last great king with an opportunity for the people to repent. Jeremiah and Zephaniah ministered during Josiah's reign. Just because King Josiah was personally a godly king does not mean that most of the people followed his faith from their hearts. To the contrary, many continued in their own evil ways even under a good king and even in the face of the renewed teaching of the Law. This continued spiritual rebellion confirmed the prophets' diagnosis of the malignant heart of mankind (for example, Jeremiah 17:9 as a summary and Jeremiah 5 as a more extended treatment). There is the promise of restoration and the reaffirmation of the Davidic Covenant with its promises of the Messiah in Jeremiah 30-33, but exile had to come first. Indeed it did for Judah as well as the Northern Kingdom after Josiah's death resisting an Egyptian effort to prop up a failing Assyria against a resurgent Babylon. Babylon was becoming powerful enough to engulf all the countries of the Middle East, including all of Israel and even most of Egypt. In fact, a large proportion of the descendants of Judah remained in Jewish communities in Babylonian territory (roughly speaking, Syria, Iraq and Iran in modern terms) or migrated within areas controlled by one of the four later Greek kingdoms portrayed in Daniel. These stayed in the Middle East or settled in various parts of Europe and most did not return to Israel until after World War 2. So the scattering after Josiah's death had consequences for over 2500 years even though a minority of the exiles did return to the Promised Land under the protection of Cyrus, the first king of the Persian Empire. Today most Middle Eastern Jews have now immigrated to Israel under its Law of Return. But the fulfillment of the promises to David expressed in 2 Samuel 7 and in Psalm 89 and reconfirmed notwitstanding Israel's unfaithfulness has only been partially accomplished in the first coming of the Messiah-King Jesus and in the regathering of Israel now in its preliminary stages. The full regathering of Israel and the direct reign of Jesus the Messiah is yet to come. But what a glorious time when it does!

— Part Two —
The Unknown Shorter Prophets

INTRODUCTION TO DISCUSSION OF
THE SHORTER PROPHETS

The Old Testament prophets placed in our modern versions of the Scriptures after Daniel and before Matthew are commonly called the Minor Prophets. I reject the name because there is nothing "minor" about them. They may be shorter than Isaiah, Jeremiah, Ezekiel or Daniel but they are anything but minor. The contemporary American church and even the church worldwide is impoverished because she is largely ignorant of what these prophets had to say to their own world and still have to say to us now. Like all of the other writers of Scriptures, these prophets were *"holy men of God [who] spoke as they were moved by the Holy Spirit."* 2 Peter 1:21. Therefore they should be read carefully and seriously. I will not attempt to explain each verse of all of these prophets, but I plan to pick out prominent themes from these shorter writings to help the reader and myself start to understand them. As a small step to recognizing their importance, I will call them the Shorter Prophets rather than misname them as the Minor Prophets.

To get context for the prophets, one tip is to note the king or kings mentioned at the beginning of most of these books and review their reign in the appropriate sections of the Kings and Chronicles. While the people did not always follow the reigning king, they usually did. There generally would be a clue to the character of the majority of the people to whom the prophet was speaking in the character of the reigning monarch.

The Shorter Prophets span a period probably 350 to 400 years in time (roughly 800 BC to somewhere between 450 and 400 BC), divided by the conquest and exile of the Northern Kingdom (commonly known as the 10 tribes and often called Israel as distinguished from Judah) by Assyria about 721 BC and the conquest and exile of the Southern Kingdom (commonly called Judah and probably including a major portion of Simeon, Benjamin and Levi as well as a sprinkling of refugees from the other tribes -- see Appendix A for further explanation of this conclusion) occurring between 605 and 586 BC by Babylon under the leadership of Nebuchadnezzar. As an introduction, it makes sense to divide the Shorter Prophets into those who wrote before the conquest of the Northern Kingdom (Amos, Jonah, Hosea, Micah and Nahum, for example), those who wrote after the fall of the Northern Kingdom and before the fall of the Southern Kingdom (most probably Joel, Habakkuk, Obadiah and Zephaniah, for example) and those who wrote after the return of Southern Kingdom under Cyrus the Persian (as prophesied in Isaiah 45, especially 45:13). These last would include Haggai, Zechariah and Malachi. There will be common themes regardless of time period, and some themes that occurred first with the conquest of the Northern Kingdom will recur concerning the conquest of the Southern Kingdom. One major difference is that the descendants of the survivors of the Northern Kingdom have not been fully identified, whereas the descendants of the survivors of the Southern Kingdom are in general known to us as Jews. The contemporary nation of Israel is populated mostly by descendants who survived the fall of the Southern Kingdom and also the second scattering of that kingdom which occurred in 70 AD under the Romans. This was prophesied by the Lord Jesus Himself as recorded in Matthew 24, Mark 13 and Luke 21.

THE GOD WHO JUDGES NATIONS

One of the easier Shorter Prophets to understand in portraying God as intervening in human affairs based on moral attributes and conduct or misconduct is Obadiah. He gave Edom a warning. In this short prophecy, verses 2-4 read in the Modern King James Version:

"Behold, I will make you small among the nations; You shall be greatly despised. The pride of your heart has deceived you, you who dwell in the clefts of the rock, whose habitation is high; you who say in your heart, 'Who will bring me down to the ground?' Though you ascend as high as the eagle, and though you set your nest among the stars, from there I will bring you down," says the Lord.

So the first reason assigned for God's punishment of Edom is pride. This punishment fell upon Edom even though this nation was descended from Abraham, so illustrious ancestry did not save them. The second reason was Edom's hostile attitude and actions toward Judah when Babylon was conquering and subduing it. Edom ignored the fact that it was descended from Esau, Jacob's twin brother. As Obadiah 8-14 says:

Will I not in that day, says the Lord, even destroy the wise men from Edom, and understanding from the mountains of Esau? Then your mighty men, O Teman, shall be dismayed, to the end that everyone from the mountains of Esau may be cut off by slaughter. For violence against your brother Jacob, shame shall cover you, and you shall be cut off forever. In the day that you stood on the other side -- in the day that strangers carried captive his forces, when foreigners entered his gates and cast lots for Jerusalem -- even you were as one of them. But you should not have gazed on the day of your brother in the day of his captivity. Nor should you have rejoiced over the children of Judah in the day of their destruction. Nor should you have spoken proudly in the day of distress. You should not have entered the gate of My people in the day of their calamity. Indeed, you should not have gazed on their affliction in the day of their calamity, nor laid hands on their substance in the day of their calamity. You should not have stood at the crossroads to cut off those among them who escaped; nor should you have delivered up those among them who remained in the day of distress.

So Edom sought to take advantage of Judah's distress, with the ultimate result that Edom was destroyed as a nation permanently. Where is Edom today? It is long gone. In fact Ishmael's descendants, the Arabs, have been granted the land in the Middle East that was in ancient times owned by the other descendants of Abraham and Lot such as the Edomites, the Moabites and the Ammonites (who have given their name to Amman, the current capital of Jordan). All of this was foreshadowed to Abraham in God's answer to his prayer on behalf of Ishmael (Genesis 21:12-13). Yet God did not permanently give the Promised Land itself to any nation other than Israel.

With the exiles of Judah and Israel have also been promises of eventual restoration, which I believe apply to Jacob's descendants both physically and spiritually. One example is the end of Obadiah starting with verse 15. Another is Joel 3:11-21. Outside the Shorter Prophets on this subject, one could study Ezekiel 37-39 and Romans 11. But for present purposes we need to grasp that God intervenes in human history to sustain the right and abase the wrong, even though those who are truly holy often suffer over the short run or even throughout their life on earth. Such interventions foreshadow the ultimate judgments of Jesus Christ, Who will right every wrong.

This whole notion of a God with moral attributes and preferences is foreign to much of American culture today. For example, the Star Wars trilogy portrays "the Force" as a morally indifferent power equally accessible to people on the side of good and of evil. This attitude is not new. Zechariah summarized the history of Israel during the prophets (1:2): *The Lord has been very angry with your fathers.* So God has pure, holy emotions and cares what people do and think. Jonathan Edwards was right when he preached his famous sermon *Sinners in the Hands of an Angry God.* Zephaniah encountered the view of God's moral indifference and denounced it (1:12):

> *And it shall come to pass at that time that I will search Jerusalem with lamps, and punish the men who are settled in complacency, who say in their heart, 'The Lord will not do good, nor will He do evil.'*

C.S. Lewis in the Chronicles of Narnia did a much better job in portraying a God Who loves good and hates evil and Who acts on His convictions. In fact, many Americans and most Europeans live as if there is no afterlife and almost no future. In intellectual circles, the idea that there is a God Who will call humanity to account -- both collectively as nations and ultimately as individuals -- is a shocking, foreign idea even though this idea is at the historical foundation of Western civilization from at least Moses forward, a period of approximately 3500 years. Even the Egyptians had a distorted view of an afterlife, so in some form this concept predates even Moses. The concept of God's justice lays behind the Flood, which long predates Moses. Zephaniah would deliver substantially the same warning to the world today, including America, as he did to Judah just before its fall to Babylon.

Zephaniah is far from alone. Jonah was instructed by God to go to Nineveh with a message of coming judgment (1:2): *"Arise, go to Nineveh, that great city, and cry out against it; for their wickedness has come up before Me."* To keep to our subject, we should deal with the controversy over the great fish that swallowed Jonah later. For now, suffice it to say that Jonah endured his ordeal because of his personal disobedience to the direct command of God to go to Nineveh. Sticking to the subject of Nineveh's wickedness, some information is found in Nahum 3:1-6. Among the sins of Nineveh were slaughter, greed and both physical adultery and adulterous worship (probably idolatry with a component of prostitution). We know from 2 Kings 17:22-41 that Assyria exiled peoples from their own lands and forced some of them to migrate elsewhere. In this case Israel was removed from the Northern Kingdom and others were forced to move there by Assyria. Even though this conduct fulfilled a judgment against Israel given by God, the cruelty of the Assyrians in carrying out the judgment of God also angered Him and provoked His judgment against Assyria in its turn. As Zechariah said later in words probably applicable to both Assyria and Babylon:

> So the angel who spoke with me said to me, "Proclaim, saying, 'Thus says the Lord of hosts: "I am zealous for Jerusalem and for Zion with great zeal. I am exceedingly angry with the nations at ease. For I was a little angry, and they helped -- but with evil intent." Therefore thus says the Lord: "I am returning to Jerusalem with mercy; My house shall be built in it," says the Lord of hosts, "And a surveyor's line shall be stretched out over Jerusalem." Again proclaim, saying, 'Thus says the Lord of hosts: "My cities shall again spread out through prosperity; The Lord will again comfort Zion and will again choose Jerusalem."
> Zechariah 1:14-17

Zechariah at the finish of this passage sounds a note of ultimate mercy and restoration for Jerusalem. We should explore this in more detail later. For the sake of continuity of the subject of a God of moral judgment, we should consider the first chapter of Micah. In this chapter the cause of God's anger is false worship, or worship of other gods. This violated the First Commandment: *You shall have no other gods before Me.* Exodus 20:3. Frequently the worship of false gods also led to other immoral conduct, including child sacrifice in the worship of false gods who supposedly so demanded. Worship of Molech, one such false deity, by passing a child through the fire is specifically denounced and forbidden in Leviticus 18:21 and Deuteronomy 18:10, although Molech is not mentioned by name in the second passage. But King Ahaz and King Manasseh of Judah both sacrificed a child (2 Kings 16:3 and 2 Kings 21:6) and the practice had become widespread in the Northern Kingdom before its fall (2 Kings 17:17). In Greek mythology, a comparable scene occurs at the beginning of the *Iliad* when Agamemnon sacrifices his daughter. Child sacrifice is especially hateful to God, but worship of anyone or anything else is enough to provoke His righteous jealousy and anger. [For a more detailed discussion of idolatry in Biblical history, see Appendix B.]

God is also angered by dishonesty and the attitude that "everything has its price." For example, consider Micah 3:9-12:

> *Now hear this, you heads of the house of Jacob and rulers of the house of Israel, who abhor justice and pervert all equity, who build up Zion with bloodshed and Jerusalem with iniquity. Her heads judge for a bribe, her priests teach for pay, and her prophets divine for money. Yet they lean on the Lord, and say, "Is not the Lord among us? No harm can come upon us." Therefore because of you Zion shall be plowed like a field, Jerusalem shall become heaps of ruins, and the mountain of the temple like the bare hills of the forest.*

Amos was rigorously impartial in pronouncing judgment on all of the surrounding nations, including his own nation of Israel. To hold an audience in the Northern Kingdom, he first started to denounce all of the surrounding nations starting in chapter 1, then Judah (starting in 2:4) and finally his own nation of Israel. There were specific reasons assigned for each judgment, many of which had to do with slavery, greed and cruelty. In Judah's case the primary reason was the rejection of God's Law. Then in Amos 2:6 the prophet turns his attention to his own nation of Israel, denouncing first sins of sex and greed and continuing in a graphic description of the coming judgment. As so often occurs today, in ancient Israel the one who speaks the truth is hated for it (Amos 5:10). Even though the people of Israel descended not only from Abraham but also from Jacob, judgment fell to such an extent that the northern tribes have not returned to the land even yet in any large numbers even though more than 2700 years have passed. From Ezekiel 37-38 we know that in the future these tribes will finally return, but we can get some idea of the fury of God from the length of time of their exile.

Habakkuk asks a difficult question: if God intervenes based on moral characteristics, then how could He raise up the Babylonians (Chaldeans) when they are even worse than the Judeans that God was judging? Consider first the word that comes from God to Habakkuk and then Habakkuk's question:

> *Look among the nations and watch-Be utterly astounded! For I will work a work in your days which you would not believe, though it were told you. For indeed I am raising up the Chaldeans, a bitter and hasty nation which marches through the breadth of the earth to possess dwelling places that are not theirs. Habakkuk 1:5-6*

> *Are You not from everlasting, O Lord my God, my Holy One? We shall not die. O Lord, You have appointed them for judgment; O*

Rock, You have marked them for correction. <u>You are of purer eyes than to behold evil, and cannot look on wickedness.</u> **Why do You look on those who deal treacherously, and hold Your tongue when the wicked devours a person more righteous than he?** *Why do You make men like fish of the sea, like creeping things that have no ruler over them? They take up all of them with a hook, they catch them in their net and gather them in their dragnet. Therefore they rejoice and are glad. Therefore they sacrifice to their net, and burn incense to their dragnet; because by them their share is sumptuous and their food plentiful. Shall they therefore empty their net, and continue to slay nations without pity? Habakkuk 1:12-17*

I have added the emphases to highlight Habakkuk's question about how a pure and holy God can not only permit people more evil to triumph but even use them to punish His own people? This question is pertinent to America today as it was to Great Britain and the Netherlands in 1940 when the Nazis were on the rise. Can America expect to endure forever? We know that the eventual answer is no, because all national governments must eventually fall to direct government by Jesus Christ. Revelation 11:15. Can America last until then as a free nation? I do not know how long America will last, but I do know that the AntiChrist will run his murderous course of Revelation 13 for 3½ years. I also can see the obvious moral deterioration of America since World War 2. It is terrible but thinkable that like ancient Judah that God might judge America for casting off its ancient faith. Even if America's possible opponents may have practices that are worse than our own, we in America have the special national sin of having known the truth and turned away from it. Peter, speaking of apostate false teachers, explained this concept:

> *For if, after they have escaped the pollutions of the world through the knowledge of the Lord and Savior Jesus Christ, they are again*

entangled in them and overcome, the latter end is worse for them than the beginning. For it would have been better for them not to have known the way of righteousness, than having known it, to turn from the holy commandment delivered to them. 2 Peter 2:20-21

America in its history has known the way of righteousness -- the righteousness which is by faith (for example, Romans 3:22). While all of God's servants are imperfect and there has always been sin throughout American society, yet prominent American teachers of truth have included such men as Jonathan Edwards, John Gano, Charles Finney (who stood strong against slavery to his great credit, although there are aspects of his revival methods and theology which are certainly subject to debate) Charles and A.A. Hodge, A.W. Tozer, Dwight Moody, Philip Newell, J. Gresham Machen, Peter Marshall, Billy Graham, Jerry Falwell, D. James Kennedy and Adrian Rogers. Among those who are still active in ministry are David Jeremiah, Michael Youssef, Charles Colson, Charles Stanley, Jack van Impe, B. Courtney McBath, Jack Hayford and Franklin Graham. Surely I have left out many others. Compared to Europe, good Biblical teaching is still abundant in the United States. Yet America by any measure is becoming salt that has lost its savor (see Matthew 5:13). While the deterioration is easiest to perceive in conduct, faith is the right place to look for the root of the rot. Habakkuk gives the great sentence quoted by the Apostle Paul that has freed so many souls from slavery to sin: *The just shall live by faith.* Habakkuk 2:4. The late President Reagan was right is saying that America was an unusual nation because it was founded for people to practice Biblical faith without government reprisal. America was a refuge of religious freedom. This was true of the Pilgrims and the Puritans of New England. It was true of the Presbyterian immigrants from Ulster and Scotland. It was true also of the Quakers and the various German groups in the Mid-Atlantic area. Some of the French Huguenots fled here when Louis XIV revoked religious toleration in France in 1685.

In colonial Virginia, where Anglicanism was the established religion, the lack of bishops meant that the local vestries exercised effective control over many congregations instead of archbishops appointed by the King as was true in England. Dutch immigrants of the 19th century to Michigan and Wisconsin sought religious freedom. People of other faiths saw both the religious and economic freedom in America and emigrated here also. But now many people have abandoned the Biblical faith of our forefathers. For example, the Ivy League universities that were founded originally on a Biblical foundation have utterly cast off their faith and attack their own roots. I know personally as a graduate of one of them and as a law graduate of a second one. In this respect America is becoming comparable to Judah in Habakkuk's time. If America should fall in similar fashion, there can be no complaint against God's justice.

But one may ask with Habakkuk: how can this happen when other nations, especially Babylon, are even worse? We have already noticed that the invaders of Judah all came to their own judgments. Jeremiah 51 is one major Scripture predicting the judgment of Babylon; Daniel 5 tells how it happened. We cannot claim exemption from punishment for our sins just because another nation or individual is worse. A thief cannot avoid a sentence for theft because there is also a murderer on the docket. God has the right to use one wicked nation to punish another, much as He used Soviet Russia to punish Nazi Germany. Beyond this, the ultimate answer is faith where we cannot understand. As Habakkuk closed in 3:17-19:

> *Though the fig tree may not blossom, nor fruit be on the vines; though the labor of the olive may fail, and the fields yield no food. Though the flock may be cut off from the fold and there be no herd in the stalls, yet I will rejoice in the Lord, I will joy in the God of my salvation. The Lord God is my strength; He will make my feet like deer's feet, and He will make me walk on my high hills.*

Nahum, in pronouncing judgment upon Nineveh for its brutality, is explicit as to the aspect of the nature of God that demands justice. His words can apply equally to all enemies of God from any nationality, even from Judah or Israel itself. Like the words of Obadiah, they were spoken at first of an enemy of Israel and can still be understood legitimately in part as a warning against the enemies of modern as well as ancient Israel. Considering that God does not change His nature (James 1:17; Malachi 3:6), the words of Nahum 1:2-9 written through the Holy Spirit speak to all of humanity, including ourselves:

> *God is jealous, and the Lord avenges; The Lord avenges and is furious. The Lord will take vengeance on His adversaries, and He reserves wrath for His enemies.*

> *The Lord is slow to anger and great in power, and will not at all acquit the wicked.*

> *The Lord has His way in the whirlwind and in the storm, and the clouds are the dust of His feet. He rebukes the sea and makes it dry, and dries up all the rivers. Bashan and Carmel wither, and the flower of Lebanon wilts.*

> *The mountains quake before Him. The hills melt, and the earth heaves at His presence, Yes, the world and all who dwell in it.*

Who can stand before His indignation? And who can endure the fierceness of His anger? His fury is poured out like fire, and the rocks are thrown down by Him.

The Lord is good, a stronghold in the day of trouble; and He knows those who trust in Him. But with an overflowing flood He will make an utter end of its place, and darkness will pursue His enemies.

What do you conspire against the Lord? He will make an utter end of it. Affliction will not rise up a second time.

To summarize the truth in Nahum that there is but one true God of absolute power and truth, consider Isaiah 45:5-7:

I am the Lord, and there is no other; there is no God besides Me. I will gird you [Cyrus, the ancient human liberator of captive Israel], though you have not known Me, that they may know from the rising of the sun to its setting that there is none besides Me. I am the Lord, and there is no other; I form the light and create darkness, I make peace and create calamity; I, the Lord, do all these things.

It is in this vein that we should understand more fully the words of our Lord Jesus: *"I am the Way, the Truth and the Life. No man comes to the Father except by Me.* John 14:6. Both the Old Testament (starting with Genesis 1:26 and including such passages as Psalms 45 and 110 and Isaiah 48:16) and the New Testament in numerous passages witness to multiple Persons within the single Godhead. Paul amplifies this. *There is one God and one Mediator between God and men, the Man Christ Jesus.* 1 Timothy 2:5. In several places in the Gospel of John, our Lord Jesus clearly used language to claim full equality with His Father. Jesus' accusers so understood him and they were correct in this part of their analysis. Where they went wrong was in their unbelief and in denying Him the worship that is His due. Luke 22:66-71; Mark 14:61-64; John 5:18; John 6:35-58; John 8:18-59 John 10:27-39. As God is the only true God, Jesus is the only duplicate of God in a human body (Colossians 1:13-20; Hebrews 1:1-6, 4:14-16; 7:20-28; 8:1-6; 9:23-28). While angels also exist for various purposes, the Holy Spirit is the only Spirit that is part of the Godhead and who since Pentecost has lived within every believer. Compare John 14:26, 16:13-14; Acts 2; 1 Corinthians 12:1-13; Romans 8:6-11; 15:13; and 1 Peter 1:2-5 among other passages. The God Who made us, Who sent our Lord Jesus to die in our place and to raise us from the dead first spiritually and then physically, and Who sent the Holy Spirit to live in us is an exclusive God Who allows no room for any other god or object of worship. It is this God who intervenes in the lives of both nations and individual people.

Without going at length into the subject of the last segment of human history, as to God's intervention in the life of nations the restoration of Israel must be noted. Isaiah 54 is one great chapter of this truth. Ezekiel 37-39 is another segment focusing on this. Romans 11:25-36 is a counterpart New Testament passage. There is also Matthew 24-25. The regathering of Israel has started by the hand of God as long ago prophesied. If you research the history of the initial establishment of Israel from 1945 to 1948, you will be left with no doubt as to God's intervention at several key points to permit the new state to survive against tremendous numerical odds. At the end, Revelation reveals that God's plans will be opposed by an unholy trinity of the Devil, the AntiChrist and the False Prophet. This opposition will fail just as every other human attempt to stop God's purposes has failed. As Assyria and Babylon are now dead and buried, so the unholy trinity will be judged without end.

THE GOD WHO JUDGES INDIVIDUALS

The Shorter Prophets also show that God controls the lives of individuals as well as nations. Jonah is an example. God first commands Jonah to go to Nineveh and warn them that their overthrow was only 40 days away. Jonah, being a patriotic citizen of Israel, disobeys God and books passage on a ship going as far away as possible from Nineveh, near the modern Gibraltar. Probably Jonah understood that Assyria, with its capital at Nineveh, would soon enough conquer his native land and exile its population. But Jonah does not get very far because of the tremendous storm that God sends to stop his ship. He finally consents to be thrown into the sea for the sake of the crew and other passengers of the ship, and the storm abates. Then God sent a great fish which He had prepared to swallow Jonah and return him to land in the direction of Nineveh. Jonah tried to run from God but he couldn't hide.

At this point many people will be tempted to stop reading the narrative because they refuse to believe the Scriptures about the great fish that swallowed Jonah. Most readers presume that this was a whale, which is one possibility. Whaling was common in America about 200 years ago; there were rare reports of human bodies being found in whales that were later harpooned and killed. Since a whale is an air-breathing mammal like a human being and not a fish that extracts oxygen dissolved in water using gills, a whale must periodically surface. There are cavities where a human being might survive for a short time within a whale somewhat as more modern naval personnel live in submarines for months. Some Biblical scholars believe that Jonah actually died physically within the great fish and was resurrected back into a mortal body as Lazarus was later, although this is a minority view. They base their argument understanding Jonah 2:6 to indicate physical death. On this view the prayer would have come after resurrection back into his mortal body. Others believe that God preserved Jonah's life within the whale until the whale expelled him to dry land. They believe that this context indicates that Jonah was as good as dead rather than literally dead. In either case, God supervised closely the details of Jonah's life.

The content of Jonah's prayers within the great fish show that Jonah was thoroughly familiar with the Psalms that had been composed and written by his time. You may wish to consult a reference Bible for more specifics; various commentators may differ on specific detailed references but will generally agree that there are copious references to the Psalms.

Many of you may ask whether I believe that Jonah was truly swallowed by a whale (or a similar type of great fish) and then lived to tell about it. Yes, as a holder of two Ivy League degrees and as a trial lawyer by training and over 30 years' experience I do believe it even though human experience says that such an event is extremely improbable. In addition to Jonah himself, there is an infinitely greater Man Who was an eyewitness to the event and Who gave His testimony to it. The Lord Jesus said:

> An evil and adulterous generation seeks after a sign, and no sign will
> be given to it except the sign of the prophet Jonah. For as Jonah was
> three days and three nights in the belly of the great fish, so will the
> Son of Man be three days and three nights in the heart of the earth.
> The men of Nineveh will rise up in the judgment with this generation

and condemn it, because they repented at the preaching of Jonah;
and indeed a greater than Jonah is here. Matthew 12:39-41 (also see
Matthew 16:4 and Luke 11:29-32)

Since the Lord Jesus was truly the Son of God, He was alive and present before Jonah was born, and even before the Creation, even though at that time He had not entered a human body. Our Lord confirmed this in John 8:57-59 under questioning by His opponents:

> *Then the Jews said to Him, "You are not yet fifty years old, and have*
> *You seen Abraham?" Jesus said to them, "Most assuredly, I say to you,*
> *before Abraham was, I AM." Then they took up stones to throw at*
> *Him; but Jesus hid Himself and went out of the temple, going through*
> *the midst of them, and so passed by.*

From the reaction of Jesus' listeners to try to stone Him we can have no doubt that they understood His claim to have pre-existed Abraham, who had lived roughly 2000 years before Jesus of Nazareth as He lived in a human body. This is no mistaking Jesus' claim. Therefore, if Jesus indeed spoke the truth, He was alive outside of a human body when Jonah lived and personally saw and heard what happened to Jonah.

The Gospel accounts witness to many other events that are physically improbable and in some cases impossible without divine intervention, but the central issue as to the credibility of Jesus Christ is whether He did or did not rise from the dead the third day after His death. Without writing an entire treatise now, I give several reasons why His claim to resurrection is in fact true:

A) Peter spoke of the Resurrection as a physical reality less than 2 months after the Crucifixion as recorded in Acts 2. If his hearers did not believe Peter's claims to be credible, how is it that Peter was not executed immediately or at least taken into custody for trial before the same Sanhedrin that had condemned Jesus Christ to death? When Peter and John were arrested later, even the Sanhedrin had to admit that a major miracle had been done in Jesus' name and that judicial body was forced to release them against its own desire. Acts 3-4. A similar sequence is recorded in Acts 5:12-42. It is no answer to say that the rulers were too mild to arrest Peter when Stephen was not only arrested but stoned to death a few short years later (Acts 6-7).

B) How did the same Peter who was so afraid of the Romans that he would deny knowing the Lord Jesus three times at the fire on the night of Jesus' arrest become the bold Peter who accused his hearers of murder in His execution during his sermon of Acts 2?

C) How was Saul of Tarsus who became Paul persuaded that Jesus was and is the Christ (the Messiah) except by being confronted by the risen Jesus Christ on the Damascus Road?

D) Why could neither the Sanhedrin or the Roman authorities ever produce the body of Jesus Christ? They could have squelched the new faith by this one simple act if His body was still in its grave. Because He had risen from the dead, this was impossible.

E) Who rolled away the stone from the tomb in the face of a Roman guard squad? The women coming to the tomb with spices were not physically capable of that. If Jesus had remained alive in His damaged human body without a transformation to another body, the damaged body would have been incapable of any exertion because the nerves controlling His hands and feet were severed in the process of Crucifixion (ignoring other injuries for which no medical treatment was given). So Jesus, even if still alive in the tomb (which supposition is ridiculous of itself because the execution squad of the Romans verified His death in addition to the facts of His massive injuries), could not have done that by human physical force.

Since the subject of this section is the Shorter Prophets, I will stop here. Lee Strobel is one brilliant reporter who started his investigation of the Resurrection as a convinced unbeliever and was compelled by the evidence to repent and change his mind. For more detail on evidentiary questions about the resurrection, his books would be well worth reading and comparing the Scriptures. Josh McDowell has also written at length on this subject.

Returning to Jonah, the testimony of Jesus Christ, now risen from the dead, is decisive as to the question of whether Jonah did or did not spend 3 days and 3 nights inside the great fish. Jesus Christ by His character is always true and He is the only eyewitness other than Jonah himself Who is capable of answering any question about the truth of Jonah's account. (The ship's crew experienced the storm and then the miraculous sudden calm but probably did not see the great fish swallow Jonah and certainly did not know what happened later.) Jesus Christ and Jonah himself constitute the necessary two witnesses to prove that Jonah indeed did spend that time in the belly of the great fish. Deuteronomy 17:6, 19:15; John 8:17. I should add that the testimony of Jesus Himself is sufficient because He is God and can speak for His Father and for the Holy Spirit as well. So yes, I believe it.

There is considerably more to the story of Jonah than the miracle of the great fish and Jonah's safe return to dry land. Consider the change in Jonah's attitude from fleeing from God's commission in chapter 1 to his prayer in Jonah 2. God's discipline of imprisoning Jonah in the darkness of the fish's belly was extremely effective in bringing Jonah from rebellion to obedience. Hebrews 12:6-7 says, *"For whom the Lord loves He chastens, and scourges every son whom He receives. If you endure chastening, God deals with you as with sons; for what son is there whom a father does not chasten?"*

Having been brought to obedience by the chastening of God, Jonah now went to Nineveh and warned of imminent judgment, which is what he should have done in the first place. The results of Jonah's preaching are astounding. An entire city from the king to the cleaning person repented, and God stayed His hand of judgment. What did not happen in Sodom, in Samaria during the Northern Kingdom nor in Jerusalem in the time of Jesus Christ did happen during this generation in Nineveh. Again, the Lord Jesus attested to the spiritual miracle described in Matthew 12:41, saying, *"The men of Nineveh will rise up in the judgment with this generation and condemn it, because they repented at the preaching of Jonah; and indeed a greater than Jonah is here."*

Jonah's rebellious streak reappears in chapter 4 because he sees that Nineveh will indeed be spared now. Whether Jonah could perceive this or not, Nineveh was going to conquer Jonah's homeland. So God again taught Jonah the lesson of mercy by a miniature demonstration with the plant that had shaded Jonah. Once more we can see God's minute supervision of Jonah's life in creating the great fish to rescue Jonah from the sea and creating the plant to shade him from the desert sun, and then the worm to kill the plant as an object lesson for Jonah. This lesson is amplified by Jesus Christ, who said, *"The very hairs on your head are all numbered."* Matthew 10:30, Luke 12:7.

We can see God's compassion on individual human beings and on a great city. The book of Jonah anticipates the command of the Lord Jesus to *"Love your enemies..."* In this case God send Jonah to his enemies' country to preach the Gospel. Perhaps a later historical example is Patrick, who took the Gospel to the people who had taken him captive as a child. In the 20th century missionary widows persisted in taking the Gospel to the Auca Indians of South America after the tribesmen had killed their husbands. There are undoubtedly other lessons to be drawn from Jonah, but I hope that this is sufficient to persuade you to read the book carefully and to search them out for yourself.

A contemporary series on cable television is the "Real Housewives" series, shot in various locations. Despite the title, the women portrayed are far wealthier than average and also more beautiful as far as the human body is concerned. Amos had his own set of similar women ("The Real Housewives of Ancient Israel?") whom he addressed in Amos 4:1-3:

> *Hear this word, you cows of Bashan, who are on the mountain of Samaria, who oppress the poor, who crush the needy, who say to your husbands, "Bring wine, let us drink!" The Lord God has sworn by His holiness: "Behold, the days shall come upon you when He will take you away with fishhooks, and your posterity with fishhooks. You will go out through broken walls, each one straight ahead of her, and you will be cast into Harmon," says the Lord.*

I am not a Hebrew scholar, but I do know that in French to address a woman as a cow expresses gross insult. In context, I think that Amos intended a similar insult to his contemporaries. These women were apparently wealthy (Amos 5:11) and oppressed the poor and also wanted to drink alcohol in luxury and so while away their time and resources. Sound familiar? God's warning to them was that their city would be destroyed and that their families would be taken captive. I would hate to be pierced with a fishhook, but apparently the conquerors used such methods to subdue their captives. On the horizon was a time of no more luxury nor drinking, but the drudgery of slave labor and the miserable violation of a concubine's life. Isaiah 32:9-14 contains a warning that is similar in many respects. Because God has not changed, the ancient warnings of Amos and Isaiah are pertinent to American society today and in particular to people who are spiritually similar to the women warned by Amos. Though cultures and technologies have changed vastly since the time of Amos, neither human nature nor God has changed.

[For a fuller discussion on money and wealth, see Appendix C.]

Still another instance of a particularized judgment inflicted by God on a particular person is found in Amos 7:10-17. This man named Amaziah was the priest of the royal idols of Bethel. Amaziah and probably the entire royal family was naturally upset about Amos' preaching, probably even more so because Amos was such an upstart. He was merely a farmer (Amos 1:1) and yet was telling the upper class what to do and to avoid! But Amos was an upstart with a commission from God Himself, Who is no respecter of persons (Acts 10:34, Romans 2:11, Ephesians 6:9). Amaziah was ordering Amos to leave the country and preach in Judah instead of Israel, and especially to be silent in Bethel, the site of the idols. An approximate modern equivalent would be an order to keep silent about the Bible in Washington, D.C. But Amos would remain faithful, and a particular judgment would fall on Amaziah. Not only would he die in exile (as he had told Amos to exile himself) but he would have to endure the day-by-day distress of the loss of his children and the knowledge that his wife was prostituting herself regularly. God's unerring anger found its individual target. When God chooses to unleash His anger, He has the ability to target an individual as with a rifle or a society as with a shotgun, or a combination of both.

THE GOD OF MERCY AND FORGIVENESS -- ZECHARIAH 3

Imagine yourself being summoned to meet your country's President. If you have a Prime Minister or a King or Queen as head of state, then substitute that person for the President. It makes no difference for my illustration. You check your clothing and the best you have is only marginally suitable, but you prepare to make do because you have no better outfit. You cannot afford enough of an upgrade to make a difference. Of course you would plan to have the outfit dry-cleaned just before you make your appearance. Now imagine that there is a fire at the dry-cleaning shop the day you are supposed to pick up the outfit and that your only suitable outfit is now soaked with water from fire hoses and is full of soot and ash from the fire. You can't go to see your head of state in sackcloth and ashes. Now what?

Zechariah 3 takes my illustration a step further. Joshua, the High Priest, is supposed to intercede before God for Israel, as did Moses and Aaron long before him. But Joshua's clothes are filthy, making him unfit to appear before God. The Hebrew word translated as "filthy" can refer to urine and feces. Imagine in my previous example that the clothes are stained beyond repair with urine and feces by reason of bodily weakness instead of filthy from soot and ash and soaked with water. There is a difference -- as human beings we are the source of our pollution mentioned in Zechariah 3, rather than an extrinsic source such as a fire in my first example. Just to make it worse, Satan was at God's right hand harping on Joshua's condition, do his worst to stop intercessory prayer at all.

As human beings, we face a like predicament with the Joshua in Zechariah 3. We all will indeed appear before God at the Last Judgment. If we believe in His Son, then we should be appearing regularly before Him on earth in prayer for others and for ourselves. And not one of us can make ourselves fit to appear before God at any time. Isaiah 64:6 confirms Zechariah 3; the prophet refers to our own righteousness as filthy in terms which could apply to tampons women discard when bloody. Here we are faced with a God-given duty which is impossible to fulfill.

As Zechariah 3 teaches, God Himself provides the cleansing and the clean clothes we need and cannot obtain for ourselves. This is pictured by the new clothes that Joshua is given and which are put on him. These enable Joshua to fulfill his office as High Priest. Similarly, in the parable of the feast each guest needed a wedding garment. (Matthew 22:11-13) The Prodigal Son was also given a new robe (Luke 15:22) as an outward indication of his new life. In several places in Revelation (4:4, 6:11, 7:9 for three examples) the saints are portrayed with white robes. We have a double need for the wedding garment: (1) As a mark of inward salvation and cleansing, and (2) As a mark that we have been accepted by God by His having placed the righteousness of Christ to our account. As Isaiah 61:10 says:

> *I will greatly rejoice in the Lord, My soul shall be joyful in my God; For He has clothed me with the garments of salvation. He has covered me with the robe of righteousness, as a bridegroom decks himself with ornaments, and as a bride adorns herself with her jewels.*

We are now dead to sin and to the Law and married to Christ Himself. Romans 7:1-4.

THE FIRST COMING OF MESSIAH — GOD COMING TO EARTH

The Shorter Prophets contain several clear prophecies concerning the coming Messiah. One of the clearest is Micah 5:2, which identifies His birthplace:

> *But you, Bethlehem Ephrathah, though you are little among the thousands of Judah, yet out of you shall come forth to Me the One to be Ruler in Israel, Whose goings forth are from of old, from everlasting.*

When the Wise Men came to Herod's court after seeing the star that signified the birth of the King of Israel, the scholars then alive had no trouble directing the Wise Men to the correct hamlet, quoting this verse. Matthew 2:1-8. But this verse says far more. The Ruler in Israel is a Person "***Whose goings forth are from old, from everlasting.***" (emphasis added) Referring back to our discussion of the presence of the Lord Jesus during the life of Jonah, the majority of the scholars who lived during Jesus' ministry would not have reacted with murderous fury at His claim of having lived before Abraham had they looked at Micah 5:2 carefully. This passage also supports the plural God revealed first in Genesis 1:26, repeated in Genesis 3:22 and amplified in Isaiah 48:16.

There are at least 3 instances in the Old Testament where many scholars believe that God assumed a form that was indistinguishable to the naked eye from a human being. One of these was Melchizedek in Genesis 14, of which much is said in the book of Hebrews. Another is the Man who wrestled with Jacob in Genesis 32. In this case Hosea provides direct support for this, saying, *"He [Jacob] took his brother by the heel in the womb, and in his strength he struggled with God."* Hosea 12:3. Hosea 12:4-5 reads: *Yes, he struggled with the Angel and prevailed; He wept, and sought favor from Him. He found Him in Bethel, and there He spoke to us. That is, the Lord God of hosts. The Lord is His memorable name.*

Since Jacob struggled with a Man, and Hosea through the Holy Spirit identifies that Man as God, the unified God (Deuteronomy 6:4) is plural within the unity. A third instance in which a divine being appeared as if human was in Judges 13, when the birth of Samson was announced to his mother. In that passage the Person is identified both as a Man and as the Angel of the Lord. In this respect Judges 13 is similar to Hosea 12:4, where the Man in the preceding verse is referred to as an angel when obviously there is only one Person involved. Many scholars therefore believe that the specific "Angel of the Lord" of the Old Testament is the Son of God before He entered an actual human body as related in Matthew and Luke. Unlike a common angel (Revelation 22:8-9), this Person received worship from Manoah and his wife. Such worship can only be given to and accepted by God Himself. By the same token, it was clearly God Himself and not merely an angel that blessed Jacob.

So we know from Hosea that Jacob wrestled with God and not just with an ordinary angel. From this benchmark we can believe that Melchizedek in Genesis 14 is probably also an appearance of the Son of God given that He received tithes (which are due to God, not to a mere man) and set out bread and wine, which centuries later became the elements of the Lord's Supper. His titles are King of Righteousness and King of Peace (Hebrews

7:2 -- compare Isaiah 9:6 which gives the titles of Messiah as Wonderful {the same title appears in Judges 13 also, supporting the idea that the Man who appeared there was in fact God}, Counselor, the Mighty God, the Everlasting Father, the Prince of Peace). Hosea 12:5 also ties in with the first part of Isaiah 9:6, so let us examine the entire verse:

> *For unto us a Child is born, unto us a Son is given; and the government will be upon His shoulder. And His name will be called Wonderful, Counselor, Mighty God, Everlasting Father, Prince of Peace.*

Isaiah identifies a Child, a Son. When has the Father ever been a child or a son? Never! So God must be plural within His unity, as Hosea 12:3 supports. When Paul wrote his explanation of the deity of Jesus Christ in passages such as Philippians 2:5-11 and Colossians 1:13-20, he wrote from a solid Old Testament foundation of which Micah 5:2 and Hosea 12:3-5 are important parts. Further, the appearances of the Son in the Old Testament are a foreshadowing of His inhabitation of a human body and His living among us in the New Testament.

Do you feel overwhelmed, as Jacob may have before he met Esau for the first time in 20 years? You may think your problems are worse, and maybe they are. But God is a God of mercy who will lay aside His glory to come to our level, as He did with Jacob, Job and Samson's parents. Jesus Christ has experienced the worst of human life. If you ask with an honest heart, He will help you too, even to the point of directing your steps from wherever you are. You may feel like Jonah in the great fish. God heard Jonah in the depths of despair and He can hear you too. *"Therefore He [Jesus Christ the High Priest after the order of Melchidezek] is also able to save to the uttermost those who come to God through Him, since He always lives to make intercession for them."* Hebrews 7:25.

Hosea also wrote (11:1), *"When Israel was a child, I loved him, and out of Egypt I called My son."* While this passage looked back to the Exodus, it also looked forward to the childhood of Jesus the Messiah, as noted in Matthew 2:15. The reason for the Father commanding Joseph to take Jesus to Egypt -- the murderous rage of Herod the Great over the thought of another king resulting in the slaughter of male babies near Bethlehem -- is prophesied in Jeremiah 31:15 and noted as fulfilled in Matthew 2:18. So Jesus Christ was in the right place to fulfill the prophecy of Hosea 11:1 at the right time.

Much of the last part of Zechariah is taken up with portions of the life of Jesus the Messiah. Zechariah 9:9 says this, *"Rejoice greatly, O daughter of Zion! Shout, O daughter of Jerusalem! Behold, your King is coming to you; He is just and having salvation, lowly and riding on a donkey, a colt, the foal of a donkey."* This was fulfilled on what we commonly call Palm Sunday as recorded in Matthew 21:1-17, Mark 11:1-11 and Luke 19:30-40. There is a miracle here in that Jesus rode on an animal that had never been broken through a huge and noisy crowd with no trouble. But riding on a donkey was a symbolic claim of authority looking back to the days of the Judges. Judges 5:10, 10:4. As prophesied by Zechariah, our Lord Jesus was presenting Himself as the King, well knowing that He would be crucified before the week was out.

Because God chose to unfold His plan gradually, He interspersed prophecies concerning His Son amid other subjects. Zechariah 11:12-13 includes a further prophecy of the last week of Jesus' life on earth:

> *Then I said to them, "If it is agreeable to you, give me my wages; and if not, refrain." So they weighed out for my wages thirty pieces of silver. And the Lord said to me, "Throw it to the potter"-that princely price they set on me. So I took the thirty pieces of silver and threw them into the house of the Lord for the potter.*

The phrase *"that princely price"* is ironic -- it is the traditional price of a slave and was the same total price as Hosea paid to redeem his wife out of the slave market (Hosea 3:2 -- Hosea paid half of the price in grain instead of coin). This prophecy was fulfilled by people who had no thought of fulfilling Biblical prophecy. Judas and the Temple leadership negotiated their price of thirty pieces of silver, unwittingly fulfilling this prophecy. Matthew 26:14-16, 27:3-10. (The reference in Matthew to Jeremiah is probably an allusion to Jeremiah 18, but as suggested in the New Schofield notes it may also be a reference to the manner of the synagogue scrolls of that day, in which Jeremiah was the first of the prophets. Zechariah 11:12-13 is the most direct prophecy.) When Judas threw the money back when he realized that he had betrayed innocent blood, the Temple priests realized that they could not take the money back into the treasury, so they bought the potter's field as a burial ground for foreigners who had no place to be buried. This field was also known as the Field of Blood. Acts 1:16-20.

Zechariah 12 contains a prophecy which mingles aspects of the First and Second Comings of Jesus the Messiah. Sticking with a portion relating to Jesus' coming in a human body like ours, we read in Zechariah 12:10 that:

> And I will pour on the house of David and on the inhabitants of Jerusalem the Spirit of grace and supplication; then they will look on Me whom they pierced. Yes, they will mourn for Him as one mourns for his only son, and grieve for Him as one grieves for a firstborn.

The word *"pierced"* clearly refers to the use of crucifixion to kill the Lord Jesus, in piercing His hands and feet. Compare Psalm 22:16. It is proper to connect the prophecy that the house of David and Jerusalem will mourn for Jesus the Messiah with the words of Jesus in the Sermon on the Mount: *Blessed are they that mourn, for they shall be comforted.* Matthew 5:4. Although Jerusalem rejected the Lord Jesus when He came the first time, they will mourn that rejection and worship Him when He returns the second time. Just after death, the body of Jesus was pierced again by a spear to confirm that He had actually died. John 19:34.

A similar mingling of the First and Second Comings of the Messiah occurs in Zechariah 13:7. *"Strike the Shepherd and the sheep will be scattered."* Matthew 26:31, Mark 14:27. The disciples scattered when Jesus was arrested. In fact Jesus persuaded the guards to take Him peaceably and voluntarily in exchange for the guards permitting the other disciples to flee. If one reads John 18:1-8, one can perceive that the guards lacked the power to arrest Jesus against His will (they fell backwards in His presence). The guards must have been astonished to see Jesus heal the ear of the man whom Peter had cut with a sword (Matthew 26:51-54; Mark 14:47; Luke 22:49-51; John 18:10-11) -- they were so astonished that they took no action against Peter even though he had offered armed resistance and had wounded one of the guards. All of this was to fulfill the prophecy of Zechariah. Zechariah 13:8-9 refer to events connected to the Jewish War or to the Second Coming.

Malachi was the last recorded prophet until John the Baptist. To our best knowledge there was a gap of over 400 years between the end of Malachi's ministry and the start of the preaching of John the Baptist, the last prophet before the ministry of the Lord Jesus Himself. When one mentions Malachi, the first things that come to most people's minds would be his denunciation of divorce and of holding back tithes from the Lord. Yet he also witnessed to the coming of the Messiah, proclaiming in Malachi 4:2:

> But to you who fear My name The Sun of Righteousness shall arise with healing in His wings; and you shall go out and grow fat like stall-fed calves.

This prophecy has been fulfilled by the Lord Jesus. His healings cannot be counted. In addition to the many and varied individual healings,

Jesus healed uncounted masses of people too. Matthew 12:15, Luke 6:19, Matthew 14:36, Mark 3:10, 6:56. Of course the spiritual healings should be added to the physical ones; Mary Magdalene (Mark 16:9) immediately comes to mind. So do Zacchaeus the money-grubbing tax collector (Luke 19) and the woman Jesus met at the Jacob's well at Sychar (John 4). Perhaps the most dramatic of all was Legion, the demon-possessed man who lived naked in a cemetery. Mark 5:1-20; Luke 8:26-40. As to the meaning of the last clause in Malachi 4:2, I would suggest that it refers to the abundant life that our Lord Jesus promised and that He actually gives to His people regardless of earthly fortune. *"I have come that they may have life, and that they may have it more abundantly."* John 10:10.

[There are various sources for additional Old Testament prophecies fulfilled by the coming of the Lord Jesus Christ. This selection is at best a sampler. Alfred Edersheim's Life and Times of Jesus the Messiah *is well worth reading. Arthur W. Pink is another authority on this subject, and there are many others.]*

PROPHECIES OF THE SPIRIT AND OF THE CHURCH

Acts 15 records the first church gathering to consider two related major doctrinal issues: can Gentiles be saved from their sins and enter the Christian church? If so, what are the requirements for them? Reading the chapter, three distinct positions seem to emerge.

1. Certain teachers from James (but not James himself) claimed that a Gentile must become a Jew and obey the Mosaic Law particularly with regard to circumcision (at least concerning males) in order to become a Christian. Acts 15:1 The speakers appear to advocate that salvation is at least partially earned. This position was rejected totally by the council at Jerusalem.

2. Certain others sought a compromise position in stating that a Gentile can be saved and become a Christian but thereafter must conform to the Law of Moses. Acts 15:5.

3. Others, especially Paul, taught that a Gentile may become a Christian without obedience to any portion of the Mosaic Law relating to ceremonies, such as circumcision. Peter expressed this view as recorded in Acts 11 after the conversion of Cornelius recorded in Acts 10. Peter

sided with Paul at this conference. But Peter later waffled on this stance in Antioch, as is recorded in Galatians 2:11-16.

These three views were debated at the council. As we study portions of the Shorter Prophets, we should note that James appealed (Acts 15:14-17) to the prophet Amos to settle the controversy:

> *Simon (i.e. Simon Peter) has declared how God at the first visited the Gentiles to take out of them a people for His name. And with this the words of the prophets agree, just as it is written: 'After this I will return and will rebuild the tabernacle of David, which has fallen down; I will rebuild its ruins, and I will set it up, so that the rest of mankind may seek the Lord -- Even all the Gentiles who are called by My name,' says the Lord who does all these things. (quoting portions of Amos 9:11-12)*

So it was a passage from Amos that settled the first great doctrinal controversy of the early Church. So much for calling these prophets minor!

James, the half-brother of our Lord Jesus Christ, described the Israel of his own time as a ruined tabernacle. The trials of the Lord Jesus Christ are clear evidence of the spiritual depths to which the leadership in Israel had fallen. As portrayed in the Gospels, the Saducee leadership of the Temple disbelieved totally in the supernatural. The Pharisees accepted more of the Old Testament Scriptures as a matter of doctrine but were so legalistic that they forgot about justice, mercy and faith. The Herodians were collaborators with the Roman authorities with no sense of the kingship of God, and the Zealots were violent terrorists like the two men crucified at the same time as the Lord Jesus. James' description was accurate even though there was a faithful remnant.

What is the rebuilt Tabernacle of David? Clearly it is the New Testament church, which has survived through the centuries. At Pentecost and at

Jerusalem, it was initially composed of Jews, but we know that our Lord Jesus' design for the church included "all nations." Matthew 28:19. This was already coming true by the time of the church conference in Jerusalem described in Acts 15. Peter had already preached to the household of Cornelius (Acts 10-11) and Paul and Barnabas had already taken their first missionary journey to Cyprus and to parts of Asia Minor, both areas that were predominantly Gentile with Jewish minorities. (Acts 13-14) The doctrine of the church and of the spiritual gifts that empower the church is elaborated in most of Paul's epistles, most especially in 1 Corinthians 12-14, Ephesians 1-2 and Colossians 1:18-29. The officers of the church are expounded in 1 Timothy 3 and Titus 1. This listing is not meant to exclude other passages but to give highlights to help you research Biblical teaching about the Church in more detail. Peter himself participated in the outreach to bring Gentiles into the Church and personally witnessed the gift of the Holy Spirit to Gentiles. (Acts 11:15-18) So this teaching is consistent with Peter's actions as well as with the words of Acts 15.

What is the implication of this teaching to understand our relationship with the Epistles of James and of 1 Peter? Both of these letters start with a greeting to the "dispersed", which is the term for the scattering of the Jews that persists in part even today after the re-founding of Israel. Does this mean that James and 1 Peter are primarily intended for Jewish believers only? The Biblical answer is a clear "No!" Starting with James 1:1, are we to understand that James was excluding believers within the land of Israel (they would not have been literally "scattered" or "dispersed") when he wrote this letter? James' own ministry was centered in Jerusalem; it would be strange to interpret his language to exclude those to whom he ministered on a daily basis. James refers to the "twelve tribes", and yet there would have been very few members of the tribes of the fallen Northern Kingdom who would have read his epistle near the time it was written because almost all of those tribes had been dispersed by the

Assyrians centuries earlier. [See Appendix A for more detail.] In contrast, 1 Peter 1 is written to "pilgrims of the dispersion" in a specific geographic area, much as most of Paul's epistles. One's first impulse from the word "dispersion" is to suspect that Peter's readers were exclusively Jewish, in line with the fact that Peter's primary ministry was to the Jewish people. But Peter tells his readers that they were "not a people" in 1 Peter 2:10. From Abraham and especially from Moses up to Philip's preaching in Acts 8 to the Samaritans, the Gentiles had been generally excluded from the most precious promises of God. (Ephesians 2:11-13; Romans 3:1-2, 9:1-5; see also the statements of the Lord Jesus to two Gentile women who did receive His blessing in Matthew 15:21-28, Mark 7:24-30 and John 4:21-26). According to Hosea 1-2, Israel would fall from being God's people to the unbelieving position of the Gentiles, who had never to this time been the people of God (although there were rare exceptions individually and in exceptional national instances). The end of Hosea 2 promises restoration to unfaithful Israel, but Gentiles can also be included within the description of Hosea 2:23. The bride in Hosea 2 pre-figures the Bride in Revelation, which is clearly the Church composed of believing Jew and Gentile alike. So Peter's readers in 1 Peter 2:10 who had been "not a people" had been either unfaithful Israelites or Gentiles and most probably some of both. This matches with Ephesians 2:11-22 and in particular with the "one new man" of Ephesians 2:15. It also matches the figure of the olive tree of Romans 11:13-25 in which believing Jews and believing Gentiles are to be found in the same root (perhaps an allusion to Isaiah 11:10, the Root of Jesse). By the same token, we are spiritually part of the "twelve tribes" addressed by James in accord with Romans 2:28-29:

> *For he is not a Jew who is one outwardly, nor is circumcision that which is outward in the flesh; but he is a Jew who is one inwardly; and circumcision is that of the heart, in the Spirit, not in the letter; whose praise is not from men but from God.*

And again it is written in Romans 3:27-4:1:

> *Where is boasting then? It is excluded. By what law? Of works? No,*
> *but by the law of faith. Therefore we conclude that a man is justified*
> *by faith apart from the deeds of the law. Or is He the God of the Jews*
> *only? Is He not also the God of the Gentiles? Yes, of the Gentiles also,*
> *since there is one God who will justify the circumcised by faith and the*
> *uncircumcised through faith. Do we then make void the law through*
> *faith? Certainly not! On the contrary, we establish the law.* **What**
> **then shall we say that Abraham our father has found according**
> **to the flesh?** *(emphasis added)*

So Abraham is our father. In Romans 4 Paul goes on to expound both Abraham and David as our spiritual forbears as being justified by faith and not by works of any kind. This is true without regard to human ancestry. For our present discussion, we need to establish that James and 1 Peter apply to the entire Christian Church and not merely to a small segment of it. In fact, the entire Church is *"one body [subject to] one Spirit, just as you were called in one hope of your calling; one Lord, one faith, one baptism; one God and Father of all, who is above all, and through all, and in you all."* (Ephesians 4:4-6)

Therefore we can and should conclude that the precious promises of James and Peter are shared by the entire church and each and every true member of it. The promise of wisdom in James 1:5 is for us. The undeserved blessings of 1 Peter 2:9-10, derived from Hosea 1-2, are ours:

> *But you are a chosen generation, a royal priesthood, a holy nation,*
> *His own special people, that you may proclaim the praises of Him who*
> *called you out of darkness into His marvelous light; who once were not*
> *a people but are now the people of God, who had not obtained mercy*
> *but now have obtained mercy.*

Hallelujah!

James in Act 15 went on to prescribe certain necessary practical requirements for Gentile converts to maintain a good witness to all those who were familiar with the Law of Moses -- especially Jews but also Gentiles who had become proselytes to Judaism. Gentiles were required by the terms of the letter from the council to avoid sexual immorality (a requirement of conscience amplified by the Law of Moses and particularly the Seventh Commandment), to avoid things polluted by idols (compare 1 Corinthians 8 and 1 Corinthians 10:19-33 for a fuller explanation of this basic principle -- the main purpose of this command was to avoid giving unnecessary offense), to avoid eating meat from strangled animals and to avoid eating meat with blood remaining in it. The emerging church of both Jew and Gentile (which Paul describes more fully in Ephesians 2:13-22, for example) is the first fulfillment of the prophecy of Amos that David quoted.

When Paul in Romans 9:22-29 showed that Jew and Gentile were together in one Church, he quoted from Hosea and Isaiah:

> *What if God, wanting to show His wrath and to make His power known, endured with much longsuffering the vessels of wrath prepared for destruction, and that He might make known the riches of His glory on the vessels of mercy, which He had prepared beforehand for glory, even us whom He called, not of the Jews only, but also of the Gentiles? As He says also in Hosea: "I will call them My people, who were not My people, and her beloved, who was not beloved." And it shall come to pass in the place where it was said to them, '"You are not My people," there they shall be called sons of the living God. Isaiah also cries out concerning Israel: "Though the number of the children of Israel be as the sand of the sea, The remnant will be saved. For He will finish the work and cut it short in righteousness, because the Lord will*

make a short work upon the earth." And as Isaiah said before: "Unless the Lord of Sabaoth had left us a seed, We would have become like Sodom, and we would have been made like Gomorrah."

The references are to Hosea 2:23 and 1:10, and to Isaiah 10:22 and 1:9.

Isaiah is not one of the Shorter Prophets, but one should note his emphasis on the salvation of the Gentiles. He wrote somewhat later than Amos and expanded the idea originally expressed in Amos, as in Isaiah 11:10, 42:1-12 and Isaiah 49:6. Moses also exhorts the Gentiles to rejoice with Israel when God destroys Israel's enemies in Deuteronomy 32:43. This basic principle underlies the Christian community's support for the national existence of Israel as a preparation for God's deliverance of Israel both nationally and spiritually.

Peter quoted the prophet Joel during the very first Christian sermon on the original Day of Pentecost, explaining that the miraculous languages heard and understood by the Pentecost pilgrims were a fulfillment of Joel 2:28-32:

But Peter, standing up with the eleven, raised his voice and said to them, "Men of Judea and all who dwell in Jerusalem, let this be known to you, and heed my words. For these are not drunk, as you suppose, since it is only the third hour of the day. But this is what was spoken by the prophet Joel: 'And it shall come to pass in the last days, says God, That I will pour out of My Spirit on all flesh; Your sons and your daughters shall prophesy. Your young men shall see visions; Your old men shall dream dreams. And on My menservants and on My maidservants I will pour out My Spirit in those days; and they shall prophesy. I will show wonders in heaven above and signs in the earth beneath: Blood and fire and vapor of smoke. The sun shall be turned into darkness, and the moon into blood, before the coming of the great and awesome day of the Lord. And it shall come to pass that whoever calls on the name of the Lord shall be saved.'"

Once again we can see the significance of these Shorter Prophets. While some of the extraordinary signs in the heavens and on earth may also refer to the Second Coming, we do know about the sun being turned to darkness for 3 hours while Jesus was on the Cross. Matthew 27:45. But plainly Peter preached that the witness from the Upper Room in multiple languages that people had never studied or learned was a fulfillment of Joel's prophecy. Although the predictions were veiled before the death of Christ, the Church as a united body composed of both Jew and Gentile was predicted by some of the Shorter Prophets. Furthermore, the Holy Spirit would be the vital unifying factor for the Church. 1 Corinthians 12:4-13; Ephesians 4:1-16.

Amos is not the only prophetic passage that Gentiles would come to believe in and trust the God of Abraham, of Isaac and of Jacob. As it is written in Malachi 1:11:

> *For from the rising of the sun, even to its going down, My name shall be great among the Gentiles; In every place incense shall be offered to My name, and a pure offering. For My name shall be great among the nations," says the Lord of Hosts.*

When we consider Revelation 5:8 and 8:3-4, the incense of which Malachi spoke seems to be the prayers of the saints (in the sense that Paul used the term to mean believers in general, as in Romans 1:7, 1 Corinthians 1:2, 2 Corinthians 1:1, Ephesians 1:1, Philippians 1:1, and Colossians 1:2). So today God's prophecy through Malachi is being fulfilled whenever real believers pray with a true heart.

THE RETURNING MESSIAH — GOD RETURNING TO EARTH

It is a common premise of virtually all the prophets that Israel will be exiled and eventually be returned to the land of Israel. Moses repeatedly warned that the people of Israel would be scattered from the land. Deuteronomy 4:27, Deuteronomy 28:37 and Deuteronomy 28:64 are the most direct of Moses' warnings concerning exile. Solomon when dedicating the original Temple also made reference to a time of exile. 1 Kings 8:46-50. The first of the Israelites to be exiled were the bulk of the Northern Tribes as recorded in 2 Kings 17. This is commonly dated at 722 or 721 BC. These are the "Lost Tribes" who have not returned to Israel in any organized manner, although there was a small sprinkling of them among Judah and probably in modern Israel. The Southern Kingdom was finally destroyed with Solomon's Temple by Nebuchnezzar, commonly dated at 586 BC. The first wave of exiles, of which Daniel and Ezekiel were a part, is commonly dated at 605 BC when Jeremiah was still alive. So there were approximately 20 years when Judah staggered along as a vassal state under Babylonian overlordship. Likewise the first people to return to Israel (from the descendants of the former Kingdom of Judah) started back about 536 BC, but so far as we know Zerubbabel's Temple was not rebuilt until 516 BC. So there were 70 years from first exile to first return and 70 years with no Temple. So Jeremiah's prophecy (25:11-12, 29:10) was fulfilled. It was these passages that stirred the aged Daniel to impassioned prayer in Daniel 9 when he realized that the time had run. Daniel 9:2. Then as the Lord Jesus predicted in Matthew 24, Mark 13 and Luke 21 (and also Moses' warnings of Deuteronomy 4 and 28), Judah was again exiled amidst great slaughter.

With this general background we can consider Hosea 9 and especially its conclusion in Hosea 9:17: *My God will cast them away, because they did not obey Him; and they shall be wanderers among the nations.* Zechariah 7:8-14 gives multiple reasons why God uprooted is people from the land He had promised to them. Many of the violations of the Law mentioned there involve greed as a motive, for usually it is for money that people will pervert justice. Since the people refused to listen to God and to His prophets, He refused to listen to their prayers.

There are various theories where the Northern Kingdom descendants have ended up, but it is clear that the mass of the survivors of the Northern Kingdom tribes were forcibly resettled by the Assyrians in what is now eastern Iran and perhaps Afghanistan. 2 Kings 17:6. Modern Israel has permitted immigration under its Law of Return from areas as far as China and Ethiopia under the belief that fragments of the Lost Tribes have ended up that far from the land of Israel. Israeli scholars are searching for other fragments. Other people who believe that they are part of the Lost Tribes have traced wanderings into China and then into India and other portions of Asia. It should be remembered that these migrations have been filled with peril and disaster (Deuteronomy 28:15-68; 32:15-42).

And what of the Southern Kingdom? They were exiled once by Nebuchadnezzar and permitted to return by the Persians under Cyrus. The books of Ezra and Nehemiah record the struggles to re-establish a Jewish civilization in a now desolate land, and also the disobedience of the returning people. Haggai, Zechariah (whom our Lord Jesus said was martyred in Matthew 23:35) and Malachi prophesied to the returning remnant. Esther tells the cliff-hanging story of the survival against Haman's intrigues of both the returning Jews and of those who remained behind. Had Haman succeeded, all known Jews would have been killed in the entire Persian Empire, including all in Jerusalem and the ancestors of our Lord Jesus Christ. Many descendants of those spared in Esther's time lived in communities in the cities of Iraq and Iran that existed until after World War 2 when these communities emigrated almost <u>en masse</u> to modern Israel. In fact, there were similar Jewish communities in the entire Middle East, tolerated although suffering moderate (in the very best cases) to mostly severe discrimination, under most of the Muslim dynasties after Muhammed until the 1950s. As strange as it may seem today, until 1948 it was often safer to be a Jew in Islamic-ruled lands even with the discrimination than it was in many periods of Czarist Russian history, not to mention Nazi Germany or the Spain of the Inquisition. Refugees from Spain after 1492 found relative safety in Salonika (the ancient Thessalonica where Paul ministered), now in Greece but then ruled by Muslim Ottoman Turks. England had expelled all Jews in 1290 until the time of Oliver Cromwell in the 1650s, who permitted resettlement. This action was confirmed by Charles II, his successor, in one of their few points of agreement. Even in America, we have to remember that our nation refused Jewish immigration from Germany in 1938 and that Jewish immigrants in the late 1800s and early 1900s often faced discrimination or at least ridicule when they arrived. This is one of those cases in which all sides were wrong. The wanderings were indeed caused by sin, but the nations were not welcoming nor merciful as they ought to have been. Obadiah 8-15 is an example.

Let one modern example serve as a summary of the perils experienced by generations of Jews as prophesied by Moses at God's direction by reason of their persistent disobedience. The Lord Jesus repeated the warnings.

Matthew 23 & 24 are one extended example; note also Matthew 21:33-46. And yet the human beings who inflicted these sufferings are fully responsible in turn for their sins, even though God permitted them to occur. Obadiah 9-16; Isaiah 47:6-15; Zechariah 1:1-15; Romans 9:15-33. In fact all of humanity, whether Jew or Gentile, is under sin and subject to the judgment of God unless redeemed through the blood of our Lord Jesus Christ. Romans 3:9-31.

The time of my example is the 2nd half of 1940 and the 1st half of 1941. The place is Lithuania, a new home to some Jews who had escaped the Nazi-Soviet partition of Poland in late 1939. Other Jewish communities had been there for centuries. Then the Soviets invaded Lithuania in 1940 and starting deporting "unreliable class elements" to concentration camps. So the refugee Polish Jews sought means of escape. Because of the war, westward was essentially closed. A Japanese Christian diplomat named Sugihara helped many Jews (I have read estimates varying from 2000 to 40,000 of the number that were delivered from death) to escape all the way across Russia to Japan. While a few were able to go across the Pacific Ocean to the United States before Pearl Harbor, most stayed under Japanese control. In this case the Japanese treated them relatively well despite the Hitler alliance. The Japanese government sent them to Shanghai, China for the duration of the war. Once again they would have had to flee ahead of the fall of mainland China to the Communists under Mao in 1949. While the distances and the changes in government for this group of refugees are greater and more rapid than most, the trials of this group certainly illustrate the dangers that so many Jews experienced throughout their generations of exile.

How should Christians have reacted to the wanderings of the Jewish people? They should have been compassionate and sought to witness to the coming of the Messiah, Jesus Christ, as did Paul. Now that Israel is again a nation, we should obey God's Word to Moses in Deuteronomy 32:43:

"Rejoice, O Gentiles, with His people; for He will avenge the blood of His servants, and render vengeance to His adversaries; He will provide atonement for His land and His people." Indeed the atonement has now been provided. It remains only for Israel to embrace that atonement in the person of Jesus the Messiah, as one day it will as prophesied in Zechariah 12:10 among other passages.

Candor requires that I acknowledge that many godly scholars disagree that the promises of restoration apply to all of Israel but apply exclusively to believers within Israel, and that there will never be more than a fragment of the nation that truly believes. Martin Luther is one example, although he did say that his views would be disproved if Israel was ever re-established in the Holy Land as has in fact occurred about 4 centuries after his death. But my answer is not based primarily on history but on Romans 11 itself. I interpret the promises of the Shorter Prophets as including the entire last generation of Israel based on Romans 11:25-32, which reads:

> *For I do not desire, brethren, that you should be ignorant of this mystery, lest you should be wise in your own opinion, that blindness in part has happened to Israel until the fullness of the Gentiles has come in. And so all Israel will be saved, as it is written: "The Deliverer will come out of Zion, and He will turn away ungodliness from Jacob. For this is My covenant with them, when I take away their sins." Concerning the gospel they are enemies for your sake, but concerning the election they are beloved for the sake of the fathers. For the gifts and the calling of God are irrevocable. For as you were once disobedient to God, yet have now obtained mercy through their disobedience, even so these also have now been disobedient, that through the mercy shown you they also may obtain mercy. For God has committed them all to disobedience, that He might have mercy on all.*

The quotation is from Isaiah 59:20-21. I should grant an argument from Romans 3 and 4 and also from the metaphor in Romans 11 of the olive tree that modern believers, whether Jew or Gentile, are spiritually Israel as the adopted children of God. I would agree that any believer in Christ is spiritually of Israel. We are children of Abraham, Isaac and Jacob through faith by worshiping the Son of David, their descendent and "seed." But this interpretation, standing alone, does not do full justice to the passage. The *"blindness in part"* has a time limit -- *"until the fulness of the Gentiles be come in."* We are informed that *"He will turn away ungodliness from* <u>Jacob</u>.*"* *(emphasis added)* This does not fit the Church because the Church, while yet imperfect, is already holy in principle. Ungodliness is turned away in principle at salvation (for example 2 Corinthians 5:17), and this progresses as we grow in faith and grace. Moreover, the term *"Jacob"* does not fit the Church -- I can recall no passage elsewhere where Jacob is used for the church, because Jacob is the fleshly name and describes the original birth nature of Abraham's chosen grandson. Jacob means supplanter; he was literally a heel-grabber. The name fit Jacob before his wrestling with God in Genesis 32, but afterward his name was Israel, a Prince with God. That name Israel does describe the Church. The fleshly name is used in Romans 11:26 instead of the spiritual name, indicating Israel of the flesh (national descent) rather than Israel of the Spirit. To confirm this, we are instructed that *"the gifts and the calling of God are irrevocable."* While this is true of any believer, the context of this passage points back to the covenants with Abraham (Genesis 15) and with David (2 Samuel 7). It will be through the witness of the Church that the truth will eventually come back to national Israel. Certainly so, because it will be the New Testament that will unlock the door for national Israel to the Kingdom of God. The witness of the Apostles has been echoed by the true Church through the centuries so that in God's appointed time the remnant of believing Israel will become the entire nation of Israel. As Romans 11:15 says, the fullness of Israel will be *"life from the dead."* So the entire chapter of Romans 11 is the basis upon which I interpret the promises of the Shorter Prophets to apply both to the Church and to the entire nation of Israel that survives to the return to earth of the Lord Jesus Christ. That entire generation without exception will then mourn for and worship Jesus, Who all along was, is and always will remain the Messiah and King of Israel (for further passages on the connection between the King and the Messiah as one and the same, review Psalms 2, 45 and 89, remembering that the words "anointed", Messiah, and Christ in the Greek all come from the same root).

Hosea 3:4-5 gives a succinct summary of Israel's history from Nebuchadnezzar forward:

> *For the children of Israel shall abide many days without king or prince, without sacrifice or sacred pillar, without ephod or teraphim. Afterward the children of Israel shall return and seek the Lord their God and David their king. They shall fear the Lord and His goodness in the latter days.*

For virtually the entire time from the initial fall of Jerusalem, the children of Israel lacked a fully independent national government. For the Northern Kingdom exiles, there is no known national government since. Their sacrifices never resumed after Assyria deposed King Hoshea, even for the remnant that was faithful to God (unless they escaped to Judah) rather than the images of the calves. For the descendants of the Southern Kingdom, the sacrifices stopped with the fall of Jerusalem and the destruction of Herod's Temple in 70 AD, although there were earlier stoppages in Nebuchadnezzar's time, during the time of Antiochus Epiphanes and when Jesus died as the once-for-all Passover. To date there is no replacement Temple in the physical sense. Neither does the Levitical priesthood function. But afterward Israel would indeed be restored spiritually as well as nationally. The national restoration is in process and there is a firstfruits of the spiritual restoration, but the great harvest is yet to come. But even today there is no king and Prime Ministers rotate in and out of office frequently. "David" in Hosea 3 should be understood primarily as Jesus the Messiah, the Son of David Who is risen from the dead. In fact the Pharisees in Matthew 22:41-46 correctly understood that the Messiah would be the Son of David. How tragic it was that instead of worshiping the Son of David they ended up with the Saducees instigating Pilate to crucify Him! So close and yet so far! But Hosea 3 ends in hope. Israel will yet worship the Son of David and recognize Him as King. (John 5:17-29; Zechariah 12:10; see also Psalms 2 and 110 and Isaiah 6, noting again that the Spirit uses the plural "Us" to identify God in Isaiah 6:8. So the King that Isaiah saw is probably the Son of God before His human birth, similar to the Jesus Christ Who appeared to John in Revelation 1 after His resurrection.)

Secondarily, I do believe that King David himself will be resurrected as the viceroy of the Messiah for Israel when the Messiah rules personally the entire earth after Armageddon, although I would not be 100% sure that this interpretation is correct. If this is true, I am sure that King David would be delighted with such close fellowship with his King.

As the Shorter Prophets have spoken concerning the wanderings and troubles of Israel, they have also spoken concerning its restoration to the land of Israel and its reunification. Ezekiel 37 is perhaps the most picturesque prophecy in terms of the dry bones coming to life, but the Shorter Prophets are also clear about this, particularly at the end of their prophecies. Hosea 14 is one instance. Joel 3, which has aspects of events which occurred during the first scatterings of the Northern and Southern Kingdoms, also has prophecies which reach forward to the final regathering of all of Israel into its ancient land. Joel 3:12-13 is echoed in Revelation 14:14-20. Amos 9:14-15 is succinct, with God speaking:

I will bring back the captives of My people Israel. They shall build the waste cities and inhabit them. They shall plant vineyards and drink wine from them. They shall also make gardens and eat fruit from them. I will plant them in their land, and no longer shall they be pulled up from the land I have given them," says the Lord your God.

In this vein also consider the close of Micah (7:18-20):

> *Who is a God like You, pardoning iniquity and passing over the transgression of the remnant of His heritage? He does not retain His anger forever, because He delights in mercy. He will again have compassion on us and will subdue our iniquities. You will cast all our sins into the depths of the sea. You will give truth to Jacob and mercy to Abraham, which You have sworn to our fathers from days of old.*

Zephaniah 3 recognized the contemporary sin of Jerusalem and yet promised regathering, restoration and deliverance, with their Lord their King in their midst. Zephaniah 3:15-17. Zechariah 12, 13 and 14 have similar promises, recognizing that the time for their fulfillment will be a time of great conflict as well. In this respect Zechariah is similar to Revelation (for example Revelation 13 & 14). Our Lord Jesus, the rejected Messiah, predicted that the spiritual house of Jerusalem would be left desolate, but not forever -- but *until you say "Blessed is He Who comes in the name of the Lord."* Matthew 23:39. The reverent crowds quoted this verse when Jesus was riding into Jerusalem on what is today called Palm Sunday. Matthew 21:9. The reference is to Psalm 118:26, just after the prophecy, *The Stone that the builders rejected has become the chief cornerstone.* Psalm 118:22. So Israel will eventually *mourn the One Whom they pierced, as one mourns for an only son.* Zechariah 12:10. Then Israel will no longer be desolate spiritually but alive and invincible!

What about you? Do you reject or receive the Messiah? Will you worship Him now while you can do so voluntarily? Or will you wait until

He forces you to worship Him unwillingly (Philippians 2:10-11)? To Jew and Gentile alike He offers eternal life. *To as many as received Him, to them He gave the right to become the children of God, to those who believe on His name, who were born not of blood, nor of the will of the flesh, nor of the will of man, but of God.* John 1:12-13

Appendices to Part Two

The Composition of the Southern Kingdom
A Historical Note Concerning Idolatry
The Place of Money in the Life of a Christian
Elijah & Elisha

APPENDIX A —
THE COMPOSITION OF THE
SOUTHERN KINGDOM

Following Solomon's reign and death, Rehoboam his son by threatening heavier taxation (1 Kings 12) triggered the division of Israel into the Northern Kingdom (often called Israel, or Ephraim or Joseph after its most prominent tribe, or sometimes Samaria, after its later capital) and the Southern Kingdom (often called Judah after its most prominent tribe). Jerusalem and the Temple remained under the control of Judah, although Jerusalem itself virtually straddled the border between Judah and Benjamin as stated in Joshua 15:8. The only two tribes clearly within the area of Judah remaining control were Judah and Simeon, whose territory was also within Judah in fulfillment of Jacob's prophecy concerning Simeon and Levi that God would *"divide them in Jacob and scatter them in Israel."* Genesis 49:7. (Levi was scattered into various cities of refuge throughout Israel. See Joshua 21.) It may be questioned whether Simeon had separate tribal organization by this time or had been absorbed into Judah. God warned Solomon that because of his unfaithfulness that his son would rule only one tribe -- Judah. 1 Kings 11:11-13.

The Scriptures are equally clear that at least the bulk of Benjamin returned to allegiance to the King of Judah instead of the Northern

Kingdom, even in Rehoboam's lifetime. This persisted into King Asa's reign and later. 1 Kings 12:21-23, 15:22; 2 Chronicles 11:1-23 and also chapters 14-15. It is also recorded that many of the tribe of Levi who had resided in what became the Northern Kingdom sided with Judah and migrated south as refugees. 2 Chronicles 11:13.

King Jeroboam, the first king of the Northern Kingdom, faced an immediate problem from his perspective even though he knew that God had given him ten tribes. With the Temple being under the control of Judah, he risked the loss of population if the northern tribes obeyed the commands of the Law concerning worship at the Temple. For political reasons King Jeroboam created a royal cult of worship at Bethel, where Jacob had had his first dream. A second site was built at Dan. This cult involved idols of a calf in direct violation of the Second Commandment. 1 Kings 12:25-33. God warned against this in 1 Kings 13. The result was that the bulk of the Levites refused to participate in idol-worship and fled to Judah, strengthening the Southern Kingdom to a point where it could defend itself even against an all-out attack by its new northern neighbor and potential enemy. Under King Asa more families from Simeon (to the extent that they were not already in Judah), Ephraim and Manasseh returned to allegiance to the House of David. 2 Chronicles 15:8-9.

By the time of King Hezekiah, after the Northern Kingdom had fallen, the House of David exercised authority over the former territory of Ephraim and Manasseh in central Israel. Assyria had exiled the population, but it is reasonable to assume that there were a few escapees along the way and some Northern Kingdom families that were able to flee the Assyrians to either remote hiding places or across the border to Judah. Some families of Judah may have moved into vacated territory. At this point the Kingdom of Judah probably had a small sprinkling of all the tribes with larger remnants of Ephraim and Manasseh. The bulk of Levi, Simeon, Benjamin and Judah would have been the largest proportion.

Centuries later after Judah had been exiled and the population was allowed to return, Anna of the tribe of Asher, a prophetess, added her witness to the infant Jesus Christ as Redeemer. Luke 2:36-38. The Apostle Paul was of the tribe of Benjamin; he was born outside of Israel and educated within Israel.

With Judah having been scattered again in 70 AD and restored to statehood in 1948, it is probable that the modern citizens of Israel are probably mostly composed of descendants of Judah, Levi, Benjamin and Simeon with some representation of Ephraim and Manasseh with a sprinkling from other tribes. It should also be noted that there are probably almost 1 million residents of Israel of Arab descent from Ishmael, some of whose forbears remained in Israel in 1948 despite the fact that their leaders called on them to flee before the Arab attack on the new state of Israel. The total would represent well over 10% of the population. There are also Palestinians who were in the 1967 territories when they changed from Arab to Israeli control. The process of regathering the children of Israel is far from complete and probably considerably less than half done as I write, although nobody knows for sure how fast it will proceed nor how far along we are in the process.

As a comparison, the Northern Kingdom population was transformed by the Assyrians, who exiled the Israelite tribes and imported other subject peoples into the northern part of Israel. 2 Kings 17:5-41. The resulting mixed population came to be known as Samaritans, whose descendants lived in part of the old Northern Kingdom in the time that the Lord Jesus walked the earth. Because of their mixed origin, the Samaritans were wrongly detested by most Jews in His time on earth. Our Lord Jesus rebuked this prejudice, not only in the story of the Good Samaritan but also in ministering in the Samaritan village of Sychar (John 4). That particular village gave a far greater response to Jesus' preaching than many of the towns around the Sea of Galilee. The Samaritans as a whole proved

Thomas D. Logie

to be quite receptive to the Gospel when Philip, one of the first deacons, preached to them. Acts 8. Although the Samaritan population suffered severely during the Jewish War from 66-70 AD, it is believed that there are perhaps 700 descendants of the Samaritans alive even today. The bulk of the population of Israel today is descended from the Southern Kingdom (Judah, Levi and Benjamin predominantly) with a substantial minority of Arabs descended from Ishmael.

APPENDIX B —
A HISTORICAL NOTE CONCERNING
IDOLATRY

Even though God has warned most solemnly concerning idolatry, it was present within Israel during the Exodus (for example, the Golden Calf -- see also 1 Corinthians 10:7) and later in Israel's history. For example, see Judges 18. Idols of calves reappeared at the very beginning of the Northern Kingdom. Asa, the third king of Judah, faced a situation in which his grandmother worshiped an idol. King Asa's response was to remove his grandmother from her place as queen mother. 1 Kings 15:13. This was a step in the right direction which reflected Asa's basic faithfulness but stopped short of the prescribed penalty under the Law of Moses, which was death. Deuteronomy 13:6-16. King Jehu of Israel did indeed burn Baal worshipers to death, but he did not uproot the shrines at Bethel and Dan that Jeroboam had set up at the inception of the Northern Kingdom. As we read the history, Jehoshaphat (2 Chronicles 17:6) Hezekiah (2 Kings 18:4-5) and Josiah (2 Chronicles 34:3-7, 2 Kings 23) all suppressed idolatry. There can be no doubt that these kings acted at God's command. Does such a command to enforce an immediate death penalty for worship of a false god apply today?

Several considerations indicate that current governments do not have such a commission from God, and neither does the Church. The church is not itself a political body and the parable of the tares (Matthew 13:24-30, 36-43) indicates that the separation of wheat and tares is the work of angels and not of humans. This work is done at the end of the age and not immediately. Further, one must recall the special covenant relationship between Israel and God which has not been repeated with any other nation. Moses gave the Law to Israel. While we also are forbidden to commit idolatry, the immediate punishments of the Mosaic Law with respect to the worship of God were never intended to be administered by Gentile governments of any description. I would counsel that a Gentile government must concern itself with the 2nd table of the Law which deals with relationships among people, not with the 1st table which deals with relationships between God and people. Paul, when writing about human government in Romans 13, quotes the Sixth through Tenth Commandments but makes no mention of the first five. Romans 13:9.

As a practical matter, we cannot count on godly leaders in government. The very powers that a government would use to enforce worship of the true God can also be used to suppress true worship, and in the long run they would be so used. Even Israel often had evil rulers even despite its special covenant relationship with God. The brutal treatment by Manasseh of Isaiah is one example in Biblical times. The Inquisition, Nazi Germany and Communist governments in the 20th century are more recent examples. If Jesus Christ were ruling directly and personally on earth, He can be trusted with absolute power in all spheres, but it is folly to entrust powers to control religious worship by force in the hands of sinful human beings. The examples of Stalin and Mao should be enough to warn against any attempt to permit any government to intrude into worship. Modern Iran is another contemporary example. In the times of Jesus Christ, the Roman Empire was developing its cult of Emperor-worship as a counterfeit to the true worship of Jesus Christ. The Roman Empire did not hesitate to persecute both Christian and Jew for refusing to worship the Emperor. Government enforcement of the Law against idolatry must wait for the personal return of Jesus Christ.

There is more to the commandment against idolatry than the basic prohibition against worshiping an image or object or using an image or object in the process of worshiping God. People can and do idolize entertainers, sports players and teams, spouses ("worshiping the ground he/she walks on") governments, nations and dictators. Most insidious of all is the worship of oneself. We sometimes call this narcissism after the Greek mythological character who could not stop gazing at his own reflection. Only the Father, His Son Jesus Christ and the Holy Spirit are worthy of worship and unquestioning obedience. Yes, there is secondary authority such as human government, but such secondary authority is limited within bounds described in the Holy Bible. Such authority is normally to be obeyed within its limits, but no authority has the unqualified finality of the authority of God. To take one example, Peter and John refused to obey a government command to stop preaching in the name of the risen Jesus Christ. Acts 4:13-21. They defied that order practically every day of their lives.

The persistence of idolatry throughout Biblical and human history should warn us that the impulse to worship something or someone visible is embedded in sinful human nature. We must resist the temptation to commit idolatry in any form and indeed kill such remaining tendencies within us. (Romans 8:12-13) Until we have been transformed and can see Jesus Christ face to face, we can never have a visible object of worship. As it is written:

> ... that the genuineness of your faith, being much more precious than gold that perishes, though it is tested by fire, may be found to praise, honor, and glory at the revelation of Jesus Christ, _whom having not_

seen you love. Though now you do not see Him, yet believing, you rejoice with joy inexpressible and full of glory, receiving the end of your faith-the salvation of your souls. 1 Peter 1:7-9 (emphasis added)

And after eight days His disciples were again inside, and Thomas with them. Jesus came, the doors being shut, and stood in the midst, and said, "Peace to you!" Then He said to Thomas, "Reach your finger here, and look at My hands; and reach your hand here, and put it into My side. Do not be unbelieving, but believing." And Thomas answered and said to Him, "My Lord and my God!" Jesus said to him, "Thomas, because you have seen Me, you have believed. Blessed are those who have not seen and yet have believed." John 20:26-29 (emphasis added)

The first two Commandments mutually interlock. The First Commandment outlaws idolizing any human being or combination of human beings except Jesus Christ Himself as well as outlawing any division of worship with anyone except God Himself. The Second Commandment reinforces the First by outlawing objects and pictures as objects of worship or veneration. Our full and final love and devotion is to God Himself in all His glory, including all three Persons of the Godhead. For those of us who are married, our love for our mates is to reflect our love for God and have similar qualities even though we understand that both we and our mates are flawed. (Ephesians 5:22-33) Those of us who are adult and unmarried and able to live alone comfortably have a rare gift from God to be able to serve Him without a mate on earth. (1 Corinthians 7 discusses this in detail.)

APPENDIX C —
THE PLACE OF MONEY IN THE LIFE
OF A CHRISTIAN

If you were to consider the Lord Jesus' command to the rich young ruler to give his possessions to the poor and then to follow Him (Matthew 19:21) in isolation from the rest of Scripture, you might get the impression that physical poverty is the way to have fellowship with God. For a particular individual this may be necessary, but is this true for all Christians? One may try to argue this from historical examples, but as with other subjects there is no substitute for grappling with the Scriptures themselves.

The prevailing popular opinion in the time of our Lord Jesus' life on earth was that physical wealth was a sure sign of favor from God. Our Lord Jesus repeatedly corrected this illusion. When our Lord Jesus commented on the reaction of sadness by the rich young ruler, He said:

> *Then Jesus said to His disciples, "Assuredly, I say to you that it is hard for a rich man to enter the kingdom of heaven. And again I say to you, it is easier for a camel to go through the eye of a needle than for a rich man to enter the kingdom of God."*

> *When His disciples heard it, they were greatly astonished, saying,*
> *"Who then can be saved?" But Jesus looked at them and said to them,*
> *"With men this is impossible, but with God all things are possible."*
> *Matthew 19:23-26*

In Luke16:19-31, our Lord gave an instance when the pauper Lazarus was taken to everlasting joy while the rich man was taken in everlasting torment, starting with his burning tongue. The Lord Jesus also used an example of a rich farmer who lived only for retirement, not for God. Luke 12:16-21. Our Lord commended the poor widow who put her last mite into the treasury more than any of the wealthy contributors. Mark 12:41-44; Luke 21:1-4. Our Lord's half-brother James also faced a tendency on the part of the Jerusalem church to favor the rich over the poor and warned against it, noting that rich men were the ones who caused legal trouble for the members of the church. James 2:1-9. James also warned against focusing one's life on riches instead of the will of God (James 4:13-17) and against trying to get ahead by holding back employees' wages (James 5:1-6).

While in many passages "the poor" are mentioned without any discussion of the reasons for their poverty, Proverbs gives several ways in which some people bring poverty upon themselves. Rather than expound each of these verses individually, I will list them to help you search them out for yourself.

<u>Laziness:</u> Proverbs 6:9-11, 10:26, 12:24, 12:27, 13:4, 15:19, 18:9, 19:24, 20:4, 20:13 21:25, 22:13, 24:30-34, 26:13-16
Paul commanded in 2 Thessalonians 3:10, *If anyone will not work, neither shall he eat.*

<u>Adultery and allied sexual sins:</u> Proverbs 5:1-23, 6:23-35, 29:3
From my legal experience, I can surely attest to the truth that adultery has impoverished many. Divorce generally is costly to both parties even when

adultery is not involved or at least not proved. The emotional toll often triggers additional monetary losses.

Waste and inefficiency: Proverbs 10:5, 13:23, 21:5

Proverbs 13:23 also points out that lack of justice creates waste in addition to individual sin. From modern history we can observe that nations that have fairer justice systems as a rule generate more wealth than those that do not.

Refusal to hear instruction: Proverbs 1:7, 5:21-23, 8:10, 12:1, 13:1, 15:5

These verses and others like them apply to spiritual instruction as well as to employment and economics. Considering entry-level employment, a basic qualification is the willingness to hear and obey instructions relating to employment. Some people are unemployed because they develop a pattern of either being late or unready to work or unwilling to work at the task set by the supervisor. At the same time, learning and advancement is impossible if the student or employee will not pay attention to the instructor. It should also be noted that alcohol in any significant quantity and marijuana reduce memory function and are likely to hinder both education generally and following directions in particular.

"Get rich quick" schemes: Proverbs 28:22 (compare 1 Timothy 6:9-10)

Drunkenness & gluttony: Proverbs 23:21 (so-called recreational drugs such as methamphetamine, cocaine and marijuana can be included in this principle)

Uncontrolled anger: Proverbs 22:24-25, 29:22

Gossip, excess talking: Proverbs 14:23

Any employer or client needs to be able to count on confidentiality. Therefore, controlling one's speech is an essential part of keeping a job or otherwise earning money.

Lack of generosity, selfishness: Proverbs 11:24

Others clearly are poor or even incapable of work through no direct fault of their own.

The Lord Jesus told us that we will always have poor among us. Matthew 26:11. In this He was not distinguishing between those who are poor by reason of self-inflicted wounds and those who are poor for other reasons. We have both. Some people are incapable of competing in the modern work force by reason of age, ill health or other special challenges. In many countries, oppressive government, high tax rates and lack of social mobility are substantial barriers to anyone who desires to escape poverty. And certainly any Christian who is able should desire to provide enough for his family, regardless of the economic and social system which he may face. 1 Timothy 5:8.

So far, we can say that poverty is certainly not desirable for its own sake but sometimes is a consequence of one's own sin. Yet it is also true that both our Lord Jesus and James, His half-brother, perceived that the some rich people were oppressive and uncompassionate and that some obtained riches by fraud. Solomon had anticipated modern fraud in Proverbs 11:1, 16:11, 20:10 and 20:23. Yet a business run honestly is commended in Proverbs 11:1 and 16:11.

Our Lord Jesus never did condemn riches outright. Certainly Job, David and Solomon were wealthy. Our Lord used a parable that commended investment of wealth for a return and condemned a total lack of enterprise. Matthew 25:14-30. Clearly the parable can be applied to spiritual gifts as well as to money, but the passage commends business enterprise and condemns excess caution grounded in fear. Well-judged investments are treated as examples to imitate. It was prophesied that our Lord would be buried with the rich (Isaiah 53:9), which was fulfilled by Joseph of Arimathea and Nicodemus, both rich men. John 19:38-42. The spices that Nicodemus brought to the grave were very costly, showing that he was quite wealthy. One of Jesus' supporters was the wife of Herod's steward, who was a man of great authority and quite wealthy. Luke 8:3. His wife apparently gave financial support to Jesus Christ from her spending allowance. So some wealthy people have done great good which they could not have done without wealth.

I am indebted to Bo Bounds, a former pastor, for making a point in a sermon that there is a place for "the costly and the beautiful" in the worship of Jesus Christ. One example was the pouring out of the costly ointment worth about 9 months' wages on the body of our Lord Jesus shortly before His death. Matthew 26:6-13; Mark 14:3-9, John 12:1-8. Jesus did have one garment which was too good to tear up, so the soldiers rolled dice for it instead. John 19:23-24. Solomon's Temple was fantastically expensive for its time, made of the very best materials. Its beauty and grandeur was intended to convey visually the greatness and worthiness of God. However, this can be taken too far today as expensive buildings may absorb money that should go for missionary outreach and poor relief. We should remember that both Solomon's Temple and Herod's Temple were destroyed by God acting through militarily skilled but harsh empires. God has no need of buildings. Nevertheless, there is a time and place for the proper use of wealth in the worship of Jesus Christ.

One may ask me about inherited wealth as distinct from wealth that a person has earned himself or herself. *He who has a slack hand becomes poor, but the hand of the diligent makes rich.* Proverbs 10:4. But the Scriptures view preparing an inheritance for children and even grandchildren as right, not as greedy in itself. *A good man leaves an inheritance to his children's children, but the wealth of the sinner is stored up for the righteous.* Proverbs 13:22. The Scriptures also warn that an inheritance can easily be squandered. There is a sinful tendency to spend unearned money quickly and wastefully. *An inheritance gained hastily at the beginning will not be blessed at the end.* Proverbs 20:21. The story of the Prodigal Son (Luke 15:11-32) is an instance in which a premature inheritance nearly destroyed a man. Studies have shown that most people who become suddenly wealthy manage the new wealth badly and lose or spend it all in a few years. This includes lottery winners, and some sports figures and entertainment people, among others. But the potential for good is there if the money is used wisely.

> If you should receive wealth, seek wisdom from God as to how to use it, as Solomon did when he first became King of Israel. 1 Kings 3:5-15.

Even considering the pitfalls of sudden wealth, there is no justification for the cries of some that inheritance is fundamentally unfair and should be taxed into oblivion. For those parents who can, it is a duty to provide for their families even after death if God puts this within their reach. In social terms, inheritance is a bulwark against dictatorial economic control. Moses' Law expressly provided for inheritance. Number 27:1-11; Deuteronomy 21:15-17. A large inheritance can be spiritually dangerous, but it can also be a source of tremendous good. In any case it should have the protection of law.

What are proper purposes for wealth beyond the needs of the day? A first priority is the care of family members who are financially unable to care for themselves without fundamental fault on their part. 1 Timothy 5:8. We have already seen that investment is a legitimate use of such money from the Parable of the Talents. Matthew 25:14-30. In fact, investment can do great social good by fueling both innovation and employment. Direct relief for the poor is also good so long as most of the help actually reaches the poor instead of being consumed in administration. Care must be taken not to subsidize wicked practices such as drug usage or drunkenness. The rich young ruler was told to give his goods to the poor. Matthew 19:21 -- read Matthew 19:16-26 for the complete context. Christians and others have long contributed to the healing arts to the good of humanity as a whole. Saving for a reasonable retirement is appropriate -- we should not plan to burden our children if we can avoid it. To the contrary, we should hope to store up an inheritance for them if God permits. Proverbs 13:22; 2 Corinthians 12:14. Employers are not condemned in Scripture, although they are warned to treat employees fairly and courteously. Employees have a general duty of obedience. Ephesians 6:5-9.

In the usual course of history, Christianity has not been popular in the upper crust of society because Christianity is an unrelenting opponent of pride and arrogance in anyone. Most rich and powerful people like to strut and flaunt their positions. As Paul wrote in 1 Corinthians 1:26-29 through the Holy Spirit:

> *For you see your calling, brethren, that not many wise according to the flesh, not many mighty, not many noble, are called. But God has chosen the foolish things of the world to put to shame the wise, and God has chosen the weak things of the world to put to shame the things which are mighty; and the base things of the world and the things which are despised God has chosen, and the things which are not, to bring to nothing the things that are, that no flesh should glory in His presence.*

But Paul himself was one of the most brilliant men intellectually of any age. There have been wealthy Christians who have been good stewards of what the Master gave them. Job in ancient times was an outstanding example. Jay van Andel and Rich DeVos were businessmen who professed and lived Christianity in the last half of the 20th century in the United States. Watchman Nee was both a businessman and an outstanding Christian witness in China before and after the Communists took over. He suffered severely but steadfastly for his faith and his confiscated business. The fact that many wealthy people misuse their wealth is not a good reason for government to seize it. It is an illusion to believe that government would do better over the long run even if a country happens to have a wise ruler who truly cares for his people above himself, which is rare among the powerful. Wise government does not last if there is no system to restrain the institutional power of government. Scripture and later history alike (for example 1 Samuel 8 and 1 Kings 12) testify that government will do more damage than private individuals in misusing money. So the Christian church should thank God for those of wealth and intellect who are called to love and serve Jesus Christ even though they are relatively few. The church should pray for those who are in authority (1 Timothy 2:1-4) and pray that political leaders will have enough sense to permit freedom in matters of both faith and economics. In some countries a political system designed to restrain government has been a great blessing.

Most Christians outside the United States face at least official harassment if not worse and many must function under laws and economic rules designed to preserve government power rather than designed to permit spiritual, intellectual or economic growth without strict government control. In some countries there is explicit discrimination against Christians just because they are Christians. Some modern preachers teach a doctrine which echoes the old idea that wealth is a certain sign of God's favor and that a faithful Christian will inevitably become wealthy in this life. Note the shocked reaction of the disciples in Matthew 19:23-26 when the Lord Jesus explained that it is hard for a rich man to enter the Kingdom of God. Often the prosperity of the Christian is spiritual rather than economic; often the Christian's treasure is in heaven rather than on earth. (Matthew 6:19-34) We should remember that whatever we teach as Christian doctrine must be transportable from a wealthy country such as the United States to a leper colony in India or to a refugee camp along the Moei River in Thailand with no electricity or to a country such as Iran where converting to Christianity may risk a death penalty.

The Apostle Paul in 1 Timothy 6:6-19 discusses the topic of wealth as it may connect to the Christian life. The passage reads as follows:

Now godliness with contentment is great gain.

For we brought nothing into this world, and it is certain we can carry nothing out.

And having food and clothing, with these we shall be content.

But those who desire to be rich fall into temptation and a snare, and into many foolish and harmful lusts which drown men in destruction and perdition.

For the love of money is a root of all kinds of evil, for which some have strayed from the faith in their greediness, and pierced themselves through with many sorrows.

But you, O man of God, flee these things and pursue righteousness, godliness, faith, love, patience, gentleness.

Fight the good fight of faith, lay hold on eternal life, to which you were also called and have confessed the good confession in the presence of many witnesses.

I urge you in the sight of God who gives life to all things, and before Christ Jesus who witnessed the good confession before Pontius Pilate, that you keep this commandment without spot, blameless until our Lord Jesus Christ's appearing, which He will manifest in His own time,

He who is the blessed and only Potentate, the King of kings and Lord of lords, who alone has immortality, dwelling in unapproachable light, whom no man has seen or can see, to whom be honor and everlasting power. Amen.

Command those who are rich in this present age not to be haughty, nor to trust in uncertain riches but in the living God, who gives us richly all things to enjoy.

Let them do good, that they be rich in good works, ready to give, willing to share, storing up for themselves a good foundation for the time to come, that they may lay hold on eternal life.

The immediate previous context involved the denunciation of proud and argumentative people who harbored the old illusion that riches equate to godliness. So Paul untwists the false into the true: *godliness with contentment is great gain.* The gain of godliness combined with contentment far outweighs earthly wealth without godliness and contentment. Earthly wealth without God's blessing on it brings troubles in its wake. For American examples, consider the wealthy recluse Howard Hughes as an extreme example -- and his wealth was earned legitimately rather than by fraud as in the case of Bernie Madoff. Michael Jackson was at one time fabulously wealthy but plainly was spiritually bankrupt and died seeking joy through drugs. Elvis Presley had a similar end a generation earlier. Far better to be content with food and clothing as Paul states than to live the life of the spiritually bankrupt, whether rich, poor or in-between.

Being content with food and clothing does not mean that seeking profit is sinful. Our Lord Jesus Himself approved investment for profit, as we have seen earlier in Matthew 25:14-30. But if we devote our whole life to economic profit, we are inflating something that can be good in its place into an idol and probably violating at least the Tenth Commandment against covetousness at the same time. So often that covetousness ripens into a violation of the Eighth Commandment against theft as well. James warns against making profit our main goal in life in these words (4:13-17):

*Come now, you who say, "Today or tomorrow we will go to such
and such a city, spend a year there, buy and sell, and make a profit."
Whereas you do not know what will happen tomorrow. For what is
your life? It is even a vapor that appears for a little time and then
vanishes away. Instead you ought to say, "If the Lord wills, we shall
live and do this or that." But now you boast in your arrogance. All
such boasting is evil. Therefore, to him who knows to do good and does
not do it, to him it is sin.*

Solomon said this in Proverbs 27:1, *Do not boast about tomorrow, for
you do not know what a day may bring forth.* In the last 10 years (give
or take) I have seen the old General Motors stock drop from about $90
per share to virtually worthless. Enron's drop was even faster. So was
the implosion of AIG, of Bear Stearns and of Lehman Brothers. Fannie
Mae and Freddie Mac have had losses nearly as great. In England, the
Royal Bank of Scotland has had a near-failure similar to Citicorp in this
country. Earthquakes have wiped out tens of thousands of homes in Haiti
and in Chile in 2010 alone. In Biblical history, even good kings suffered
financial losses as discipline from God. 1 Kings 22:48; 2 Chronicles 20:36-
37. Since we know that even the shrewdest financiers can be burned, we
cannot count on our wealth, whether of gold, real estate, stocks, bonds
or any other asset you can name. Our trust must be in God Himself. We
should all wish that the slogan on our coinage were actually true of most
Americans: IN GOD WE TRUST.

This part of the teaching of Paul could be summarized by Proverbs
23:4-5: *Do not overwork to be rich; because of your own understanding,
cease! Will you set your eyes on that which is not? For riches certainly make
themselves wings; they fly away like an eagle toward heaven.* So we need to
steer between laziness (or other sin) which causes poverty and shame and
overwork which misdirects our life toward a goal of riches which cannot
satisfy the soul and may even damage the body.

If we do have wealth, we are commanded in 1 Timothy 6:17 to enjoy it as from God and to be willing to share with those who lack. Even though we may have abundance, we are still stewards of God and remain dependent on Him. Even if we are financially secure now, we never know when we may need to be on the receiving end. 2 Corinthians 8:1-15. We should remember that in our hour of need that we will receive the measure that we have shared in times of prosperity. Matthew 7:2, 12; Mark 4:24; Luke 6:38. We are not to trust in the riches but in the God Who has the power to give or withhold them. We should also note that Paul does not condemn the rich just because they are rich. Some, such as Job, are prospered by God from His generosity. Not all rich people are hardhearted as was Nabal (1 Samuel 25 -- he died of a heart attack at the thought of his wife being generous with David when he was fleeing from Saul).

However, we are warned strongly against the love of money. Money must be our tool, not our master. Matthew 6:24. Demas left Paul, *having loved this present world* (2 Timothy 4:10). Bunyan pictures Demas as having fallen down the shaft of a silver mine to his death. As we know from medicine and from Scripture, either misuse of wealth or poverty can kill. Let us pray to God for our daily bread (or ration) and for the wisdom to use properly what He gives us.

Let us attempt a summary of Biblical teaching about money even though we know that our summary will be imperfect and incomplete. At least this summary may be a quick reference to help someone get started in the Scriptures on this subject.

A) Most believers are not going to be rich on earth, but earthly prosperity is not sinful of itself. Jesus Christ Himself was not wealthy; he owned no real estate and did not even rent any during His ministry. Matthew 8:20; Luke 9:58.

B) There is no special virtue in poverty unless it is connected with a specific calling from God unique to that person. Often poverty is the result of laziness or some other sin with financial repercussions. However, not all poor people are poor because of specific sin on their part. In economies which are not free, many people are kept poor by evil government. (Proverbs 28:15 -- in contemporary times Cambodia under the Khmer Rouge and North Korea are especially terrible examples, as was Soviet Russia under Stalin and China under Mao. This is not a complete list.)

C) God condemns the idle rich, the arrogant and proud rich, the dishonest rich and the wasteful rich, but He does not condemn the rich indiscriminately.

D) Christians hold their assets, whether few or many, as stewards of God and under His direction.

E) Christians should tithe their income or more, but should also remember that justice, mercy, faith and love are the greatest issues to be confronted in this life. Matthew 23:23, Luke 11:42

F) Christians should be generous within their means. Proverbs 11:24

G) Christians should not begrudge the wealth of others, unless it was obtained by fraud or similar illegitimate means. Envy is always sinful. Proverbs 14:30, 23:17; Titus 3:3; 1 Peter 2:1. In the modern world, it is often necessary to amass large sums of capital to conduct research and to translate new technology into useful products that can make life physically easier for everyone. Someone will and should make a fortune in the process as a reward for the labor and risk.

H) Debt is undesirable and to be avoided where reasonably possible. Proverbs 22:7. Once debt has been incurred, whether wisely or not, it should be repaid on time or as close as possible. The idea of "strategic default" when someone is capable of paying the debt is wrong. *Better not to vow than to vow and not pay.* Ecclesiastes 5:5. A future lender facing a history of "strategic default" has every right to draw the inference that the prospective borrower is less than honest. This is unwise financially and not an appropriate witness for a Christian.

I) The Law of Moses did have a bankruptcy system embedded within the Jubilee. Leviticus 25; Deuteronomy 15:1-11. While it is not desirable, a Christian may resort to bankruptcy if he is genuinely unable to pay his or her debts and cannot reasonably expect to be able to pay. One of the purposes of bankruptcy laws is to restrain the most aggressive creditor from taking all that the debtor has to the detriment of other creditors who may have been more willing to forbear.

J) If reasonably possible, a Christian should restrain his or her consumption in favor of savings for times of need and for family inheritance. However, an inability to save because of low earning power should not bring any reproach so long as the person works to his ability and is frugal.

K) Children should take care of impoverished elderly parents as they can before resort is made to the church or to charity. 1 Timothy 5:16

L) Our praise of God must not depend on whether we are financially prosperous or not. As Habakkuk 3:17-19 says,

> *Though the fig tree may not blossom, nor fruit be on the vines;*

> *Though the labor of the olive may fail, and the fields yield no food;*

> *Though the flock may be cut off from the fold, and there be no herd in the stalls*

> *Yet I will rejoice in the Lord, I will joy in the God of my salvation.*

> *The Lord God is my strength; He will make my feet like deer's feet, and He will make me walk on my high hills.*

APPENDIX D —
ELIJAH & ELISHA

In our main volume we bypassed spiritual application of the personal lives of Elijah and Elisha for the sake of historical flow. There is enough profitable material to write a book on either or both of these two great prophets of God. I am not called to write such a book now, so I will try to give a few tidbits for you to launch your own studies on the personal qualities of these men and of their lives. As with all of my writing, please do not accept my statements blindly, but rather search the Scriptures for yourself to see whether what I am saying is true or not. Further, please allow for the fact that my sketch is very much incomplete.

Elisha sought and received a double portion of Elijah's spirit, so one would expect parallels between the two. (2 Kings 2 gives the details.) Elijah foretold the downfall of Ahab and of his posterity through the wrath of God, while Elisha arranged the commissioning of Jehu to accomplish this judgment. Elijah anointed a King of Syria who harried Israel, while Elisha blinded a Syrian army attacking Israel as prophesied by Elijah. And Elisha wept because of the coming Syrian king who would do terrible damage to his own people Israel.

Both prophets lived during judgments of God upon Israel administered through nature. I would approximate the length of the drought in Elijah's time at nearly 3 years (1 Kings 18:1), although if one counts back to the normal dry season before the drought started it could have been closer to 3½ years since rain had fallen. The Scripture does not give an exact duration. In giving advance warning to a faithful woman, Elisha spoke of a famine of 7 years' duration (2 Kings 8:1). Both prophets were protected by God, but in different ways. Elijah was hidden first by the Brook Cherith and then in Zarephath, where Elisha was protected publicly by 2 female bears and then by fire from heaven. Elijah was carried bodily from earth to heaven without death; Elisha died from disease (2 Kings 13:14).

Elisha imitated God in being no respecter of persons. Although he was an Israelite, he healed Naaman the Syrian of leprosy but inflicted leprosy upon Gehazi, his own servant, for taking an unauthorized fee from Naaman. (2 Kings 5) More than this, Gehazi was attempting to spoil a picture of the free grace of God in healing the soul from sin by changing Elisha's free healing into a financial transaction in which Naaman paid for his healing from leprosy, the disease most symbolic of sin. If Gehazi survived for long, he would have had to beg for free grace in the form of charitable alms on a daily basis because he could no longer live in society and work with his disease. There are great lessons here:

(1) Ultimately national origin (or skin color) does not matter in valuing a person;

(2) God's mercy, healing and grace are free and cannot be earned or obtained by money;

(3) God's mercy is received in submission and obedience rather than earned by effort. Naaman received his healing in immersing himself in the Jordan River seven times -- seven is the number of completion just as in our culture a Game 7 in an athletic series is so often the most dramatic. So the seven immersions of Naaman symbolize complete surrender.

(4) Sometimes the greatest miracles -- and in that time the healing of a leper was a miracle of the highest order -- start with the faith and witness of a person of the lowest rank. In this case it was a female slave of Naaman's wife who had been captured in war that started the chain of events that led to the healing of Naaman by mentioning Elisha as a prophet of God to Naaman's wife.

Still another example of grace starting with the lowest of the low is found in the siege of Samaria described in 2 Kings 6:24-7:20. The King's deputy, like most of the kings of this era except the faithful Jehoshaphat of Judah, had no abiding faith in God. Neither did they have spiritual vision or insight to perceive the angels fighting for Israel even though Israel was unfaithful (2 Kings 6:13-18, describing the previous siege of Dothan). In this respect I believe that the true situation today is parallel -- I believe that God is defending and preserving Israel even though Israel is currently unfaithful to Him. Deliverance in Elisha's time came not through the King's deputy, nor through the King himself, nor through his army. *"Not by might, nor by power, but by My Spirit," says the Lord of Hosts.* Zechariah 4:6. Deliverance came from the Lord of Hosts Himself through the witness of the lepers, who were the most despised of society and found themselves in no-man's land between the Syrian army and the besieged city. Theirs was the desperate faith of those with nothing left to lose. They survived, while the king's deputy of no faith was trampled to death by the people rushing out to get food which was now in abundant supply.

Both prophets had great faith from God and in God. Elijah called fire from heaven to accept his sacrifice; Elisha called fire from heaven to consume two companies of soldiers intent on arresting him. Elisha had no doubt that God would heal Naaman's leprosy and equally believed that God would punish Gehazi with that leprosy. Each prophet raised a person from the dead. (1 Kings 17:17-22; 2 Kings 4:8-37; 8:1-3). Both were able through the power of God to miraculously supply oil to a widow to sustain her family. (1 Kings 17:11-16; 2 Kings 4:1-7) It was this God-given faith that enabled both to stand firm against all opposition. If we need more faith, then with the father of the demon-possessed child let us pray: *"Lord, I believe; help my unbelief!"* Mark 9:24.

— PART THREE —
On Christian Masculinity

In modern Western culture, we are rapidly losing the idea of masculinity. One indication is the growing number of children growing up without fathers for substantial portions of their lives before they become adults. Another is the decrease in the percentage of young men in higher education. In the current (fall 2008-2010) recession, men have been disproportionately impacted compared to women. This has struck at the traditional male role as primary breadwinner in families.

In the case of less-educated men, the long-term decline in jobs that require more physical strength than mental acuity has been accelerated by the recent decline in construction work. Going back to Depression days, pipelines and roads would be done mostly by unskilled labor. Ditchdigging was the proverbial employment of last resort, as it was in Biblical times (Luke 16:3 specifically, Luke 16:1-13 for context. The dilemma of the steward will be quite modern though spoken by Jesus Christ almost 2000 years ago). But who digs ditches today by hand in Western society? One skilled backhoe worker does this work instead. This example can multiplied thousands of times and can affect women as well as men. Consider self-service cash registers in retail stores and how they will reduce openings for cashiers. Recent legislation in the health care field has further accelerated the trend over the last 2 centuries of replacing unskilled labor with machines because employers foresee that total costs of employees will rise even if nominal wages do not. Even surgeons can sometimes operate more precisely by robot than by hand. Robots do not require either Social Security or health care plans. Even in war there is the increasing use of drones and robots. Unskilled workers of both sexes are being affected, but men will probably be affected the most.

Christian churches are not meant to run the economy. But churches are called upon by God to help teach new believers -- children or adult -- how to act once they have believed the Gospel and have begun to be transformed by the power of God's Word and Spirit living within him or her. Because the entire concept of masculinity is being blurred in Western culture, I plan to focus on men. I do not believe that men are more precious or more important to God than women, but I have to be realistic as to my own limits as to the subject matter I can cover with any clarity. This is not intended to be a balanced presentation between men and women, but it is focused on men.

A comparable book could readily be written on Christian femininity, although there is one difference: one perfect Man, Jesus Christ, has walked the earth, whereas there never has been a perfect woman since the Fall of Adam and Eve. If I ever were to attempt to portray Christian femininity, I would have to start with a composite of such godly women as Sarah, Hannah, Deborah, Ruth, Abigail, Huldah, Esther, Mary the mother of Christ Jesus as to His manhood, the Syro-Phoenician woman, the woman with the issue of blood, Lydia, Dorcas and some of the women who ministered to the Lord Jesus. Proverbs 31 and the witness of the woman at the well in John 4 might need to be added, and surely others could add to my list with profit. One could also add negative examples such as Jezebel, Sapphira and Herodias and her mother, who caused John the Baptist to be martyred. At this point I do not sense the Spirit's call to try this, but I would encourage someone who believes that the Holy Spirit would help to make such an effort for the profit of the Christian church.

At least one Scripture is aimed especially at men, although this idea is lost in some translations. I have consulted Ricker's interlinear *Textus Receptus* and several translations of 1 Corinthians 16:13-14 and will offer my own version based on John Darby's translation: *Be vigilant; stand fast in the faith; behave like men; be strong. Let all things you do be done in love.* A few modern translations insert the idea of bravery in place of masculinity in my phrase *"behave like men."* Bravery and courage are indeed Christian virtues, but I still object to those translations because they remove the essential idea of masculinity from the original text. Even in Bible translation there is a modern tendency to de-emphasize masculinity. But the idea is present in the original text. So what is the Biblical idea of masculinity?

Jesus Christ, the sinless Son of God, is the gold standard of masculinity.

Single or married?

The Lord Jesus had the unusual attribute of not being sexually interested in women. However, He made it plain that His own life without sex was not a requirement for a godly life. Just after His teaching on divorce, in Matthew 19:11-12, our Lord Jesus taught concerning singlehood for men:

> But He said to them, "Not all can accept this saying, but only those to whom it has been given. For there are eunuchs who were born thus from their mother's womb, and there are eunuchs who were made eunuchs by men, and there are eunuchs who have made themselves eunuchs for the kingdom of heaven's sake. He who is able to accept it, let him accept it."

The Apostle Paul, also a single man, amplified this teaching in 1 Corinthians 7:1-4:

> *Now concerning the things of which you wrote to me: It is good for a man not to touch a woman. Nevertheless, because of sexual immorality, let each man have his own wife, and let each woman have her own husband. Let the husband render to his wife the affection due her, and likewise also the wife to her husband. The wife does not have authority over her own body, but the husband does. And likewise the husband does not have authority over his own body, but the wife does.*

The ability to live a single life well is a precious gift and is to be accepted by those to whom it has been given, but it is an exceptional gift. The norm for adult men is marriage and has been since the beginning of the church. Consider Paul's historical testimony in 1 Corinthians 9:3-6:

> *My defense to those who examine me is this: Do we have no right to eat and drink? Do we have no right to take along a believing wife, as do also the other apostles, the brothers of the Lord, and Cephas? Or is it only Barnabas and I who have no right to refrain from working?*

So Peter (Cephas) and the other apostles and the half-brothers of the Lord Jesus such as James and Jude, including the Apostle John and the others, were married men. In fact Peter was married before he was ever called to be Jesus' disciple. (Mark 1:30-31) Marriage was the norm among Jesus' closest disciples even though He never married personally.

If you examine the qualifications for elders and deacons in 1 Timothy 3 and Titus 1, you will find tests that relate to their leadership of their wives and children. This is not intended to disqualify single men such as Paul, but it does indicate that marriage is a normal characteristic for church leaders so long as the church exists. Any teaching that disqualifies married men from church leadership flies in the face of Holy Scripture. By the same token, no man who is having serious trouble at home should be an elder or deacon at least until those troubles are resolved for the long term. It is in resolving family problems and conflicts that most church leaders learn how to lead a church. So a man following God's design for masculinity can be either single or married, but he must be faithful to the requirements of his marital status. If single, he can have no sexual relations with anyone and he must seek to keep his mind pure of sexual desire as well. Our Lord Jesus said, *"He who looks upon a woman to lust after her has already committed adultery with her in his heart."* Matthew 5:28. If married, he must desire his wife and no other. The Tenth Commandment forbids coveting a neighbor's wife or even his servant in old society. Further, Solomon from his own bitter experience warns married men in Proverbs 5 and Proverbs 6:21-35 to stay away from immoral women and to cling to our own mates with delight.

Even though Jesus Christ was not sexually attracted to any woman, He was able to and did relate to women with compassion as no one else did in the contemporary culture. Indeed none has matched Him at any time. Mary Magdalene, delivered from seven demons (Mark 16:9), was a woman salvaged from the human garbage dump by Jesus of Nazareth. So was the Samaritan woman of John 4 -- she was going to Jacob's well in the heat of the day to avoid facing her neighbors who were well aware of her sinful relationships with men. The Syro-Phoenician woman (Matthew 15:22-28; Mark 7:24-30) received both instruction and compassion from Jesus. Mary and Martha (John 11), who had just lost their brother Lazarus, worshiped Jesus and received their brother back to life. So many in that culture acted as if women were mares for breeding -- an attitude that persists even today in polygamous cultures and certainly persisted in slave societies for many centuries after Jesus died and rose from the grave. Jesus Christ was helped in His ministry by women (Luke 8:2-3). Paul received help from Lydia

Thomas D. Logie

(Acts 16:13-15). It has been said that women were last at the Cross and first at the Tomb. If we are to imitate our Lord Jesus as a man, we must value women highly and treat them kindly precisely because we are men.

We should be so taken (1) with the love of God and then (2) with the love of our wife (if married) that desire for any forbidden lust is simply driven out of our hearts and minds.

What of same-sex sexual attractions? They are *verboten*. From Creation itself we observe that God made male and female human beings to join with each other. The careful design of human anatomy should leave no doubt even to the person who does not have access to the Holy Scriptures. Then we have the voiceless witness of the area where Sodom and Gomorrah once flourished to the point that Lot made his home there in order to get rich. Even 4000 years later the region is still barren. It is literally the lowest place on earth, about 1200 feet below sea level at the Dead Sea. Genesis 18-19 makes it clear that God sent two angels to deliver Lot and destroy the entire region. Romans 1:18-32 and 1 Corinthians 6:9-11 make it clear that same-sex practices as well as adultery are incompatible with the holiness of God. So a man who truly seeks to walk as a disciple of Jesus Christ can either have one wife or be completely single unless and until he marries. There are a few special men who can live well as single men, but the clear majority are better off in marriage to one woman. This was the case even among the 1st-century Apostles.

Endurance

There is much more to the Biblical ideal of manhood than sexual purity, even though this is vitally important. Again looking at Jesus Christ as our highest example, we observe that a man is able to endure pain, although none of us can endure the pain that He did. Faithful military service and "playing hurt" in an important sporting event are two physical examples of this in our world. Some men may be physically puny but moral and intellectual giants. In agriculture George Washington Carver was such a person. But Jesus on the Cross endured far more than the physical pain of crucifixion, as ghastly as that was. He endured separation from His Father and His Father's wrath as His Father poured out the penalty of our sin upon His Son. His Father for those terrible few hours treated His Son as if He were the Devil Incarnate instead of the incarnate Son of God. Jesus generally addressed God as Father throughout the Gospels because of their relationship to each other. But on the Cross we hear, *"My God, My God, why have You forsaken Me?"* (Matthew 27:46, quoting Psalm 22:1) There is formality instead of the usual intimacy. The intimacy and fellowship were restored as Jesus was about to die. *"Father, into Your hands I commit My spirit."* Luke 23:46. The suffering for our sins was now complete. The price for our salvation was paid in full.

I can only suggest what we as Christian men can learn from Jesus Christ on the Cross under pressure that we cannot fathom:

1) Even if we feel isolated from our heavenly Father, this is not truly so. As Jesus' isolation was temporary, so ours will be also. Keep the faith and repent where necessary.

2) Jesus carried out His Father's plan to redeem His people in the face of every temptation (for more detail, read Luke 4 and Matthew 4 and also Matthew 16:21-23) that Satan could devise and of unimaginable pain. If the Father has given us a plan, continue pressing to the objective that He has set.

3) Jesus endured patiently, looking for the victory at the end. In Hebrews 12:1-2 we read (I have added the emphasis):

> *Therefore we also, since we are surrounded by so great a cloud of witnesses, let us lay aside every weight, and the sin which so easily ensnares us, and let us run with endurance the race that is set before us, looking unto Jesus, the author and finisher of our faith, **who for***

the joy that was set before Him endured the cross, despising the shame, and has sat down at the right hand of the throne of God.

He also instructed us to endure necessary persecution with joy even though we naturally shrink from it. *"Blessed are you when they revile and persecute you, and say all kinds of evil against you falsely for My sake. Rejoice and be exceedingly glad, for great is your reward in heaven, for so they persecuted the prophets who were before you."* Matthew 5:11-12. So we can have joy in all circumstances, even when we simultaneously feel pain and sorrow.

If one prefers an example short of the perfection of Jesus Christ, Job is a Biblical example of a man who bent under the storm but did not break. Even though he lost 10 children and his entire fortune, he maintained his faith in God even when his wife suggested that he curse God and die to "get it over with." Job 2:9-10. I have written a short volume, Endurance, published by Trafford Publishing Company for a more expanded treatment of this topic.

4) Jesus was tender. Consider that He took time on the Cross to arrange for the future care of His mother through His disciple John. (John 19:26-27) Another example of this tenderness is Jesus weeping with Mary and Martha over the death of Lazarus. John 11:35.

5) Jesus was a forgiving Man. He prayed for His executioners (Luke 23:34), and His prayer was answered. (Luke 23:47, Mark 15:39) This is but one example of the power of Jesus Christ as a man of prayer.

Other examples of Jesus' power of prayer

Our Lord Jesus on at least one occasion prayed all night. Luke 6:12. In his narrative Jesus followed that night of prayer by calling His disciples. This certainly sets an example of sustained prayer before a critical decision, whether it be a marriage, a major hiring, a major purchase, a job or matter of comparable importance. As one continues in Luke 6, one reads of a tremendous healing time (Luke 6:17-18) just after the time of extended prayer. Matthew 14:23 records an extended time of prayer on the mountain just after the 5000 men and their families were fed. The sequels included Peter walking on water and another time of healing. None of us will equal the power of the Lord Jesus in prayer, but as disciples of our Lord Jesus we -- men and women -- must make sure that prayer becomes and remains a major part of our lives. For a married man, gentleness with his wife is an important foundation to effective prayer. 1 Peter 3:7.

A full analysis of Jesus' prayers might be a book by itself. Besides His prayer for the execution detail at the Cross, there are at least two other examples of His praying on which we as men should reflect. One is the resurrection of Lazarus found in John 11. In verses 33-41, there are references to Jesus groaning within Himself and then the statement of thanksgiving in John 11:41-42: *"Father, I thank You that You have heard Me. And I know that You always hear Me, but because of the people who are standing by I said this, that they may believe that You sent Me."* Our Lord Jesus had perpetual access to His Father. While we are in no sense Jesus' equal in holiness, we as His children do have perpetual access to the Father through the Holy Spirit Who lives within us. Romans 8:15-26. So we must be men and women of prayer.

The other example is John 17, Jesus' prayer for His people just before He was arrested in Gethsemane. In John 17:20-21, the Lord Jesus expanded His prayer for His immediate disciples to include us too, who have believed through the witness of the disciples recorded in the New Testament. Jesus' prayer is still being answered today even though it is nearly 2000 years old. The intensity of that prayer was so great that Jesus actually sweated blood. Luke 22:44.

Paul exhorted in 1 Timothy 2:8, *"I desire therefore that the men pray everywhere, lifting up holy hands, without wrath and doubting."* In this passage the term "men" is specifically masculine. In my own case prayer is some of the hardest work that I undertake. I might feel drained after 15 minutes. Though many would find it strange, I find it easier to write than to pray. But I cannot escape my share of the church's work of prayer; if I could escape it, I should nevertheless pray even though it is hard work to share in the blessing of prayer. I do not believe that Paul was excluding women from prayer. Instead, he was exhorting men to be men of prayer, knowing the masculine tendency to prefer things "more practical" than prayer. But *"the fervent prayer of a righteous man avails much."* James 5:16. In truth prayer is extremely practical.

So many times our failures can be traced to three causes: (1) Lack of prayer (James 4:2); (2) Lack of holiness in prayer (James 4:3); and (3) Lack of faith in prayer (James 1:5-7 -- see also Matthew 7:7-11, where the verb tenses exhort persistence in prayer, as does also Luke 18:1-8). So we must be men of prayer.

Humble

Though born the Son of God, Jesus Christ was the humblest of all men, as Moses was in his generation the meekest man in all the earth (Numbers 12:3). We are given a picture of the humility of Jesus in John 13, when Jesus after supper washed the feet of all the remaining disciples after Judas had departed on his treacherous scheme of betrayal. This was customarily the work of a slave. Jesus' humility is discussed in Philippians 2:5-11, where He obeyed His Father to the point of dying on a cross like a common criminal -- though He was in truth the Son of God. Here we are beyond human comprehension -- how could the Creator willingly subject Himself to death at the hands of a conspiracy of His rebellious created human beings, all infinitely inferior to Him? In fact He did, displaying a humility so deep we cannot fully understand it.

James (4:6) instructs us that *"God resists the proud but gives grace to the humble."* So we as men must be humble even though we cannot match the Lord Jesus in this respect.

Compassionate

We have already touched on Jesus' compassion in the section on His dealings with women. But our Lord Jesus because of compassion fed two multitudes and healed sick people beyond counting. Both of these strands of His compassion come together in Matthew 14:14-21:

> *And when Jesus went out He saw a great multitude; and He was moved with compassion for them, and healed their sick. When it was evening, His disciples came to Him, saying, "This is a deserted place, and the hour is already late. Send the multitudes away, that they may go into the villages and buy themselves food." But Jesus said to them, "They do not need to go away. You give them something to eat." And they said to Him, "We have here only five loaves and two fish." He said, "Bring them here to Me." Then He commanded the multitudes to sit down on the grass. And He took the five loaves and the two fish, and looking up to heaven, He blessed and broke and gave the loaves to the disciples; and the disciples gave to the multitudes. So they all ate and were filled, and they took up twelve baskets full of the fragments that remained. Now those who had eaten were about five thousand men, besides women and children.*

Since the 5000 men present do not include the women and children who would also have been present, a reasonable estimate of the number of people fed would be about 20,000 -- roughly the entire stadium attendance for a major league baseball game in a secondary market such as Tampa Bay or Detroit. And unlike the concession operators at a modern baseball stadium, Jesus started with 5 loaves and 2 fish brought by one boy and had no commercial source to increase His supply. Jesus Christ used His power as God-on-earth to meet the needs of his hearers and of his neighbors in healing and feeding them. As God gives us ability, we are meet our neighbors' needs as God gives ability, especially of the soul but also of the body where needed. James 2:15-16; 1 John 3:17-18.

There will be other instances of Jesus' compassion in the section on truth, so further discussion of His compassion can be found there.

Commanding

We see a hint of Jesus' powers of leadership when He commanded his hearers to sit down in groups of 50 and 100 (Mark 6:39-40) when He fed the multitude. When we observe Jesus calling His apostles, there was never any question or even and issue of refusing His call. Even hostile soldiers sent to arrest Him testified to His powers of leadership. In John 7:44-47 we read:

> *Now some of them wanted to take Him, but no one laid hands on Him. Then the officers came to the chief priests and Pharisees, who said to them, "Why have you not brought Him?" The officers answered, "No man ever spoke like this Man!" Then the Pharisees answered them, "Are you also deceived?*

The officers were powerless to arrest Jesus at this point because that time had not yet come. Yet there was no visible use of force. The power of His speech was sufficient to deter the soldiers and disarm them as effectively as if Jesus had seized their weapons. Another set of soldiers sent to Gethsemane also were unable to arrest Jesus until He gave permission. Until the disciples were given safe-conduct, they were unable to advance to Jesus and in fact fell to the ground. John 18:6ff. Even Peter was left at liberty although he had wielded a sword and wounded a man. When that was arranged, then Jesus permitted them to arrest Him according to their wishes and the wishes of the High Priest, but most fundamentally because that arrest was a link in Jesus' own plan to become the true and enduring Passover for the sins of all of His people for all time.

If Jesus was commanding before His death, then how much more commanding He is now! After His resurrection He said, *"All power is given to Me in heaven and on earth."* Matthew 28:18. Hebrews 1 also presents the risen Christ as all-powerful. He now *"uphold[s] all things by the word of His power"* (Hebrews 1:3 -- compare Colossians 1:16-17). At a future time He *"[l]ike a cloak ... will fold them up"* (Hebrews 1:12). The very Creation that Jesus Christ now sustains He will one day fold up in favor of a new heaven and a new earth (Revelation 21:1).

We as men do not have such power as He has. However, we do need something of the quality of command that Jesus had. This is not bullying. The quality of command in Him was blended with the tenderest compassion and the deepest humility. In our case we need also to recognize our own fallibility. But even with the burden of fallibility we must lead after we have listened, though with gentleness. We must take responsibility within our families. We must lead, although there will be times that God will lead us to follow our wives' advice, as Abraham followed Sarah's wishes with respect to Hagar and Ishmael (Genesis 21:1-12).

Truthful

Jesus Christ was and is *"the Way, the Truth and the Life."* (John 14:6) Nobody can come to God except through Him. One common thread in Jesus' dealings with people was that He was truthful, and in the process He exposed the sin of those who resisted Him and even those who sought to approach Him. Truth is not always pleasant, but it is necessary in our dealings with people. Nobody is capable of exhausting the wisdom of the Lord Jesus in dealing with people. There are times when the truth may be postponed, especially where one has a continuing relationship.

Nathan did wait until God knew that David was ready to hear the truth about what he had done to Uriah. God waited seven years to deal with Nebuchadnezzar. But postponement cannot mean that sin and serious issues can be swept under the rug. In this day, it seems more prevalent to ignore issues that should be confronted than to confront issues too soon.

For an executive summary, here is a table showing how Jesus Christ communicated the truth to various people. This is not an exhaustive list. Some short comments will follow. But in no case did Jesus ignore sin completely. He often corrected compassionately, but correct He did.

Syro-phoenician woman	Jesus sent to Israel, not to Gentiles	Mark 7:25-30
Samaritan woman	living in sin with a man not her husband; salvation is revealed in the Jewish Messiah, not in the Samaritan tradition	John 4
Woman taken in adultery	She was guilty of adultery -- go and sin no more	John 8:1-11
Rich young ruler	You're covetous and need to give away your wealth	Mark 10:17-25; Matthew 19:16-24
Simon, the Pharisee host	no courtesy or compassion	Luke 7:40-47
Simon Peter, the Apostle	You're being used as the Devil's tool to tempt Jesus!	Matthew 16:22-23

Simon Peter, the Apostle	You denied Me just as I warned you.	Luke 22:54-62; restored in John 21
Contemporary Jewish leadership	You are snakes, vipers (symbolically showing the control of the Devil)	John 8:31-44; Matthew 23 especially v. 33; Matthew 12:34

Jesus' treatment of the Syro-Phoenician woman seems harsh at a quick glance. She was a Gentile, and the Lord Jesus confronted her with the truth that the true God is the God of Israel. Moreover, Jesus Himself was sent to the children of Israel and not to Gentiles. While there were rare exceptions noted by Jesus Himself in Matthew 12:41-42, in general God's revelation to humanity came through Israel starting through Abraham. Most of what we know prior to Abraham was revealed through Moses. Two more partial exceptions could be noted: Job, and Nebuchnezzar of Babylon, the actual human author of Daniel 4, which Daniel transcribed and included in his prophecy. As Paul later wrote:

> *What advantage then has the Jew, or what is the profit of circumcision? Much in every way! Chiefly because to them were committed the oracles of God. Romans 3:1-2*

Yet Jesus' challenge brought out and intensified the woman's faith rather than destroying it. She humbled herself in taking the place of a dog instead of a child of the family. She persisted in her petition to Jesus, and He answered with the miracle she requested. When she went home, the demon had been cast out of her daughter.

The Samaritan woman was in a similar position to the Syro-Phoenician woman in being outside of Israel, and she was living a sexually immoral life to boot. So it is easier to understand why Jesus challenged this woman in John 4:16-18. But in John 4:22 Jesus challenged this woman in the same way He had challenged the Syro-Phoenician woman, telling her that

"Salvation is of the Jews." Once again, with rare exceptions (for example, the centurion in Matthew 8:5-13), the only worshipers of the true God when Jesus walked as the Son of Man on earth were Jews, and a minority of Jews at that. But this awful state of affairs was about to end, and both the Syro-Phoenician woman and the Samaritan woman were harbingers of the mighty and blessed change about to come.

The Lord Jesus violated convention in dealing with women directly as individuals in the first place. Once He broke that barrier, He faced obstacles frankly and confronted both women with their sin. When another desperate woman seeking healing touched the fringe of His garment, Jesus brought her immediately to public confession of what she had done. Luke 8:43-48. With Jesus Christ truth is vital.

The case of the woman taken in adultery is somewhat different because the Lord Jesus did not seek her out. Scribes and Pharisees dragged her to Jesus in an effort to trap Him. As with the previous women, our Lord Jesus dealt with this woman with both compassion and truth. Whatever He wrote in the dirt caused the witnesses to withdraw from the scene, leaving no witnesses against the woman. Under Jewish law, without two witnesses there could be no conviction for adultery (Deuteronomy 17:6). So the woman was spared a probable death sentence. Yet our Lord did not ignore the truth of the charges but sternly warned her to *"go and sin no more."* John 8:11.

In all three of these situations our Lord Jesus blended compassion and truth in dealing with these women. As men and as husbands, we are to imitate Him, realizing that we will not reach His standard. There is a time and place for correction by a husband of his wife, but it must be done with compassion, remembering that his wife is of his own flesh (Ephesians 5:22-33) and a weaker vessel (1 Peter 3:7). How are women generally weaker? Not in intelligence nor in faith nor love. I would suggest that in addition to sheer physical strength women tend to be weaker in withstanding chronic stress, although there are exceptions to the general rule. Correction by husbands ought to be occasional and not a constant habit. *Love covers a multitude of sins.* 1 Peter 4:8; see also James 5:20; Proverbs 10:12, 17:9.

The rich young ruler made a real effort to walk according to the Law and to avoid obvious sin. Like the Apostle Paul (Philippians 3:6), this young man was blameless under the Law, or at least the first nine Commandments that involve outward action. The rich young ruler apparently recognized Jesus as Lord (Mark 10:17) and thought the matter urgent enough to run instead of walk. But Paul admitted that the Tenth Commandment against covetousness exposed and inflamed his sinfulness (Romans 7:7-8). So it was with the rich young ruler -- at the moment that Jesus Christ confronted him he was unwilling to kill his covetousness by giving away his wealth. He would not exchange his wealth for the true riches of knowing Jesus Christ intimately. In truth, Jesus' counsel was the right remedy for this man's soul. It is not a universal command for every Christian to give up all possessions. We do not know the ultimate course of the rich young ruler's life. Did his sadness lead to repentance, or did he cling to his fleeting riches to the exclusion of truly obeying Jesus as Lord? We will know for sure only at the Last Judgment.

As men we may have to make similar choices, if somewhat less radical. We may need to give something up to help the church, help the poor, or simply to spend and save wisely. Many a man has damaged his family by spending on "toys" instead of the long-term needs of his family or the needs of others. There are even rare occasions where a man must give up all on earth to serve the Lord of heaven and earth.

Simon the Pharisee invited Jesus to eat with him on the one hand and extended no courtesies on the other. He did not provide water to wash Jesus' feet nor any anointing for His head. He provided no greeting either. This is puzzling conduct for which I can suggest two contrasting motives. One is that Simon set out to snub the Lord Jesus from the outset. The other is that Simon felt pressured by other Pharisees to keep his distance from Jesus of Nazareth after he issued the invitation but was too embarrassed to withdraw it. There are indications of such pressure in other passages of the Gospels, such as John 3:2 (Nicodemus came by night most probably to avoid being seen at this initial stage of his life with Jesus Christ), John 9:20-24, 31-34 and Luke 4:17-30. Perhaps there is another explanation that I have missed -- the Scriptures do not give a definite explanation. But what Simon did not provide, a woman with an evil past but now filled with love did supply. Jesus frankly acknowledged the extent of her sin and yet forgave her all of it. Simon neither asked for nor received forgiveness, at least on this occasion. Apparently Simon could see the woman's sins clearly but was blind to his own. (Compare Matthew 7:1-5) Whether Simon was ever willing to listen or not, the Lord Jesus told him clearly that he needed to learn to forgive, to love and to have faith. The sin of pride can blind the inner eye of the soul so thoroughly that one may be under the illusion that he or she needs no repentance or forgiveness. Matthew 6:14-15, 22-23.

We cannot believe that we are immune to the need for the Savior's truthful correction because we are His brothers and sisters and children of God. Simon Peter is a prime example. He had just reached a spiritual pinnacle by receiving revelation from God that Jesus is the Messiah and Son of God. (Matthew 16:15-17) And then only a few verses later Peter is resisting the truth that Jesus the Messiah must go to the Cross. Jesus' reply as recorded in Matthew 16:23 was severe:

> *But He turned and said to Peter, "Get behind Me, Satan! You are an offense to Me, for you are not mindful of the things of God, but the things of men."*

Peter in fact had become temporarily a tool of Satan, echoing the temptation of Christ by the Devil recorded in Matthew 4 and Luke 4.

The Lord Jesus corrected Peter without a word after His first trial. Peter had boasted that he was willing to lay down his life for the sake of his Lord. John 13:37-38. Peter had been willing to take up a weapon to prevent His arrest -- Peter still resisted the necessity of the Cross. (John 18:10-11) But a few hours later, Peter had denied knowing Jesus three times when challenged. (John 18:15-27; Luke 22:54-62) One look from the Lord Jesus was enough to convict Peter of his sin, but it took special attention from the Lord Jesus (John 21) and then the filling of the Holy Spirit (Acts 2) to make Peter ready to exercise leadership.

Our Lord Jesus was plainspoken about the hypocrisy of the religious leaders of His day. Matthew 23 is one extended denunciation. John 15:22 shows that there was no excuse for their blindness. John 8:44-45 is perhaps the most pointed summary:

> *You are of your father the devil, and the lusts of your father you will do. He was a murderer from the beginning, and did not abide in the truth, because there is no truth in him. When he speaks a lie, he speaks of his own: for he is a liar, and the father of it. And because I tell you the truth, you do not believe me.*

These words were not spoken behind the back of the targets, but to their faces. Our Lord Jesus was no coward. With courage He told the truth in their hearing.

In several other similar passages, our Lord Jesus called His determined enemies *"vipers."* (Matthew 12:34, 23:33 -- John the Baptist had used the same word in Matthew 3:7, also recorded in Luke 3:7.) This particular word has two implications: deadly poison and alliance with the Devil, who after all used the serpent to deceive Eve. The serpent's punishment in Genesis 3 was to crawl on the ground. Hence most people have an instinctive fear of snakes even today from that ancient memory.

There may be occasions where we may have to act as Jesus did, but we first must remember that we ourselves are sinful, while Jesus was perfect. We have to remember Matthew 7:1-5 and consider also James 1:22-27. Before we can stand up to evildoers, we must first judge ourselves honestly according to truth, both of doctrine and of acknowledging our own actions and even secret thoughts. In the immediate context of the Lord's Supper, Paul wrote in 1 Corinthians 11:31-32, *"For if we would judge ourselves, we would not be judged. But when we are judged, we are chastened by the Lord, that we may not be condemned with the world."* Before we can effectively take truth to others, we must apply the truth to ourselves.

Forgiveness

Hand in hand with truth and correction must go forgiveness. Our Lord Jesus exercised His prerogative to forgive sin on many occasions. Two instances that we have already considered are the woman at the well in John 4 and the woman who adored Him at the house of Simon the Pharisee. We as men must also forgive. Just after giving the Lord's Prayer Jesus commented: *"For if you forgive men their trespasses, your heavenly Father will also forgive you. But if you do not forgive men their trespasses, neither will your Father forgive your trespasses."* Matthew 6:14-15; Mark 11:26.

Men of Praise to God

David (a man after God's own heart -- 1 Samuel 13:14) was definitely a man who praised God as a matter of habit. A brief study of the Psalms that he wrote will establish this. Psalm 8 is but one example. Psalm 119 is an extended praise of God. It is recorded that Jesus and the disciples sang a hymn (most likely Psalm 118, but we cannot be certain) before they left the Upper Room for Gethsemane. Matthew 26:30; Mark 14:26. Jesus certainly approved the praises of God coming from the people on Palm Sunday.

Mark 11:9-11; Luke 19:37-40. So praise of God and encouragement of our families and church should be another characteristic of us men.

One of the strongest statements of this truth is found in Habakkuk 3:17-19:

> *Though the fig tree may not blossom, nor fruit be on the vines; Though the labor of the olive may fail, and the fields yield no food; though the flock may be cut off from the fold, and there be no herd in the stalls, yet I will rejoice in the Lord, I will joy in the God of my salvation. The Lord God is my strength; He will make my feet like deer's feet, and He will make me walk on my high hills.*

Peace, calmness, composure

Minor illustrations of this quality can be drawn from the world of sports. Older fans who saw Bart Starr, Roger Staubach, or the late Johnny Unitas play would attest to their calm under pressure on a football field. The late Tom Landry surely showed this quality as a coach. My father has said that "Nothing perturbs Rivera," referring to the New York Yankee closer Mariano Rivera. Peyton Manning as a quarterback shows the same type of disposition today. There are surely many others. While these examples pale in comparison to the Lord Jesus Christ, they are genuine examples in a limited part of life which may make it easier to grasp this part of Jesus' character, which Christian men should desire to make part of themselves.

Disciples and enemies of the Lord Jesus alike marveled at His peace and calm. This can be seen visually in His ability to tame instantly the wind and the sea. When His disciples were in the midst of a night storm on the Sea of Galilee, Jesus was sleeping. In a panic they woke Him up. Instantly Jesus calmed the storm and the water. (Mark 4:35-41; Matthew 8:23-27, fulfilling Psalm 107:29-30)

Pilate was amazed at the ability of the Lord to remain silent in the face of a capital charge. Matthew 27:12-14. When nailed to the Cross, Jesus *"reviled not again"* when insulted by the priests. (Matthew 27:39-44; 1 Peter 2:21-24, especially verse 23) Instead He bore our guilt in accord with His Father's plan. As Isaiah 53:7 says, *"He was oppressed and He was afflicted, yet He opened not His mouth. He was led as a lamb to the slaughter, and as a sheep before its shearers is silent, so He opened not His mouth."*

Working to a plan

Our Lord Jesus in human flesh had one major mission: to sacrifice Himself at precisely the right time to be the permanent atonement for all the sins of His people for all time and eternity. All the details of His life fit into this mission. The Virgin Birth was necessary to acquire a human body to sacrifice. The many miracles that He performed proved His perfection and His Deity. His ministry had to be the length prophesied by Daniel (9:24-27) and start at the age when Levites began their priestly ministry. The moment of His death had to be the exact moment that the Passover should have been sacrificed on the precise day prophesied by Daniel in his prophecy of 69½ weeks of years to the "cutting off" of the Messiah. So Jesus unfolded His identity gradually, starting with the miracle of turning the water into wine at Cana (John 2) and climaxing with the public resurrection of Lazarus (John 11). Then came the final debates during the week that Jesus was examined as the Lamb of God before He gave His life. I have skipped many details, but this is enough to show that Jesus worked to an overall plan as a carpenter would plan his end product, whether a chair or a house.

At the same time Jesus was always able to react perfectly to unexpected events, such as having the Pharisees and scribes interrupt His lesson by dragging an adulteress into His class. He was never taken off stride by anyone, whether His worst enemies or by a desperate, unrestrained person seeking His aid as a last hope from utter tragedy. Within His plan, He always had flexibility to deal with the moment. For us His perfect balance between organization and flexibility is impossible, but we can still learn from it and grow in grace. We cannot see Jesus yet, but we can and should listen to the Holy Spirit Whom Jesus sent to the church in His place.

A Decisive Leader

When Elijah confronted the priests of Baal on Mount Carmel, he challenged the people of his own time and still challenges us today: *"How long will you vacillate between two opinions? If the Lord is God, follow Him. But if Baal, follow him."* 1 Kings 18:21. Baal-worship is long dead, but there are plenty of substitutes. Some worship themselves or some idea of collective humanity. There is no shortage of other gods besides the God of the Bible. In Jesus of Nazareth there is never a hint of any other true god except His Father. Jesus Himself claimed and proved His equality with His Father by His life. (For instances of his claims to deity, consult John 5:20-47, John 6:28-69, John 8:12-59 and all of John 10. Jesus also received worship even in His body of flesh. Matthew 2:11, 8:2, 9:18, 14:33, and 15:25 are examples from the first gospel. The guards who scourged Him worshiped Him in jest, but the centurion and the execution squad worshiped Him in truth. Mark 15:16-20; Mark 15:39, Matthew 27:54)

The Lord Jesus calls us to undivided loyalty. When He called His disciples, they came as recorded in Matthew 4:18-22 and similar passages. Matthew 8:19-22 reads as follows:

> *Then a certain scribe came and said to Him, "Teacher, I will follow You wherever You go." And Jesus said to him, "Foxes have holes and birds of the air have nests, but the Son of Man has nowhere to lay His head." Then another of His disciples said to Him, "Lord, let me first*

go and bury my father." But Jesus said to him, "Follow Me, and let the dead bury their own dead."

There can be no half-hearted following of Jesus Christ, just as there can be no half-hearted commitment to our mates and families. The modern-day fear of permanent commitments is a symptom of grave spiritual rot. When the Lord Jesus calls us in our modern day to repent and to follow Him, this is a call to all-out commitment immediately. *Today, if you hear His voice, do not harden your heart as in the day of provocation.* Hebrews 3:15ff., quoting Psalm 95:7-11.

When one reads the Gospels, Jesus led with certainty from day to day. He as a Man did pray frequently. In the Garden of Gethsemane He did have to face the revolting prospect of being made sin and being treated like garbage when He truly was holy. He had never been separated from His Father from all eternity past. So He could wish that the bitter cup of separation from His Father and physical death at the hands of inferiors could pass from Him, but He knew full well that He must drink the cup to its dregs. His prayer in John 17 reflects this certainty. Jesus paused in prayer as an example to us, showing us an example of prayer under extreme stress.

Jesus Christ is also a decisive leader in a different sense. Beyond providing a perfect and everlasting atonement for our sins, He is aiming at the total destruction of Satan. Hebrews 2:14. His healings and resurrections of others (as well as His own resurrection) were preliminary steps to this ultimate purpose, which will be completed when the Book of Revelation has its final fulfillment. Great generals in the past knew that decisive results could be achieved only by destruction of the enemy. Jesus Christ has already destroyed Satan's kingdom beyond repair and will complete its total destruction in due time. He will not stop until final victory is won.

In our own lives strongholds of sin must be destroyed, not accommodated. Even if Satan makes a truce with us he will never keep it. It is war to the death. Jesus will lead us to nothing less than total victory in the end, even if on earth our prospects are entirely gone.

My sketch of Christian masculinity is imperfect. I am emphasized the issue of truth because our culture is especially unbalanced in seeking to assuage feelings in the face of reality. (Compare Isaiah 30:10, Psalm 55:21, Proverbs 5:3-4, 2 Timothy 4:3) This takes my portrait somewhat out of balance in the interest of trying to correct for our severe cultural bias in Western societies. We men in this life will never completely fulfill all of these attributes, let alone those I have overlooked. But we must keep fighting spiritually within ourselves to put our remaining sin to death. Romans 8:12-13.

This sketch is further incomplete because I have not focused on Christian virtues that apply equally to both men and women. To study those in detail, I would suggest 1 Corinthians 13 with its exposition on love, Galatians 5:17-24 for the contrasting study of the works of the flesh and the fruit of the spirit, and 2 Peter 1:5-11 for its structure of Christian virtues. Surely Proverbs can teach both men and women much about practical living. But this particular study is intended to focus primarily on things that apply especially to men. Christianity is not unisex. One could reasonably say that this entire chapter is an attempt to enlarge on Genesis 1:27: *So God created man in His own image; in the image of God He created him; male and female He created them.* Contemporary Western culture is doing its worst to obliterate the differences between the sexes, even to the point of discussing artificial reproduction and gene selection as an alternative to natural conception instead of just a means to cure disease or overcome infertility. But among Christians this must not be so. For example, Deuteronomy 22:5 forbids a man to wear woman's clothing and likewise forbids a woman to wear a man's clothing, to the end of preserving the God-created distinction between male and female. Masculinity and femininity are God-given and God-designed gifts to humanity and should be modeled by Christians to an unbelieving world. If this makes us radically different from our culture, so be it! The French were right in this saying, *"Vive la difference!"* Better still, we should give thanks to God for the differences although they will not persist into our final resurrection bodies. Matthew 22:23-32.

— PART FOUR —
Spiritual Warfare: A Modern Story of Divorce, Death and Remarriage

Introduction

The following short story is based on real events and real people, with numerous fictionalized dates, names, locations and other details. Time intervals between one event and another are accurate. Any story told from human perspective will fall short of the absolute truth as God knows that truth because He knows not only all events but all thoughts and temptations, whether embraced or resisted, within each of us. The same story told from the viewpoints of different people will have differences in perspective and emphasis without anyone attempting to distort or conceal the truth. When one then adds the possibility of either unconscious or conscious distortion and concealment to protect oneself or others, one can realize how even our best efforts to tell the whole truth about subjects such as marriage, divorce, death and remarriage can fall short. So this story is not the final judgment on the real events and the real people on which this story is based. That can come only when Jesus Christ renders His judgment.

Then why write this? Because divorce and death of a mate are battles which many people must face. This is one case in which Matt and Carolyn were able to triumph over their troubles and even over the Devil through the power of Jesus Christ working through people. How this happened and what they were thinking might help someone with a similar struggle.

The predominant viewpoint in this short story is masculine. In stories of love and marriage, this is unusual. But there is value in this. All human perception is imperfect short of Jesus Christ. However, on subjects like this we can get closer to the whole truth with both an honest male and honest female perspective than with either one alone. Since modern male perspective on love and marriage is uncommon, a story like this is important as an "after-action" report in spiritual warfare just as battlefield reports after the fact are important to the military.

Much later Matt would reflect that Jeanne had introduced him to solid Christian writing such as Luther's Bondage of the Will and to Spurgeon's sermons. He should always be grateful for that and especially for their children. But this was not at the forefront of Matt's mind during the crisis itself. At the time Matt was wrestling with anger that he could not express in public but only in prayer to God. He was angry that the name of Jesus Christ was being dishonored and also in having to cope with severe emotional pain and numerous practical problems stemming from the separation.

In spiritual warfare, eventually every Christian will share in the final triumph of Jesus Christ over the Devil. As an old hymn says, "And when the war is fierce, the battle long; steals on the ear the distant triumph song. And hearts are brave again and arms are strong, Allelujah." There are times even on earth when believers are granted by God the privilege of routing evil. Revivals come that way. This story is based on real-time skirmishes between Christians armed with the armor of God (Ephesians 6:10-18) and the Evil One. If you are faced with spiritual warfare like Matt and Carolyn or much more intensely like Job, you can recover and win through the power of Jesus Christ. *Blessed be the God and Father of our Lord Jesus Christ, the Father of mercies and God of all comfort, Who comforts us in all our tribulation, that we may be able to comfort those who are in any trouble, with the comfort with which we ourselves are comforted by God.* 2 Corinthians 1:3-4.

Prologue — Election Day 1991

Matt Galloway and Joe Jensen were both Republican candidates for local office. Each had helped the other in both the nomination and the election process. Neither was favored. Matt Galloway indeed lost his race to unseat the incumbent prosecutor with about 42% of the vote. In a stunning upset, Joe Jensen defeated a well-known incumbent for a county supervisor's seat. The prospect of rising property taxes squeezing long-time residents was a major reason for the surprise. When Matt went to the local radio station to give his concession statement, he was told that nobody knew where to find Joe. So Matt called Joe at his home from the station when Joe was about to go to bed. Joe's mother Carolyn answered the phone. Joe was the most surprised man in the county when Matt congratulated him. "Why?" Joe asked.

Matt replied, "Because you just won by seven votes." Joe at first thought Matt was joking. But this was no joke. Joe now had the responsibility of being one of 5 supervisors dealing with spending and school construction plans too big for the county tax revenue. Matt would go back to his private law practice and representing indigent criminal defendants.

Sunday, 7:00 PM -- Kingsville (about 6 months later)

Matt Galloway was surprised and displeased to see his wife Jeanne leaving their apartment above his law office. "Where are you going?" he asked. Jeanne answered that she was going down the street to the tavern connected to a fashionable restaurant. Alcohol was on the menu. Matt had already warned Jeanne about driving under the influence on an earlier occasion when he had smelled alcohol on her breath when she had come home late. She was not driving this time, but Matt was concerned about intoxication. But inside he was almost resigned to his wife's leaving rather than interacting with him. He was tempted but squelched the temptation to say, "Go ahead and go where you want. I don't care." When Jeanne had left, Matt whispered in prayer, "Lord, that's dangerous!" He felt cold inside. Later that week, he would view this as a premonition.

May 14, 1992 -- Kingsville, 5:05 PM

Matt Galloway had completed his work for the day. He was hurrying over to the travel office to buy an inexpensive travel package to Niagara Falls and Canada for a much-needed vacation with his wife. He had discussed with Jeanne for weeks his view that they needed to get away for a short time to re-connect their marriage. There had been strains for some time. Both children were out of the house. Their son David was finishing his second year of college. Their daughter Deidre had graduated from high school the previous June and had been married the previous July. She was living with her husband and his aunt and uncle. Then the telephone rang one more time. He was tempted to let it go, but what if were a client with a really important phone call? With considerable irritation he reversed his steps and grabbed the phone. "Mr. Galloway speaking, may I help you?"

"This is Mrs. Dillon, the tenant at your house. Your wife just came here and asked permission to stay. She wanted to stay here and leave you. She also admitted that she was having an affair. I told her no, but I thought you should know."

"Thank you for the call. I'm sorry that you wound up in the middle of this, but I thank you very much for telling the truth. I will have to deal with this when she comes in."

That was the end of the vacation plan. Two weeks earlier Mr. Galloway had received a phone call from a friend's son telling him that Mrs. Galloway had been at a saloon being overly friendly with one of his relatives. He had confronted her and she had denied any wrongdoing. Matt had accepted her denial on the basis that there was only one witness, which is insufficient in Scripture to establish truth on an issue of importance. (Deuteronomy 17:6) He had maintained his relationship with his wife on that basis. Now there was a second, totally independent witness with a similar warning which went beyond the first one because it indicated actual adultery. If true, this was life-threatening behavior and an issue which could not be postponed for the intended vacation 2 or 3 months later. The timing was especially awkward with David scheduled to arrive home that night from college.

May 14, 1992 Kingsville, 6:30 PM

Matt was downstairs in a vacant portion of the building that served as a law office with other rental space and an upstairs residence when Jeanne came in. She seemed upset. Matt confronted her immediately. "I just got a call from Mrs. Dillon telling me that you admitted to her that you committed adultery. This is the second witness within two weeks. Jeanne, tell me the truth!"

Jeanne confessed, "Yes, it is true. I want to live elsewhere but have no place to go."

Matt asked, "What about your parents?" But Jeanne had not talked to them yet. So as a temporary measure Jeanne was going to move a couch downstairs and use the shower when Matt was out of the upstairs apartment, but the couch might remain upstairs for a night or two to allow time to get curtains in the vacant section.

May 14, 1992 10:50 PM

David had come home and learned of the separation. Jeanne had come into the bedroom where Matt already was trying to go to sleep. David came too. Was reconciliation possible? Matt did not desire reconciliation now that he knew the truth about the adultery, but he did not entirely rule it out. He laid down several conditions for any serious consideration of reconciliation: (1) That Jeanne resume studying the Bible with him, which she had dropped many years earlier before the children were born. He also wanted joint prayer; (2) That Jeanne stop going out at night and stop drinking totally; (3) That Jeanne stop watching soap operas and similar television that is poisonous to Christianity, (4) That Jeanne would attend church with Matt, and (5) That Jeanne stop her opposition to Matt's tithing. All connection with the adulterous partner must be severed totally. He also wanted Jeanne to resume her high-protein and low-sugar hypoglycemia diet in order to reduce her mood swings; this was an additional reason for his concern about alcohol beyond normal intoxication.

Jeanne was not happy with Matt's response and was not willing to commit to anything. Jeanne seemed to be asking for acceptance without any change of behavior. Matt refused. David asked his mother a classic question from Campus Crusade: "If Jesus were to ask you 'why should I let you into my heaven?', what would you say?"

Jeanne responded, "Oh, I made that decision a long time ago, about 29 years ago."

At this Matt became truly alarmed. "That is one of the classic wrong answers to that question. Salvation is not merely a one-time decision but results in a changed and holy life. Besides, you well know (referring to Jeanne's previous instruction when they first married) that salvation is at bottom the choice of God and not the decision of human flesh." He felt his blood feel cold at the implication that his spouse of over 22 years had not only committed adultery but may have been self-deceived as to the state of her soul and in danger of not just God's punitive discipline but of damnation because her faith was hollow and false if her answer was the full extent of her faith. Neither David nor Jeanne saw him weep, but God did in the privacy of what had been the marital bedroom.

Matt finally drifted off to sleep and awoke alone in the morning. He showered quietly and prepared for work without disturbing Jeanne or David.

May 16-23, 1992 -- Doctor's appointment

The arrangements had been completed for Jeanne to sleep in the previously vacant portion of the building. The discussion with a pastor at Matt's church was basically the same as the night of the separation. There was some discussion of financial matters because Jeanne thought that Matt spent too much on computers and software to maintain his law practice. Matt estimated that 80% of the computerizing money was well spent and that 20% did not save enough to justify the cost. In those days before the Internet was available to most computer users, being one's own purchasing agent and systems operator was difficult. Matt in fact was substituting hard-won knowledge as a computer user for sheer computer power in order to minimize expenditures and still run the office efficiently. But the pace of the sole practice combined with the necessity of handling many indigent defense cases meant that there could be no turning back on modernizing the back-office of the practice. Jeanne was used to old-fashioned paper systems and was having trouble understanding computers. Matt had started in the early 1980s because he saw no other way to compete with larger firms. There was no progress either on Matt's ideas to restructure the marriage. More than that, Jeanne was not willing to promise to remain faithful from now on. Matt was thankful that at least Jeanne was honest rather than deceptive. He also believed that he had a clear course charted for him rather than uncertainty.

The next day Matt began drafting a property settlement agreement between Jeanne and him. For some time he had been concerned about

Jeanne's conduct and in his mind had been thinking through contingency plans in case Jeanne left. These plans were in the nature of plans that first-class military organizations draw up to prepare for the unexpected without any intention of actually using them. It was not that Matt ever wanted to have to carry them out. They were not committed to either paper or to a computer file before the separation. Since Jeanne several years ago had become unable to keep regular hours for a job, it was obvious that Matt would have to take sole responsibility for the properties and for the family debts. (The agreement finalized the next month was largely along these lines.) In May 1992 Kingsville had not yet recovered from the closing several years earlier of the largest employer, so real estate prices remained depressed from levels reached at the end of the Reagan Administration in early 1989. Winter unemployment levels were over 13%; summer levels were around 7%. So there was no immediate equity in the real estate, but Matt thought that with patience there could be equity in the long run. (In the actual event Matt did make a substantial long-term capital gain, but most of it did not come until several years later after considerable work and renovation to the office building.) Matt believed that to maintain his reputation for integrity and -- above all -- to keep faith with his creditors as a Christian should to the limits of his power, he had to take both the risks and the responsibility. He was particularly concerned that Jeanne had approached the tenant with her scheme, which could have jeopardized the rental income vital to keeping the secured payment, taxes and insurance current. Fortunately, the tenant family was not so disturbed as to seek other premises. Matt believed that he had to trust God to bring him and the children through this crisis, although he thought the marriage was probably beyond salvage given Jeanne's continuing adultery. Matt did admit to himself that he had no emotional desire to "hang on" at this point. He was in prayer between his church and work time, but Matt was reasonably sure that his only sensible course was to bury the dead marriage as decently as he could with as little fanfare as possible. Joseph, the legal father of Jesus Christ, was his model; he wanted to put Mary away quietly until he learned that the Holy Spirit was the biological Father of Mary's child Jesus. Matt reflected that at least he was spared the agony of uncertainty.

A RETROSPECT FROM MATT'S VIEW

Over the weekend Matt took stock of the lowlights leading to the collapse of the marriage. He realized that he himself was a sinner and that whatever good was in him was due to the grace of God. *"But by the grace of God I am what I am ..."* 1 Corinthians 15:10. His thoughts flashed back to the time when Jeanne was pregnant almost 20 years before with David that she refused to study the Bible with him but could give no reason. He had tried to persuade her and even hold her on the couch, but it was no use. One pastor had questioned Jeanne's salvation in Jesus Christ during that time, but Matt had then thought that the pastor's concerns were excessive though honest and serious. He and Jeanne were able to discuss them then. But Jeanne would not join with the children in Bible study at any time thereafter, although into the children's teen years she would go to church faithfully, sing hymns in the car and occasionally pray with Matt. Jeanne agreed that the children should go to Christian school and loyally supported Matt in his political activism as a community pro-life leader, although she seemed tired in the last year or so. Jeanne had always been slow to get up in the morning, and this had grown to the point by the time David was about 10 that Matt had to see personally that the children got to school on time most days.

Matt recalled a chaotic weekday in Kingsville when he went home to get a raincoat on an overcast day before he drove to Bankruptcy Court. When he picked up the raincoat, he noticed that his brother-in-law was unexpectedly present. So Matt turned his car around and discovered that

Jeanne's family wanted to take Deidre away for counseling without even consulting him. She was about 11 at the time; David was about 13. Jeanne was not home because of some car trouble. Matt returned home to prevent Deidre from being snatched and through the grace of God was able to handle the court matter over the telephone from the house. After this Matt felt the terrible necessity of giving an emergency instruction to his children in the event that family members tried again to take them away: as a last resort they might have to kick someone in the knee to prevent being seized. Matt was careful at the same time to instruct the children to continue to love and respect their maternal relatives, painfully conscious of the mixed message involved. He emphasized that this was for an emergency only. Matt thanked God that there never was another attempt to take away either one or both of the children. When the crisis had finally broken, both were legally adults and the split would not have the same day-to-day impact as it would have had about 6 years earlier.

In retrospect, there was a major milestone about 3 years before the separation when Jeanne had spent the tithe money from the checkbook without discussing the matter with Matt beforehand. Up to this time Jeanne had handled the checkbook details. She was good at this and enjoyed it. But Matt took action; he opened a second bank account in his name only and deposited the tithe money in that account from his office salary. It occurred to him that Jeanne might be tempted to dip into the rent revenue needed for mortgage payments and building maintenance, so Matt set up a third checking account in his name only and made the rent deposits into that account. From here he made the necessary payments related to the real estate directly to the appropriate people. Matt was thankful that the cash flow was sufficient to cover the obligations. Jean continued to handle the joint account where most of Matt's salary from his law practice was deposited; she was not cut off from most of the family money. Jeanne resented the new arrangement even though she still handled the joint bills. Matt understood this but thought that this was a minimal measure necessary to preserve financial integrity. He believed that Jeanne could be tempted again now that she had spent the tithe money once. Matt had desired until the telephone call from the tenant to take Jeanne on a vacation to repair their marriage's foundation, but in retrospect he viewed the altered financial arrangement as a milestone toward the destruction of the marriage.

Jeanne had hectored Matt from time to time about getting a "real job" with a regular salary. Matt's response was that the sole practice was the way that the Lord was providing for the family, and that He had never failed them yet and would never break His promises. Very early in the marriage Matt had tried to get staff work on Capitol Hill. He was told that he was a good candidate but never got an offer. Matt learned later that Jeanne's brother had discouraged his acquaintances from hiring Matt from good motives. He knew that the hours of work were terribly destructive to family life and did not want Matt away from home so many hours. In fact the brother was right -- Matt was needed at home to help with the children during the evening. When Matt found out years later, Matt regarded this as the Lord's way of keeping him out of spiritual peril. In fact one Congressman for whom Matt had hoped to work had turned out to be homosexual, which would have been a horrible mismatch. *For My thoughts are not your thoughts, neither are your ways My ways, saith Jehovah. For as the heavens are higher than the earth, so are My ways higher than your ways, and My thoughts than your thoughts.* Isaiah 55:8-9.

Jeanne had also changed Deidre's school behind Matt's back when she was in 7th grade. Deidre had been enrolled with David at an academic private school with respect for the Scriptures. Deidre found the work hard but was making solid progress. Jeanne had decided on her own to shift Deidre to public school without telling Matt; she gave finances as her reason. So Jeanne dressed Deidre in the school uniform. Jeanne later had Deidre change clothes and took her to the public school. Matt caught the deception within a week, but it was too late to put Deidre back with David. Because of the decadent morals of the public school system (for example, one student poll showed that 88% of the high school students even then were "sexually active"), Matt felt compelled to switch Deidre to a Christian school even though there were relatively few students. Matt felt that he could not fully trust his wife, but he thought that her judgment was poor and that she was rebellious against him (and disobeying God as a byproduct) rather than imagining that she would one day directly defy God Himself and commit adultery. In retrospect, Matt realized that this was another major step toward the destruction of the marriage.

After the school changes, it often took tremendous effort to get Deidre to school on time at any school she attended. Neither Jeanne nor Deidre would cooperate consistently. Instead, Jeanne wanted Deidre to see boys of her age during school hours. This made Matt furious. He was severely critical with Jeanne, although there were no curses. Deidre also got cigarettes with her mother's help. In an effort to stop this, Matt threatened to turn his own wife in to the authorities for contributing to their daughter's delinquency if she did not stop. That seemed to help temporarily, but this too had its long-term price.

There was also a running disagreement over David's college applications. David was a top-tier student. Matt wanted him to apply to several strong academic schools both in and out of state. Jeanne wanted him to apply only to the prestigious state university. Matt had reservations because of the spiritual reputation of the professors and because of the heavy party atmosphere there. Jeanne's parents lived a few miles away in town, and she hoped that David might live with them while attending school. Matt had reservations about this, especially because of ongoing family strains between both children and their grandparents. Also, this would have cut David off from healthy portions of campus life. The grand-mother had been involved in the attempt to take Deidre out of the house. Jeanne stalled for over two months in typing the applications, and Matt finally paid his former secretary to get the typing done on four applications.

One day during David's spring vacation Matt had a trial cancel, so he had no appointments that day. He told David that he would take him unannounced to both in-state campuses on their "off" day so that they could see what each campus was like without window dressing. Jeanne did not come. Matt and David arrived at the first campus about 8:00 AM, at which time there were already large numbers of students going either to breakfast or to early classes. That impressed Matt. They both looked at the student newspaper. The campus was easy to navigate and they had heard that there was an active Christian ministry on campus. When they drove to the more prestigious campus, David's father was impressed with the library but horrified with the student newspaper despite its technical quality, with frank photographic coverage of a same-sex love-in on the central lawn of the campus. He recognized the college President as a former hardline left-wing activist of his own generation. David also saw the sin in the love-in. They reasoned together that as an educational matter the vigorous computerization on the first campus could offset the advantage of the older university in library volumes. The campus computer network and e-mail were just beginning to jell. Both agreed that the less prestigious choice was better balanced ideologically and probably as good academically. It was modernizing faster and had healthier food. When David was accepted in both schools, the clinching factor was that David was taken into the special academic program and a special academic dormitory at the lesser-known school. He received an academic scholarship to boot. Like a scholar-athlete who responds when a school pursues him vigorously, David responded to the school's pursuit and decided to go there, with the full approval of his father and the reluctant acquiescence of his mother. Once David made his final choice, Jeanne did cooperate fully and even showed some of her former enthusiasm when the day came. Jeanne said that Campus Crusade's help with the suitcases was an answer to prayer.

Then just about a year before the crisis it was Deidre's turn to decide on college. She was completing her last year in the public high school because Deidre was out of other options. Without Jeanne Matt took her to a college in North Carolina, which Deidre liked because of its practical and environmental emphases. Deidre was accepted and Matt sent the $300 deposit to hold her place. So far Matt was working through his overall plan of getting the children situated and then concentrating on repairing the relationship between him and his wife. For this and other reasons, Matt was also running for the local prosecutor's office -- this would finally give the regular salary that his wife craved. It would also open the door to public service. But God did not choose to permit this plan to work. Matt had a rude jolt when Deidre and Jeanne told him 5 days before the nominating meeting that Deidre was pregnant. Deidre could probably graduate from high school before she would "show." But college would be a problem with a delivery during the first year.

There was no initial consensus in the family of what to do, but Matt didn't care about a consensus. The Holy Scriptures give specific instruction about this situation, and that instruction is to be obeyed, not questioned. Matt found out that the father was willing to marry Deidre, which made obedience much easier. Deuteronomy 22:28-29 reads, *If a man find a damsel, a virgin, who is not betrothed, and lay hold on her, and lie with her, and they be found, then the man that lay with her shall give unto the damsel's father fifty [shekels] of silver, and she shall be his wife, because he hath humbled her; he may not put her away all his days.* Matt was not interested in the money, but he was interested in Deidre's honor, in her child and most of all in doing what is right in God's sight. So he paid for the marriage license and signed for his daughter to marry. This was required because she was not yet of age. He also arranged for the pastor and for a modest reception.

Although the father of the child later became an alcoholic and bolted, the change in Deidre from the marriage in time became obvious. She had passed from rebelling against God to obeying Him after this major step of obedience in marrying the father of her child. Deidre never did get to the college where she was accepted. But in by-passing any thought of abortion and in doing what the Scriptures teach, she grew from a rebellious teenager to a young woman with faith in God. That was more important than a college education once a choice had to be made.

Matt continued his campaign and won the party nomination. He ran respectably but not well enough to win the general election. So there was still the solo law practice as provision.

But Matt did not want to hold a pity party and rehash grievances in his mind. He tried to understand Jeanne's viewpoint even though he could see no excuse for adultery, especially repeated adultery without a real desire to stop.

He was aware that Jeanne never felt secure with his solo law practice. For her, faith was regularly an issue, especially in financial matters. Matt urged her to pray and commit the family finances and provision to God. With no open door in the employment world, Matt believed he had no other option but to trust God where he was. But Jeanne was restless and Matt found no way to satisfy her in this respect.

Jeanne was extremely outgoing, to the point where she made Matt appear introverted even though he was enough of an extrovert to engage in the rough-and-tumble world of politics. She was in her element in political conventions and similar large gatherings. But Matt could be comfortable alone also, and Jeanne could not. She needed contact on the telephone if nobody was around. Contact with her children would not satisfy her in this respect. Matt used to say that Jeanne's perfect job would be where she saw 10,000 new people each day, but there were no such jobs near Kingsville and few such jobs anywhere. Perhaps Jeanne would have liked to work at a large convention center or stadium, Matt thought. But the same characteristics that suited Jeanne for such public work (if available) also made deep relationships such as family very difficult for Jeanne. Matt and Jeanne worked together to rally support for pro-life and conservative candidates in the nominating and election process in their area, but Matt did not have an element of life between large political gatherings that met Jeanne's desires for extensive human contact.

The legal profession with its emphasis on client confidentiality and preservation of secrets was an especially poor match for Jeanne that limited her participation in the office. She could and did handle billing tasks, but Jeanne did not press to be Matt's secretary despite her excellent typing ability. She probably sensed her mismatch with highly confidential material -- Matt used to tell job candidates that a law office is the civilian equivalent of the CIA in terms of secrecy. Jeanne was excellent at broadcasting information but lacked discretion to keep secrets.

Matt reflected that Jeanne did not find him fun. Matt preferred to get to bed at a reasonable hour and to get up promptly in the morning. Sometimes he even had to be in court at 8:00 AM. No coffee for him! Jeanne liked to stay up late and sleep in. When she did wake up, she insisted on multiple cups of coffee even though this was bad for her hypoglycemia. A slow start did not work during the school year with children at home, and in Matt's experience the vast majority of trouble arose when sensible people would be in bed. Kingsville was too far away to go to the big city for nightlife even if it were affordable. So Jeanne felt stranded much of the time. While neither Matt nor Jeanne used drugs nor smoked, to Jeanne there was a shortage of fun. Matt was able to enjoy being with the children when there was time to play. He was a baseball umpire and coach. He also did most of the parental supervision of education. Jeanne would go also to children's activities, but she did not derive the same enjoyment as did Matt. Jeanne did encourage Deidre to have a very active social life with boys, which Matt viewed as dangerously premature and eventually a contributing factor in her pregnancy. For Matt, perceiving the problem was easier than finding a solution. What he wanted was for Jeanne to find more joy and spiritual satisfaction from the worship of Jesus Christ and church fellowship, which he hoped would displace Jeanne's need for temporary merriment.

Jeanne thought Matt tense and uptight. Matt did not agree -- he viewed himself as intense rather than tense. Matt had confidence -- the very word is compounded from two Latin words meaning "with faith." He was calm rather than jittery. Matt wanted to do things right and wanted to instill the same desire in the children. Jeanne was that way with financial records but not in other parts of life. She thought Matt too strict in general, with himself, with her, with the children and with others. Having responsibility for parts of the lives of others as an attorney, Matt believed that he could not change professionally and was also mindful of the account that he would give to God for his family. Again, Matt could see the outlines of what Jeanne thought but had not come to a ready solution either before or at the time of the crisis.

An illustration of these differences arose when the family saw a Christian counselor after the aborted attempt by Jeanne's family to remove Deidre. Early in the counseling Matt suggested that he and Jeanne do two things together after dinner: (1) Take a walk together -- just the two of them; and (2) Read the Bible and pray together before sleep. Matt said that this would revolutionize their marriage. Jeanne reacted as if Matt was being weird. Nothing came of the suggestion nor of the counseling itself, although Matt did not blame the counselor.

Later on, Matt also reflected that he may partially misunderstand Jeanne because he assumed that there was always some internal logic to how she reacted. This was not necessarily true. Matt himself was highly logical, but some people may not be logical at all. For example, an alcoholic may be reacting logically (even though wrongly) to suppress intenal pain through drink instead of "taking it to the Lord in prayer" as the hymn teaches. But people sometimes may react on whim to "feel good" for the moment. If Jeanne was among them from time to time, there would be no logical key to unlock her thoughts or motivations at least until she returned to logical thought. God would understand, but without some logical key Matt would have no way to interpret her actions into a coherent picture of her. Yes, the Holy Spirit could give supernatural warning or understanding, but when this is necessary we are beyond any realm of human understanding.

For Matt, feeling good should be derived from achievement, which in turn is derived from the grace of God as He begins to enable human beings to meet responsibility. Feeling good is not itself a target, but achievement in meeting God-given responsibilities is a target which will allow us a large amount of good feeling with thanksgiving. For example, children should aim at excellence in school which will yield recognition and ultimately financial reward in the form of scholarships. If pride is avoided and thanksgiving to God substituted for natural pride, there will be legitimate joy. David had experienced this; Deidre would later grasp this but had not at this time. Pastors who lead well according to the Scriptures should in time reap this as the Word and example they spread brings good fruit. Jeanne did not appear to understand this. In Matt's book, an underachieving person should not feel good but should rather repent of sin and show more diligence in the future. But Jeanne did not accept this cycle of discipline leading to improvement either for herself or for Deidre. (Compare John 15:1-9) Jeanne wanted fun for herself and Deidre whether they achieved well and lived Biblically or not. This was a major gap between Matt and Jeanne that was sensed and understood even though it was probably not discussed then in these terms.

On later reflection, Matt would add that initial joy with salvation is entirely the gift of God, with no human responsibility. That initial joy should always remain even if it may be obscured from time to time, as in Job's case. God's mercy and grace is the source of all joy; we can never deserve to be joyful. But side by side with the joy of God's free grace can exist also the joy that God graciously permits us through spiritual achievement as a co-laborer with Him. (1 Corinthians 3:5-9; 2 Corinthians 5:10) When God chastens, *"Weeping may endure for the night."* But when the chastening brings inner righteousness, *"Joy comes in the morning."* (Psalm 30:5). Still a third joy and greatest joy yet to come is the everlasting joy of heaven and perpetual complete fellowship with the Father, the Son and the Holy Spirit. This is given by pure grace, but joy of rewards in heaven can be achieved through incentives that God chooses to give His undeserving people through His grace.

There was one final factor emerging: the influence of Jeanne's mother. There was some old history. Jeanne's parents had lent Matt and Jeanne a few thousand dollars early in the marriage, and Matt and Jeanne had signed a note and made some payments. But the economy had gone into recession, Kingsville's largest employer had closed and the children's needs had grown, squeezing Matt's legal income and the budget. Matt had suggested that they sell their house and pay off the debt when it was sold. But both Jeanne and her parents refused and the matter was left to rest for the time being. It may have been festering even though Matt did not realize it. Years later Jeanne had told Matt that her mother had offered money to assist Jeanne to leave. Matt had politely but firmly confronted her over the telephone about trying to break up the marriage. His mother-in-law denied it, which may conceivably have been true at the time. Matt was more inclined to believe his wife than his mother-in-law. It later did "come out" that the mother-in-law after that phone call dangled money toward Jeanne to push her over the brink to leave the marriage, and this time (taking the previous story as true) Jeanne had taken the bait.

Jeanne told Matt a few days after the first admission of adultery that she was feeling feverish and needed to rest in the old marital quarters during the day while Matt worked. She surprised Matt by asking him to arrange for a doctor's appointment and to go with her. Matt agreed to do so and to pay for the appointment. At the appointment (about 10 days after the initial breach) Jeanne was found to have a simple urinary tract infection and nothing more. Matt was relieved both for his wife and for himself. At least he probably had not contracted an STD from his wife, although AIDS testing could not be done until mid-November.

May 25-26, 1992 and following

The separation came at a particular awkward time because both Matt and Jeanne had been elected as delegates to the state Republican convention. Both would attend in the same county delegation and support the same candidates. Matt took an older assistant pastor and his wife in his car. This was their first experience in politics. Matt and Jeanne were cordial but otherwise stayed away from each other. Jeanne's mother, although not a delegate, showed up to make sure it stayed that way. Jeanne talked about her situation freely, where Matt stayed quiet and concentrated on the convention business. Some of the delegates expressed sympathy to Matt; he thanked them and said that God is always good. Matt had a good time talking with the pastor and his wife and playing Christian music in the car. The pastor's wife was an accomplished musician and enjoyed that especially.

Shakespeare was basically right that the entire world is a stage and we are its players.

> *You are our epistle written in our hearts, known and read by all men;*
> *clearly you are an epistle of Christ, ministered by us, written not with*

ink but by the Spirit of the living God, not on tablets of stone but on tablets of flesh, that is, of the heart. 2 Corinthians 3:2-3.

Matt adapted this concept to Kingsville and the surrounding area, where he was living in a figurative goldfish bowl because of his public stance as a Christian, as a pro-life leader and former political candidate and as a lawyer. Since his wife had left him, Matt reasoned that he would have to show the world how a Christian copes with adultery and divorce, as he had started doing at the political convention. Some of Matt's principle weapons in his inner warfare were Bible study, prayer, Christian music (especially cheerful music because Matt did not need to stew over his situation) and heavy physical exercise.

With the convention behind him and Jeanne's separate living quarters being fully ready, Matt's next concern was to complete a Marital Settlement Agreement. Jeanne was fully recovered from her infection. She received the assistance of two local lawyers and a banker as she considered the draft. She did request some additional money from Matt not in the original draft, which Matt agreed to provide over four payments. The 1991 tax refund was to be divided equally. So the agreement was signed without a fuss. The following month Jeanne took her furniture and other personal property to her parents' home and left Kingsville. She only returned to visit friends occasionally.

In the meantime, Matt was coping with his anger by Bible study, reading, prayer, Christian music and vigorous physical exercise. He was turning his anger on his own fat because he could not express it in public. God was the only one he could tell in full. Matt did chuckle a bit when a couple of motorists honked at him when he was running. His mental image was a chess game in which the Queen has turned traitor, which does not occur in chess but sometimes does in real life. He was in the process of losing about 40 pounds. He also stepped up his worship and mid-week church attendance to fill the void of the loss of his wife. He kept up his legal work. At times Matt was exhausted at the end of the workday; on other occasions he was so fueled by anger that he felt driven to bicycle up a mountain with an average grade of nearly 4.5% for 6 miles with a second similar slope to follow if there were enough time before dark.

Matt was pleasantly surprised when the pastor permitted him to continue teaching Sunday School for adults despite the separation. Preparing to teach Revelation to experienced adults is a good way to keep one's mind off other troubles.

Matt knew that he was under attack by Satan. In terms of his character, he imagined that he was defending Fort Integrity, his spiritual equivalent of Masada or of a fortress that is the linchpin of an entire defensive line. By analogy next to Christ Himself integrity was the linchpin of Matt's life. This was shorthand for resistance to temptation -- toward sexual sin, toward bitterness toward God and even toward being unwilling to forgive and pray for Jeanne. That last was the hardest -- Matt came as far as to ask God not to lay any sin against him to Jeanne's charge, as Stephen had prayed when dying (Acts 7:60). The dishonor to God's name stemming from the sin and its public nature Matt left to God Himself.

Matt knew that in one sense he deserved what was happening, in that his sin actually deserves the Lake of Fire forever. Compared to that, the pain of adultery and divorce is a picnic. *"Against You, You only, have I sinned, and done this evil in Your sight."* Psalm 51:4 Even though David had murdered Uriah, in this sense his sin was against God Himself. So Jeanne's sin did not exceed what Matt knew he deserved. At the same time Matt knew that God was permitting this disaster for Matt's own good (Romans 8:28) and would make a way of escape so that he could bear this trial (1 Corinthians 10:13). So Matt felt great pain but not despair.

The Satanic attack on Matt's soul was heavy and by a force which would ordinarily be overwhelming, yet God would and did sustain Matt. At one choir rehearsal in October Matt knew that he should sing as a solo in church the following Sunday morning "A Mighty Fortress Is Our God." Various other church members were under different forms of spiritual attack. Several services in a row had strong blessing upon them. This was one. Matt never felt quite so pressured after that solo. Instead of mostly absorbing and parrying blows, he was fighting back against the Devil.

Democratic Nominating Convention -- 1992

John and Carolyn Jensen were in bed at their daughter's home in Minnesota. They were living a few miles east of Kingsville at the home of their son, but they were visiting their daughters about 600 miles away. John, 65, had not been feeling well that day and had fallen asleep. Carolyn was still watching President Clinton deliver his acceptance speech for nomination by the Democratic Party, even though she was a Republican. Suddenly, Carolyn her a rattle and called for her daughter to call 911. But there was nothing to be done. John had departed the earth suddenly.

In retrospect, John probably had a premonition of his death. When Carolyn checked the trunk of the car, John had brought his Masonic suit for his burial. Most of John's friends and relatives still lived near their daughters. In the midst of her grief, Carolyn at least was spared the necessity of arranging for a funeral while hundreds of miles from the place of death and burial. Since she worked for a missionary and relief organization headed by her son, there was no problem in re-arranging her work schedule.

John had been a private man. He was thoroughly honorable and worked hard so long as his body would permit. In the main Carolyn had tended to the home and children as they grew up. She had the major say in decisions such as living in town or in the country. But both believed in bringing up children who are morally straight. John had approved when Carolyn got the kids involved with the Young Republicans. Carolyn had on her part been a loyal wife.

Their major differences had been in spiritual matters. John had originally been a Lutheran, following the pattern of his family of Scandinavian descent. Carolyn had had no family pattern because she had not been raised by either her father or her mother. But at two of her childhood residences she had been exposed to the Holy Scriptures, and these had become implanted in her heart by the Holy Spirit. By the grace of God Carolyn had *"accept[ed] with meekness the implanted word, which is able to save your souls."* James 1:21. At first the family attended John's Lutheran church. But when Carolyn saw the pastor smoking before the service as she walked in with the family, she recoiled and refused to attend there again. Not even visits from church leaders could persuade Carolyn to change her mind. Neither could her husband, who wound up not attending any church. So she found a tiny Bible-believing fellowship and attended a church 50 miles away to see to the children's Biblical training as well as her own soul's nourishment.

The result of this spiritual division in the marriage was a long-lasting crimp in the intimacy of the marriage. John withdrew spiritually to the privacy of the Masonic Lodge while Carolyn carried on with her small Biblical fellowship and took the children there. John grew to tolerate the pastoral visits of Carolyn's pastor and his wife, although he kept his distance when they came to the house. In time the couple worked out a lasting truce from arguing over the subject but not any agreement. But Carolyn did honor John's wishes for a Masonic funeral. Months after John's death, Carolyn did find and read a brief written statement of faith in John's handwriting. She was comforted by this. Meanwhile the children loved both parents but spiritually followed the leadership of their mother -- and above all of the Holy Spirit.

About two months after her husband's death Carolyn believed that she had a message from the Holy Spirit that she would meet a younger man and that he would cherish her. She had no clue of whom or when.

She did not share this with her children but did with a close female friend of her own generation. Matt knew nothing of this at the time and was not divorced yet. Neither had Carolyn met Matt except in passing in the course of politics or when Matt met with Joe at his office. In hindsight, she perceived Matt as the fulfillment of this message.

If one were to try to compare the two marriages, John's and Carolyn's marriage had less drama and did last "until death do us part." They were of an older generation where divorce was less accepted. Matt's and Jeanne's marriage had more obvious stress and strain. Both marriages ended up with the partners disunited over church attendance, although in the case of Matt and Jeanne this had taken about 15 years. In each case marital intimacy suffered and in both cases there was a mixture of grief and sadness with some relief. While this sounds contradictory, it takes much sustained emotional energy to maintain a marriage without spiritual unity. When such a marriage becomes impossible to maintain, there is often a sense of relief mixed with the grief and loss because that energy need no longer be spent to maintain a difficult marriage. Instead, that energy must be expended on dealing with the loneliness of being single again after a long marriage. In Matt's case this was over 22 years and in Carolyn's case over 35 years. But a feeling of relief on Matt's and Carolyn's parts co-existed with the fact that Matt and Carolyn had loved their mates.

Matt felt from the beginning that his "trusting muscle" was undamaged by the figurative bullet he had taken when Jeanne confessed and departed. He believed that God remained in control and had some good purpose, although he knew no specifics yet. Within 2 weeks of the separation after studying 1 Corinthians 7 and praying he had concluded that God probably would not remake his emotional nature to make him comfortable as a single man. Matt still believed that marriage is the best state for most men and women, and further was assured from his study of 1 Corinthians 7 that remarriage was permissible for one who had valid Biblical reason

Thomas D. Logie

-- especially adultery (Matthew 19:1-10) -- to be "loosed from a wife." (1 Corinthians 7:27-28) But he believed that he needed to have his HIV test results and have the divorce finalized before he could make serious plans over his future. But Matt was not afraid to trust another woman, as so many of his divorce clients had been gunshy of the opposite sex for some time after the separation. Some were injured permanently. The fault was divided between him and his wife -- none of this was God's fault. So for several months Matt was largely on hold although keeping an eye out for a possible future mate. In the wisdom of God this time permitted more of the spiritual wounds to heal before Matt considered remarriage.

After the divorce was final before Christmas 1992, Matt prayed specifically for a wife in line with Genesis 24 that He would select a wife for him as Abraham's servant had been charged with the responsibility of selecting a wife for Isaac. In turn that servant had prayed for a sign from God concerning the watering of the camels, which God answered in the person of Rebekah.

Carolyn did not have the peculiar wounds of divorce. The human soul was not designed to endure divorce any more than the knee or the elbow was designed to bend backwards or sideways. Modern television has given us gruesome illustrations from football of the physical injuries that can occur when a joint is forced to bend the wrong way. Tim Krumrie's injury in a Super Bowl is probably the most famous, along with Joe Theismann's career-ending injury against the New York Giants on a Monday night. Often the psychological injuries from divorce are analogous. But Carolyn instead endured the death of her husband.

Carolyn seemed somewhat numb after her husband's death, but she carried on her work for the missionary organization and lived quietly in a separate apartment at her son's house east of Kingsville. She saw her son and her son's four children frequently when she was at home. Carolyn became somewhat concerned that her son was spending so much time with her that he was not spending enough time with his own wife.

Perhaps her son Joe shared those concerns. He had known Matt from their political cooperation. So in mid-December he called Matt and asked whether Matt would take his mother out for lunch. Joe indicated that Carolyn needed fellowship. By this time Matt's divorce was about to become final and Matt knew that all of his tests indicated that he was free of disease. So he said yes. Matt had encountered Carolyn briefly when he saw her son on political matters but did not know her well. He did make two observations during the conversation: (1) That he was more than 12 years younger than Carolyn; and (2) That he was decidedly masculine and that these facts would have to be taken into account if matters ever went beyond lunch. He thought it only fair that Carolyn's son know these things before the outset.

Christmas is often a hard time for those whose families are broken. Carolyn had some buffer because she was with one of her children and four of her grand-children. In Matt's case this was not true. His divorce had just become final. Deidre was with her husband's family and David was headed for a college missionary conference right after Christmas and was stopping in that night on the way. Matt's parents were 300 miles away; with work it was impractical to drive the round trip. So Matt was alone for a cold Canadian clipper. The bank display read 2°. Nevertheless Matt felt a surge of angry energy and ran through town, across the bridge and all the way to a new subdivision under construction. There was practically no traffic. The round trip run was about 10K. Then Matt went to an early Christmas dinner with his pastor and family. The dinner seemed subdued to Matt, but he was thankful for the pastor's thoughtfulness. Matt and his son played one-on-one basketball that night, with David winning at the end.

With court schedules and Christmas holidays, the lunch did not occur until December 31. It might seem strange today, but at the time both the law office and the missionary office were open and work was being done. The schedule was light enough that Matt had some flexibility behind the normal 1 hour for lunch on this day. Matt drove up in his nearly new Toyota Corolla -- a modest car for a lawyer -- and invited both Carolyn and her son to lunch, as originally discussed. But the son cited his workload and backed out. Matt was happy to take Carolyn alone and escorted her to the car and then to the local cafeteria with its salad bar and luncheon spread. Carolyn had seen Matt pass the front desk where she worked; Matt had once given her a catalog of discount computers. Carolyn noted that Matt was old-fashioned in opening the car door and the restaurant door for a lady. She also noticed that Matt said a public grace in the restaurant thanking God for the food.

Both Matt and Carolyn were stiff and awkward for the first 15 minutes. As they ate, Matt and Carolyn began discussing the Scriptures and then they began to loosen up. The meal became enjoyable for both. Matt realized that Carolyn loved the Scriptures, which was rare. He returned Carolyn to her work over an hour later and then returned to his work down the street and then to his apartment. After work he prayed about his encounter. Matt thought that God's answer lay in Carolyn's love of the Bible. He should therefore try to meet Carolyn again.

On Carolyn's side, she started under the misapprehension that Matt had no car. She was unsure how Matt would take her to the restaurant. Matt was not the best dresser in the world, but he was courteous and well-spoken. Carolyn had heard a rumor that Jeanne intended to secure her inheritance from her family by a sham divorce from Matt and then remarry him, but it was clear enough that Matt had no intent of living with Jeanne again. Matt exceeded her expectations, which were modest enough.

Matt and Carolyn attended a Sunday night service with Carolyn's family at Matt's church. For the first time in several years Matt had had a woman worshipping with him. That felt good. He was also surprised to see Carolyn completely at home holding and rocking her youngest grand-child. Matt was surprised and pleased to see the whole family come to church and enjoy the service.

The following night Matt called her at her apartment. They talked for over an hour. Carolyn was flying the next day to see her other children and grand-children, so any meeting would have to wait at least a week. Because of a snowstorm, Matt called the next day to make sure that Carolyn had actually left. She had. But when Carolyn heard about Matt's call, she suspected that she would hear from him again soon after she would return to her apartment. She was right. The change in her disposition made Carolyn's daughters wonder what was going on, but Carolyn had nothing concrete to report with only one lunch meeting and one church service so far. With so little to go on, she said nothing.

Matt had political business with Carolyn's son shortly after she returned. With Carolyn back, they saw each other when Matt came to see her son. As they saw each other, their eyes locked for 10 to 15 seconds. Carolyn finally lowered her eyes, but that incident made a lasting impression. Matt was also impressed with their silent communication and believed that the locked eyes were a test of spiritual strength. To be a husband, he must be able to lead, although not to dominate. Yet as a highly logical man Matt would not make decisions based predominantly on such an incident. But this did confirm Matt's resolve to call Carolyn again. He did not want to approach her at work, but Carolyn would not have long to wait. That night after supper Matt called and Carolyn invited him for dinner at her apartment the following night. Matt accepted for the nearest Thursday night.

Matt wondered what kind of food Carolyn would make. He himself knew enough about cooking to survive and have some kind of balanced diet, but that was about it. Chicken with wheat germ and granola were his staples so far as cooked meals were concerned. From his childhood

Matt disliked gravies and sauces for at least 2 reasons: (1) Too heavy; and (2) Too spicy. Matt even liked peanut butter plain without jelly. But Matt did not want to say too much before he went to dinner. Neither did he have any sense of Carolyn as a cook. Jeanne had been much more at home at an accounting desk than in a kitchen, so Matt did not know what to expect.

Matt also wondered about Carolyn's taste about music, entertainment and similar matters. They had not discussed any of those things at their first lunch.

For Carolyn, Matt was almost as much a mystery as she was to him. She had a clue that he liked chicken from the lunch. She noted the lack of sauces when he ate. She observed that he had lost weight since their casual earlier encounters; Matt gathered his trousers at the sides to conceal that they were now too big in the waist. But Carolyn had no clue as to Matt's taste in music or entertainment either.

When Carolyn served up some pan-fried chicken with green beans and potatoes, Matt was relieved and indeed delighted. Both the food and the conversation were most enjoyable. Carolyn asked him to help clean up, which he did. After supper, Carolyn brought out a tape player and put on a Steve Green tape. For Matt this was pleasant indeed. Steve Green is both an excellent musician and a devoted Christian. When Matt saw Carolyn's Bible, he suggested that they read together. So Matt taught an impromptu lesson on Psalm 1. Then Carolyn turned on the television and found *The Sound of Music,* which they both watched all the way through. During the intermission, they discussed Georg's discipline of the children before Maria came. Matt opined that most people of modern times would be excessively harsh on Georg. At least he cared about his children and did give them discipline, which is one necessary ingredient to bring up children well. Of course Maria supplied many qualities which Georg could not. But that is the way God works with couples and families. At the end of the evening

Matt told Carolyn that he wanted to see her again, and they agreed on the next night, a Friday.

This time Matt came after dinner. He did not want to burden Carolyn with preparing another meal, however much he enjoyed the first one. This time the Bible study was on Psalm 2, twice the length of Psalm 1. There was to be no television this night. When the study had been completed, Matt and Carolyn sat across a table from each other and Matt began to speak without conscious pre-planning. He told Carolyn that there was something essentially healthy about her spiritually. She loved God's Word. He loved her. Carolyn took his hand. Matt then said that he believed that spiritually they needed to marry each other as soon as possible. Carolyn was in full agreement. So in principle it was settled that quickly. But there were so many practical questions. Where would they live? In which apartment, or neither? When would the marriage take place? As to personal habits such as exercise and bodily clocks, they knew next to nothing about each other. They had much to learn about each other in a compressed time. Neither one knew much about the finances of the other. Each thought that the other had practically nothing financially. In fact, each was somewhat better off than that, though certainly not rich in wealth. But they did know two vital things: they were united in Jesus Christ and they were called to marry each other. To start on merging two lives into a joint life, that was enough.

Matt woke up before dawn the next day from a dream with one word: "warranty." That would be a strange word to most people, but Matt was a lawyer who was familiar with the Uniform Commercial Code. In his half-sleep Matt remembered the two warranties of the Code: a warranty that the goods would pass as fair average in the trade, and that the goods are fit for their particular purpose. Matt understood that the Holy Spirit was communicating with him about Carolyn. Matt already realized that Carolyn would be far better than average as a godly woman and that she was well fit to be his wife. If God warranties a car, there is no need to inquire into the model year. God's warranty by itself is enough. So Matt knew to press on ahead.

The next day Matt arrived after lunch, and Carolyn asked Matt to take them to a major shopping center. As they drove, Matt was stunned to learn that Carolyn wanted to buy him some work clothes because the ones he had did not fit well. "You don't have to do that," he said. "If we were not engaged, I would not even think of taking them. Are you sure that you can afford this and really want to do this?" But Carolyn insisted and Matt did not want to refuse a generous bride-to-be even if she really had next to nothing. Carolyn had a better sense of how people judged Matt on his appearance than he did. In his previous situation Matt had dealt with his clothing without any input from Jeanne. This was the first time he had experienced a woman shopping for a man's clothes since his mother and father visited several good clothing shops trying to find a suit that fit Matt's father just right. On that day they never did find the right fit. But Matt and Carolyn had found their fit even before they reached the clothing shop, because God had arranged it so. Because they had a short time to prepare and learn more about each other, they met each night after work as well as on weekends to talk, although at no time did they stay together or engage in any activities reserved in Scripture to married couples.

Carolyn did not want to stay in her son's house and did not like Matt's apartment either. Matt wondered how they would afford something else. Then Carolyn told him that she had a small amount of money saved that would make sense for a down payment. Carolyn's income was small, but Matt's middle-class income and length of residence in the community would provide some borrowing power because they both had a good credit history. Part of Matt's legal training and experience was in real estate. He knew Kingsville well. So during the January holiday weekend Matt tackled two projects: an engagement ring set and a house.

Matt brought Carolyn down to the jeweler to have her fitted, but then warned Carolyn that because of his political and legal prominence that they might have perhaps 48 hours before the news would be spreading through Kingsville.

Matt was wrong -- he was asked by a deputy clerk in the courthouse the next afternoon about getting married. Apparently one of the assistants at the jewelry store had tipped someone off. If the ring had not been bought on a court holiday, the word might have been out within hours instead of a day. Matt did not answer the question immediately. He walked down to Carolyn's workplace and asked her to come to the courthouse. When she did, he immediately got the deputy and requested the marriage license and paid for it. Matt decided to handle the rumor with an emphatic answer -- there was no reason to be ashamed even though this was about a month after the divorce had become final. He had not even had lunch with Carolyn until after the divorce was done. Even though the ceremony itself was modest, as far as the rumor mill was concerned this was the wedding of the year for 1993.

The house seemed more difficult. Matt took Carolyn through several neighborhoods, none of which seemed to suit. Then Matt recalled one more -- the same subdivision where he had run on Christmas Day. He arrived as the builder was leaving and honked him down. The builder showed them a "spec" house about 85% complete and still unsold. The builder was not in an ideal bargaining position with an unfinished house in the winter facing carrying charges with no income from the property. Carolyn liked what she saw. This was a split-foyer with 3 bedrooms. Matt believed that they could get better value from the builder in terms of more finished work than an absolute lowball price. So Matt negotiated for a more modest price reduction plus a finished bathroom and recreation room in the basement rather than a rock-bottom price. The builder had plentiful available labor at this slack time of year. After about a week Matt and Carolyn had reached an agreement with the builder, assuming that they could finance it. Normally Matt would have gone to a local bank, but large national lenders were taking an increasing share of the market and offering better terms. So Matt went to a local loan broker who placed loans with one of the largest New York lenders. The broker's performance was solid and professional and the loan commitment was in place in good time for the closing.

In the meantime Matt and Carolyn were arranging the wedding with Matt's pastor. He was encouraging but did note that Matt tried to do too much. He needed to step back and let Carolyn exercise her gifts in the home. This was sound advice. The church choir where Matt had sung would handle the reception.

Three days before the marriage the house closing was completed. Matt and Carolyn arranged it this way so that Carolyn would have a short time to arrange the house before Matt moved in on the wedding night. Matt was exhausted at the closing but nevertheless was able to focus on the various details of the closing and the loan. Matt also was aware that they would have to re-deed the house after the marriage to hold the house as tenants by the entireties. With some help, Matt and Carolyn moved the items from his apartment that they would use in the new house on the night before the wedding. So Matt slept on a mattress on the floor the last night before the wedding.

The wedding was February 14, 1993 -- Valentine's Day. The symbolism was apt. Both Matt and Carolyn were restraining their strong desires to live together in marriage. Matt was thankful that he had various routine misdemeanor court hearings and pretrial matters to handle. The work would take his mind off the wedding but would not be too taxing. Any difficult issues could be handled in writing before the hearing, so that any complex argument would be mapped out ahead of time. Matt did not need the drama of a jury trial or difficult argument on his wedding day. After the day's work and a quick supper, Matt put on his best suit for the wedding and drove the 15 miles to the church. There was snow on the road, but not enough to stop the wedding party and guests from gathering. Matt's parents came from 300 miles away. Carolyn's son and family were there. The wedding and reception were informal and joyous. Matt's parents came briefly to the house and then left the newlyweds alone in their new home. Although both were tired, they lost no time in celebrating their new union in Christ Jesus.

Fairy tales end with the couple "living happily ever after." In one sense this is true. Any believer in Christ will "live happily ever after" -- and much more -- as part of the Bride of Christ. But on earth the reality will be more complicated because of our own sin and because of the attacks of Satan against believers. Matt had felt this -- in fact he viewed the wedding itself as a resounding victory over Satan in that his emotional losses of the destruction of his first marriage would be more than restored with his new life.

So many times there is a spiritual letdown after a victory. Elijah was exhausted after God had consumed his sacrifice with fire from heaven that he became afraid of Jezebel and ran for his life. David had been granted an everlasting covenant by God (2 Samuel 7) and then sinned grievously in the matter of Uriah and Bathsheba. In Matthew 16 one finds that Peter perceived by revelation from God that Jesus was the Messiah sent from God and yet a short time later was used by Satan to tempt Jesus away from the Cross. Matt and Carolyn had to be vigilant after their marriage and still must be vigilant against Satan (1 Peter 5:8) so long as they remain on earth. Proverbs 4:23 has a similar idea. Our Lord Jesus gave numerous warnings to "watch", which reminds one of sentry duty. I can give a partial list: Luke 12:37-39; Matthew 24:42-43; 25:13; Mark 13:33-37; Luke 21:36. There is also 1 Peter 4:7. So Matt and Carolyn must always be on guard against a Satanic attempt to undo the victory that Jesus Christ has given them.

But even in victorious spiritual warfare on earth there is collateral damage. In this case any remaining opportunities for Matt to have a political career were destroyed. Within the pro-life movement of which Matt was a leader, there were devout Roman Catholics who honestly believed that divorce can never be justified regardless of the facts. They would no longer support Matt for high leadership for this reason. When one of them made a last-minute private appeal for Matt not to remarry, he answered her with the words of Jesus in Matthew 19:1-10 (see also Matthew 5:31-32), knowing that they knew of Jeanne's conduct because it was notorious in the entire community. They believe that Church teaching based on other passages which do not mention adultery (Mark 10:1-12; Luke 16:18) supersede what Jesus Himself said. To Matt that is an impossibility because Jesus was and still is God Almighty. No teacher can supersede what He has said. For Matt the Scriptures are clear. Matthew contains the most precise and detailed teaching, which Mark and Luke highlight the general principle against divorce but do not supply the level of detail that Matthew does. The passages are to be harmonized, not contrasted.

Since Matt was challenged on the issue of remarriage, he did privately point out that official and traditional Roman Catholic teaching on marriage claims that only a marriage consecrated by a Roman Catholic priest is a truly valid marriage. Matt pointed this out in saying that his first marriage by that standard would be invalid because it was not celebrated by a Roman Catholic priest. Logically, he would never have been validly married if this doctrine were really true. He hastened to add that both he and his friendly opponents knew better than to really accept such doctrine. In fact God gave marriage starting at Creation to the entire human race. It is not confined to His Church, however defined. Without marriage between man and woman no family life nor national life can be sustained. The very idea of civilization requires marriage between one man and one woman. Matt pointed out that his first marriage was a genuine marriage which could be dissolved, but only for reasons permitted in the Scriptures. Matt did not discuss 1 Corinthians 7:27-28 because he knew that differences in translations would blur the issue of a divorced person remarrying. (In the Greek of the *Textus Receptus*, it is quite clear that a validly divorced person may remarry without sin even though the Apostle Paul foresaw pitfalls when he wrote that epistle. But the New International Version translates from the Greek as "Are you unmarried?" the literal " Are you loosed from a wife?") Neither Matt nor his allies were persuaded, and in essence they parted ways despite occasional political cooperation.

Matt had desired to grow into being a church elder, but he now considered that this had been denied him as a consequence of a divorce. One of the qualifications for a church elder is that a person be a "one-woman man." 1 Timothy 3:2. Matt took the traditional view that a divorce means disqualification from this service because the purpose of the requirement was to preserve the reputation of the church. A stringent interpretation would serve the stated purpose. Accordingly, he did not believe that any divorced man, regardless of the circumstances, can serve as a church elder according to the Scriptures.

There was also the pain to Matt's and Jeanne's children in seeing their parents part. Matt tried to minimize this as much as he could, telling the children to love their mother even though they could not approve or imitate her conduct. He also expressed concern for her soul, especially to David -- he had heard her response to his spiritual change that first night of separation. But there was only so much Matt could do. It was a blessing that both of the children were old enough to have independent lives out of the immediate cross-fire.

Have Matt and Carolyn "lived happily ever after?" If one means perfection, the answer is obviously no. Short of Jesus Christ, there is no such thing as perfection on earth. But if one means living joyously together in Christ, then the answer is yes to the present day. May it be so always so long as they remain on earth, looking for the return of our Lord Jesus Christ! Of course there have been changes, and in the spiritual realm these have generally been for the better. The joy is still fresh, and Matt and Carolyn are far more intimate in soul and spirit than when they first married. It has helped that God has been especially merciful with regard to health.

About two weeks after the wedding Matt was passing the restroom door in the church. Two women were talking. One asked the other whether she knew Carolyn. The other said "I don't know her, but she is the best thing that ever happened to him." Matt inwardly disagreed -- his initial salvation was infinitely greater than this. But this was the greatest single blessing since that Easter Day when Matt was 8 years old.

A lawyer friend saw Matt at an outdoor community event in the spring of 1993 and told him that "Life with this woman obviously agrees with you." Indeed he was right.

Carolyn would essentially say the same, although she is not as likely to speak publicly about this. One tiny measure of her growth in her new marriage can be found in her Scrabble scores. When she married Matt, she averaged around 220. With some practice against Matt she improved to score about 350 with a reasonable draw. This was not merely the result of practice, but Carolyn's mind was growing. Matt had observed at their first lunch Carolyn's spiritual hunger. With a steady diet of joint home Bible studies her joy and comprehension multiplied quickly. *The joy of Jehovah is your strength.* Nehemiah 8:10. Carolyn had had no opportunity to go to college and even had to work her way through high school. In all probability she had the ability to be a college honors student in political science, English or history if she had had an open door in her youth. This God-given ability was now set free, and Carolyn had the time and home base to concentrate and learn first from the Holy Spirit through the Scriptures and then through her God-given abilities of observation.

Al Michaels gave his famous call at the end of the 1980 U.S.-Soviet Olympic hockey game: "Do you believe in miracles? Yes!" In a different arena, Matt and Carolyn would say the same. Strictly speaking, there are no physical miracles in this story. A true miracle is one which defies known physical laws, as when the Lord Jesus fed 5000 men and their families from five loaves of bread and two fish. This is a true miracle which is recorded in all four Gospels. Fire descending from heaven to consume Elijah's sacrifice is an Old Testament example of a physical miracle. But the accumulated improbabilities in this story make it close to a miracle and do show the hand of God orchestrating beautiful music out of adultery, divorce and death.

If one means by "living happily ever after" that Matt and Carolyn remain joyfully married and are looking together for the return of our Lord Jesus Christ, then they are in a beginning stage of truly "living happily ever after." The future climax will be the call to live with Jesus Christ forever. If given an opportunity to replay December 1996 through February 1997, would they follow the same course? Yes!

Matt wrote Carolyn a poem 2 months after their marriage that still expresses his feelings today:

Blest Carolyn! Wonderful wife!
Save only the Lord, the love of my life.
Just to consider the change in a year
To joy each day from trial severe --
From ceaseless struggle to marriage sublime,
From terrible discord to reason and rhyme.

Pilgrims single trudge in the desert;

One lacking food; the other water.
Stumbling for the next oasis,
Seeking a home with a Christian basis.

Their paths cross, and not by chance
But by a loving Father's providence!
First one lunch and then phone talk
As through their desert they together walk.

Then apart in snow's twilight--
My prayers flew with you in flight.
Safely back within one week
To a man who came true love to seek.

We met again-- my meal preferred
But the best meal was in the Word!
As I beheld your soul so fair
We rejoiced together with God in prayer.

My defense down, my heart was moved
By the hope of peace from strife.
With silent call to the Lord of Love
I spoke -- The Spirit moved
In joyful tears to pierce my fear.

As you with intrepid faith
Clasped my hand. You gave
The gift that suited my need.
And in doing so freed
Us both from emotions grave

To renewed life and joy and peace.

What now? How long to wait
The blessed joys to consummate?
Must we have a long delay?
Nay! the hand of love,
Too strong to stay,
Must strike down that prison wall
Between us and the God-sent call
To life together in Christian love.

No more stung by desert sand;
Now we dwell by God's command
In blessed Beulah land.
Freed from strife and trial long
To Christ we sing a victor's song!
Those battles harsh we still must fight
We win together in Jesus' might;
Till death should strike with futile sting
Or better yet, transformed at once
With Jesus conquering.

AFTERWORD

And what of the real-life Jeanne and countless men and women like her? Matt would acknowledge that of all people he is least qualified to judge Jeanne. In fact only Jesus Christ has that right and power. *The Father judges no one, but has committed all judgment to the Son.* John 5:22. If Jeanne repents and pleads with Jesus Christ for mercy, she will be forgiven, cleansed completely and will live in heaven forever with Christ Jesus. If Jeanne was genuinely a believer before her downfall, God will keep

His grip on His child and will lead her to true repentance and spiritual restoration. King David is an example. The earthly evidence of genuine repentance will be a life transformed from rebellion to obedience to God with faith, hope and love at the center of the new life. Such a life is always a result of God's free grace; this cannot be reached by human effort or works. If Jeanne goes down this path, the crack that widened to a yawning breach between Matt and Jeanne will finally be fully healed and full and final reconciliation will occur. If Jeanne's Christianity turns out to have been a façade and the façade is not replaced by a genuine conversion of the heart and real faith, then Jeanne's judgment (as the judgment of anyone of like character) will be an awful reminder that one cannot deceive God and that persistent rebellion against God in any form (most especially unbelief, the opposite of faith) meets with everlasting suffering and punishment. If any reader of this is either like Jeanne or proud that he or she is not like Jeanne (like the Pharisee who thanked God that he was not like the tax collector – his prayer was rejected in Luke 18:9-14), I plead with you to plead with God immediately to change you from the inside out while there is still time. *Seek the Lord while He may be found; Call upon Him while He is near.* Isaiah 55:6.

— PART FIVE —
Reconciliation

Dr. David Thomas spent his usual time in prayer for his weekly address to the students and faculty of Jerusalem University College. He was of solid and athletic build and kept in good and vigorous shape despite the natural thickening of the human body. He was about 70 with a full growth of gray-white hair and a full beard. {Dr. Thomas kept his beard to minimize offense to either Orthodox Jews or to Muslims who believe that men should not shave their beards, in keeping with Paul's teaching to minimize offense to one's hearers and thus to make it easier for them to listen to the message itself.} His baritone voice was still both musical and strong. Since Dr. Thomas was retiring at the end of the semester, this particular address was unusual in that the professors and students expressly invited students and professors from both Jewish and Arab schools to come and had used Internet communications to inform the public of the address. Dr. Thomas hoped that there would be an opportunity for questions after he had concluded his prepared remarks. While others prepared the lecture hall, placed signs and provided minimal security, Dr. Thomas pled with God for His Spirit's blessing on the teaching and the meeting as a whole. He prayed that there would be listeners who did not know Jesus Christ but who would have willing hearts to receive the truth.

When Dr. Thomas stepped out of his prayer room and to the lectern, he was pleased to see the room close to three-quarters full, meaning close to 150 people in addition to the student body and his fellow faculty members.

I should thank each and every one of you for coming and listening to me tonight. You have come from diverse and even antagonistic teachings which intellectually cannot be reconciled with one another. Our topic is reconciliation. I will discuss two aspects of reconciliation: between humanity and God and among human beings. Ultimately, these two discussions will converge.

Permit me to start with Abraham, who is one of the greatest men to have ever walked the earth by common consent. It is also agreed that Abraham recognized that each human being is under a death sentence because of his or her sins against God. With only two exceptions -- Elijah and Enoch -- each and every person who has been born as a human being has died. Abraham heard the command of God to sacrifice his son and was in the process of obeying this dreadful command because he knew that God's ultimate penalty for sin is just. He tied his son on the altar and raised the killing knife in his right hand when God spoke to Abraham from heaven and countermanded his previous order to sacrifice his son. {Note, the son is actually Isaac, but Dr. Thomas avoided a controversy with Muslims at this stage of his message by leaving each listener to imagine the son as either Isaac or Ishmael as he or she had been taught. That was not the issue for this message. Dr. Thomas picked Abraham as his starting point because he is honored by Muslims, Jews and Christians. He wanted to hold as much of his audience as possible long enough to listen to the climax of his message. In effect he succeeded even though many in the crowd grew more and more restive as the teaching progressed. The atmosphere gradually grew thicker and finally boiled over as we shall see.} From this we learn that God requires a sacrifice for sin in order for us to be reconciled to God and yet He has forbidden the sacrifice of human beings. Certain animals and birds were accepted temporarily in place of human beings created in the image of God. But even Abraham, as great as he was, was required to bring a blood sacrifice. So was Job, who acted as a family priest in sacrificing not only for himself but also for each of his children. *Without the shedding of blood there is no remission of sin.* {Hebrews 9:22} So there is a steady succession of animal sacrifices throughout the Old Testament starting with Adam's son Abel.

But these sacrifices had to be repeated over and over. From this fact it is clear that none of these animal sacrifices made any permanent peace between God and humanity in general or between God and any particular human being. {Dr. Thomas had Hebrews 9:13 and 10:1-2 in mind, but again he did not to cite expressly to the New Testament at this stage when many of his hearers did not believe that it is God's inspired Word.} These sacrifices, while ordained and required by God, did not solve the problem but only postponed the day of reckoning from year to year and from generation to generation. Sin had entered the human race through Eve and most especially through Adam and the sacrifices could not remove the sin. The fundamental division between God and man persisted.

Let us switch our attention to the problem of reconciling human beings to each other. We are familiar with the struggles between Turk and Arab, between Arab and Iranian, between various denominations of ceremonial churches professing forms of Christianity and between and among different branches of Islam, Judaism and Christianity. We see parallel tribal conflicts in Africa and racial conflicts in Southeast Asia. A new conflict has just arisen in Central Asia. Add to these conflicts issues over natural resources, economics, national territory and ideology and we have a world filled with conflict. Negotiators have struggled to achieve lasting solutions, which still seem to elude them.

From historical perspective, even individuals who profess the same faith do not always agree. For example, Ezer Weitzman ran British manufacture of ammunition in World War 1 while Walter Rathenau {both Jewish, which would be well known to this audience} mobilized the economy for the Kaiser's Germany. During World War 2, the royal house of Saudi Arabia sided with the Allies while the Mufti of Jerusalem {both Sunni Muslims, which would also be known to this audience} tried his best to help Hitler. War has always been destructive, but the increased power of modern weapons can make the killing faster and give fewer opportunities for political leaders to pull back from the brink. In fact, the prophets all agree that these problems have no lasting solution even though there may be peace in parts of the world for a generation or perhaps as much as 100 years or more in rare instances. Since the problem is worldwide, the issues must lie with humanity as a whole and not with particular nations or conflict-prone geographies. Universal human sin has made lasting peace impossible. War is not the product of weapons; weapons are a reflection of the war within the human heart and between human beings. *From where come wars and fightings among you? Do they not come from here* [gesturing to the heart], *even of your lusts that war in your members? You lust, and have not: you kill, and desire to have, and cannot obtain: you fight and war, yet you have not, because you ask not.* {James 4:1-2, although the cite was not stated in the address}

In addition to the Jewish and Islamic religions and their subdivisions, there are two other major belief systems that affect Jerusalem and the Middle East. One is atheism, which has many adherents in the European Union, especially in France. There are descendents of both Isaac and Ishmael that profess this view. The human race somehow evolved with no higher intelligence superintending it, and so as a race we are accountable to nobody unless another human being or group can make us knuckle under by force. This is in stark contrast to both Biblical Judaism and Islam, which both profess a final judgment by a power greater than humanity. Christianity is especially explicit about the Last Judgment.

In America, there are intellectual descendents of the Saducees who deny the supernatural but try to create an ethical or moral philosophy from either the Old or New Testament. Some would place Reform Judaism in this intellectual camp also.

I am not dealing in detail with any of the Eastern religions, but they do not agree among themselves either. The regime in Myanmar (or Burma) is one of oppression and not of peace. In North Korea we have a survival of a regime that deifies the government and the current Leader, whomever that might be. Along with Iran, it is one of the most belligerent in the world.

There are liturgical and ceremonial offshoots of Christianity, which stress repeated ceremonies as opposed to deep study of the Bible. Although offshoots of a church founded by the disciples of Jesus who roundly condemned both the Pharisees and the Saducees, these liturgical churches have wound up intellectually similar to the Pharisees who lived in the time of Pontius Pilate in that they stress laws and formulas over communion with the living God. Jesus condemned the Pharisees for missing "justice, mercy and faith" while paying attention to issues of lesser importance.

Some wars have been fought over money, wealth or minerals. Examples can be drawn from wars between nations or indeed wars within families. Troy was destroyed because it fought to defend an adulterous affair involving Paris, its Crown Prince. Lust for power has motivated dictators from Napoleon to Stalin to Pol Pot. Lust for land has been another cause for war. Even King Solomon with all of his wealth and all of his women was not satisfied and said that everything is vanity -- emptiness. We always want more, but if we obtain more we still are not satisfied and do not even enjoy what we have.

All this brings us to the central question for tonight: Who can reconcile all of this when both intellectual and physical conflict is apparent wherever one turns?

Isaiah does speak of a Man Who is the Prince of Peace, Who stands apart from all of this dissatisfaction and war. {Isaiah 9:6} Daniel, the greatest treasury minister who has ever served a human government, identified this Man as Messiah the Prince, the anointed Prince. David in Psalm 2 identifies the Messiah as the Son of God. Yet both David and Isaiah portray the Messiah as suffering {Psalm 22; Isaiah 53, for two examples}; some rabbis have speculated that there are two Messiahs, one suffering and one reigning as an absolute monarch. Islam acknowledges that Jesus the Messiah was born of a virgin, as prophesied by Isaiah as clearly translated in the Septuagent from Alexandria long before Jesus' birth as well as in English translations of Isaiah 7:14. Islam also acknowledges that He is sinless, in contrast to the Sanhedrin council that pressured Pontius Pilate to put Him to death. That council condemned Jesus as a blasphemer but thrust Him forward to Pilate as an alleged rebel against Rome, a charge that both Pilate and the council knew was false.

What does Jesus' life have to do with reconciliation? Jesus preached primarily to the house of Israel, but also to Samaritans and to a Syro-Phoenician woman. He pardoned a woman taken in adultery in Jerusalem and also a cohabiting woman in a Samaritan village. He healed a Roman centurion's servant as well as countless people of Israel as Elisha healed Naaman the Syrian. Both a former tax collector for the regime and a former zealot to overthrow the Roman government were among His disciples. After His death, the first-generation church was able to establish congregations with both Jews and Gentiles, especially through Saul of Tarsus who became Paul the Apostle.

Consider some of Jesus' greatest champions, ancient and modern. Paul was a devout Pharisee dispersed to Tarsus, a scholar and son of

Benjamin. Yet he received theological training from Gamaliel, one of the greatest instructors in Jerusalem, and 3 years' solitary training in Arabia before starting the major portion of his missionary work. Peter and John were fishermen and natives of Galilee. Neither were scholars. Apollos was a mighty orator but from his name must have been of Greek culture. Barnabas and Mark were Levites from Cyprus. Polycarp was Greek culturally. Jerome and Augustine were Latin. Peter Waldo was Savoyard. Martin Luther was German. Wycliffe and Tyndale were English. John Calvin was French and transplanted to Geneva. Savonarola was martyred in Italy. Some of the greatest champions of Christianity have been women. Corrie ten Boom, whose family was wiped out aiding both Jews and Gentiles in Holland in the *shoah,* is one modern example. One of the chief assistants to the Trocmé brothers in Grenoble was a Christian woman who forged ration cards for those appointed to starvation. Sugihara was a Japanese diplomat who wrecked his career to save thousands from the Nazi killing machinery. I have left out so many, but surely those who profess to worship Jesus the Messiah as the living Word of God in human flesh and revere the Bible as the Word of God in written form are the most varied set of human beings of any religious faith. This faith was spread by persuasion, not by force. A Billy Graham crusade has nothing in common with the violent Crusades of the 11th and 12th centuries. There were no Christian armed revolutions against the Roman Empire of the type of Spartacus or of Bar-Kochba. Yet those movements are dead and gone and Christianity is still here. Why?

Christianity points the way for the individual human being to be reconciled to God. We mentioned earlier the requirement of the blood sacrifice for the forgiveness of sin, and the apparent dilemma posed because God has forbidden us to offer human sacrifice. Even animal sacrifice ceased shortly after the death of Jesus Christ just outside ancient Jerusalem. Did God stop forgiving sin?

In fact the Temple and the entire sacrificial system stopped because it was no longer necessary for there to be peace between God and an individual person. The entire system of the Levitical priesthood and of their animal sacrifices was a temporary system, as Daniel {9:24-27} recognized. So did Jeremiah and Ezekiel, {Jeremiah 30-33; Ezekiel 36} who both spoke of the New Covenant under which people would receive a new heart and a new spirit within them. The real circumcision was never merely of the male organ but was of the heart {Jeremiah 17:9}, referring to the cutting away of sin and especially of rebellion against God which is natural for everyone from birth. Are we to imagine that there was no forgiveness of sin after Herod's Temple was destroyed or before Solomon's Temple was constructed? Nonsense! Even in the days of the Flood when the entire human race was exceedingly corrupt there were eight who survived in the Ark. At least Noah was deemed righteous through faith and grace. Even in Sodom and Gomorrah there was Lot, who escaped with his two daughters. Elijah thought that he was the last prophet of the Lord, but in truth God had reserved 7000 for himself. God has kept for Himself some kind of remnant even in the most wicked times.

Consider the person of Jesus the Messiah, more often called Christ from the Greek form of the same word. The Hebrew Scriptures in Genesis 1, Psalm 2, Proverbs 8, Isaiah 48:16 and Hosea 11:1 clearly state that the Father has a Son. In the Hosea passage Israel might at first glance be thought to be the Son, but that makes no sense in the other passages. In Hosea Israel is earlier portrayed as the unfaithful wife, so in context of that book the idea that Israel is God's son is not the primary meaning of that passage either, even though Israel did indeed come out of Egypt. Isaiah 7:14 prophesied that *"a virgin shall conceive and bear a Son, and you shall call His name Immanuel, meaning 'God with us.'"* I know that the Hebrew is sometimes understood as a young woman and not necessarily a virgin, but we must remember that two births are being prophesied -- one to be born to the royal house of Judah shortly, and another more important birth centuries later. So one of the two women foretold would not be a virgin at the time of the birth of her son. I am following the God-given wisdom of the Septuagint translators long before the event in using the word "virgin." This Virgin-born Son of God is presented as the precise image of His Father in a human body. Isaiah 7:14 is unambiguous in prophesying that God would come in the form of a man. The Son had laid aside His glory --like the Shekinah that formerly lived behind the veil in the Temple-- and His limitless physical strength and exchanged them for the weakness of the human body. Both physically and in knowledge He grew, yet sinless the entire time. He had supernatural knowledge that He could either use or set aside as fit His purposes from His Father. He is morally perfect and yet from experience knows our physical weaknesses and our temptations. In fact Jesus the Messiah deliberately put Himself in harm's way to pay the price of sin for His people so that His people would go free. That is why He was crucified. Though the Sanhedrin and the Romans connived at injustice and the Sanhedrin even denied that God was the ultimate King over Israel, God permitted all of this in order that His Son would pay the death penalty for sin on behalf of all of His people of every culture and background. It was no impostor on the Cross -- such a person would deserve to die himself and never could pay the price of another's sin -- such a person could never pay even for his own sin. It was Jesus the Messiah Himself Who suffered and willingly died at the precise minute of the Passover sacrifice, at the place where Abraham was prepared to sacrifice his son. So He became the one sacrifice for all time for all who would believe in Him and trust their souls to Him. Then on the third day Jesus rose from the dead in a resurrection body.

{As the crowd began to murmur Dr. Thomas pressed on in a stronger yet not strident voice to make himself heard.}

The contemporaries of Jesus the Messiah understood His claims to unite deity and humanity in one perfect, sinless package. He publicly forgave sins, a prerogative that belongs to God alone. He said that He was the *"bread that came down from heaven."* {John 6:41} He proclaimed Himself to be the Lord of the Sabbath. {Matthew 12:8} He claimed to be the Son of God. {John 5:19-28, 10:33-38} He claimed to have been alive before Abraham and that Abraham rejoiced to see Him come to earth. {John 8:54-58} Jesus used the title *I AM* that God used in speaking with Moses in the burning bush. {John 8:58} He claimed to be entitled to equal honor --worship-- with the Father. {John 5:23} He demonstrated power over Satan during His temptation. {Matthew 4:1-11; Luke 4:1-13} In fact, one could readily understand His rebuke to Satan, *"You shall not put the Lord your God to the test"* as a face-to-face rebuke to Satan's temptation of God Himself in human flesh then and there as well as a statement of general principle. When Jesus entered Jerusalem for the last time, He received worship in terms proper for God alone. {Luke 19:28-44} And when Thomas saw Him after His resurrection, Thomas worshiped Jesus, probably in the same spirit that Manoah and his wife worshiped the Angel of the Lord {Judges 13}. Jesus asserted authority over natural forces, over disease and over death itself by raising three people from the dead. And the reaction of his contemporary religious leaders -- with a few exceptions -- was to turn on Him with violence and kill Him by any means necessary, including perjury before Pilate.

If Jesus the Messiah united deity and humanity in His own person, then how did He reconcile sinful humanity to pure, sinless Deity when His presence provoked such rebellion? As Isaiah {53:4} says, *It pleased Him (that is, God the Father) to put Him to grief.* Jesus the Messiah was also the Lamb of God, Who fulfilled once and for all time all the old sacrifices such as the Passover and the sin offering. Jesus was the ultimate sacrifice that fulfilled the picture of Abraham's sacrifice of the ram in place of his son. Like the

Scapegoat, Jesus went outside the city before He died. For believers, He has paid the full price of God's just judgment on our sins, as Isaiah 53 says. In those hours on the Cross, the physical sufferings described in Psalm 22 were the climax of His paying believers' way to heaven. Before the Romans were permitted to burn Herod's Temple, it had become superfluous in terms of any sacrifices for sin that God would accept. The Glory of God had already departed, as signaled on the day of the Crucifixion by the complete tearing of the multi-layered veil from top to bottom. By the same token, the records for the Levitical priesthood were lost because God had superseded that priesthood with the priesthood of His Son Jesus after the order of Melchizedek, as prophesied in Psalm 110.

The true path of submission to God {a play on the meaning of "Islam" which would have been understood immediately by this audience} is the worship of His Son and the unqualified acceptance of God's own words, spoken from the heavens when His Son lived in His human body and now transmitted to us in written form, that Jesus the Messiah is His only begotten Son from heaven and entitled to equal worship with Himself by express and unchanging decree of the Father.

At this point the tension in the crowd burst out with competing sounds of *Allah Akbar!* and *Hear O Israel, the Lord our God, the Lord is one.* Dr. Thomas was not in immediate danger because the men in the audience turned their attention to each other rather than uniting against him. But security had to intervene to avoid a complete riot and clear the hall. No further discourse was possible in the auditorium. A few people moved toward the front and side aisles, away from the tumult, in order to avoid being swept into the tumult. Two of them went all the way to the front because they had independently of each other wanted to talk further with Dr. Thomas. In the confusion he was able to get them into a side room while the security force did its work of clearing the hall.

One of the two was a young male Palestinian engineering student, age 20. Asif did not stand out because he did not want to stand out. By nature quiet and even taciturn, he kept most of his thoughts to himself and threw himself into his studies. He enjoyed the mathematical order that he found in engineering, whether in calculus or in binary computer code. His professors could see his talent. While he had questions about his Muslim training, he kept them to himself. Prudence was second nature to him; he assumed that someone was watching him most of the time. With his father wanting him to enter into an arranged marriage, and with the divisions between Fatah and Hamas and even divisions between Sunni and the minority Shia, plus the wary vigilance of the IDF and police, his assumption was reasonable rather than paranoid even if not always accurate.

Asif blended into the background physically as well. His appearance was unremarkable and he had no obvious nationality at first glance other than being from somewhere near the Mediterranean basin. He was of medium height, slim and with a runner's natural light build. He had no scars and no combat experience in the *intafada*. He was a bit too young and not physically aggressive by nature. He had determination but not of the type that is visible on the surface.

Asif's father was polygamous; Asif's mother was his first and oldest wife. Asif resented the squabbling of his father's wives over him. He was his father's oldest child. One of his hidden questions pertained to polygamy: if God made men and women in roughly equal proportions, why is polygamy the right social system when it would leave so many young men with nobody to marry? To his keen engineering mind, that seemed inefficient as well as cruel. Asif believed that God is an orderly and efficient God, as his scientific studies revealed concerning this created world. Asif was not satisfied with the evolutionary explanation that the strongest men would take the most women and pass on the best genes. He had also observed that children of polygamous homes such as his own get little attention from their fathers because the fathers have to spread themselves among up to four wives. As his own mother aged, Asif's mother got progressively less attention from his father. As the first-born, Asif still got paternal attention and faced high expectations. Because Asif's father was skeptical that violent revolution would work, Asif was spared the dangers of growing up in an ultra-militant household. Asif's father tended to stick to his studies of the Koran and give quiet support to the *intafada* short of violence. In this way he avoided notice from either the Israeli authorities or from violent faction leaders of Fatah, Hamas or Hezbollah.

The other was a mature young Israeli student, age 19, named Yehudith. She came from a Conservative Jewish family that was intensely nationalistic as to Israel's identity but not supportive of the current Orthodox rabbinical domination over marriage and other aspects of social life. She herself was friendly but not boisterous. She loved children and animals and wanted to pursue child psychology as a career. Her father was one of the leaders at the house of worship. Her mother was a traditional Jewish housewife who concentrated her efforts at home, but she certainly held her own at the dinner table when political and social subjects were discussed. Yehudith was thankful that her parents had stayed together when the parents of many of her friends had divorced. Yehudith participated when her family observed Jewish holidays and traditions but was not inclined to any of the Orthodox persuasions in Israel. She had access to a great variety of views, from Orthodox to vigorously secular and atheist, through the Internet as well as at school. As to a man, she definitely preferred one who wanted to work in the economy to one who wanted to spend a lifetime studying the Torah subsidized by the government. Yet she did not ignore Jewish texts and had a vague awareness of Christian belief that Jesus Christ had risen from the dead and is the Son of God.

Yehudith was about 5'6" tall with shoulder-length brown hair and a friendly, open face with full lips. Her eyes were large and her skin was lighter than usual in Israel, indicating a probable European background. She was not athletic nor a drop-dead beauty, but she was a good listener who could make a person feel comfortable. Like Leah, she had weak eyesight at a distance although this same weakness made it easy for her to read tiny type. She was a good questioner. She had not been inducted into the IDF, probably because of the problem with eyesight.

During this conversation, Asif spoke in Arabic and Yehudith in Hebrew. Dr. Thomas responded in the language of the questioner. However, Asif understood Hebrew and Yehudith understood Arabic, so each could understand the other. I give the conversation in English.

Asif opened the questions:

A: When you use the term God, do you mean Allah?

Dr.: The God of the Bible is indeed the God of Abraham, whose willingness to sacrifice his son you remember each Eid. He was also the God of Noah, and Hagar herself and Ishmael were sustained by the God of the Bible. God heard and answered Abraham's prayers for Ishmael even though he said "no" to Abraham about Sodom and Gomorrah. God is truly a God of love, compassion and forgiveness as well as a God of justice, or else we would all be dead and damned. In that sense there is a clear difference between the concept of Allah and the divine revelation of God as found in the Old and New Testaments. Allah requires people to earn salvation, where the God of the Bible gives it by reason of His grace through faith. In addition, God is not inscrutable as Allah is portrayed. This idea that Allah cannot be known by humans has stimulated fatalism. In fact the living God seeks people of all varieties to worship Him and is delighted to gradually reveal Himself to willing hearts. In the end the faithful will know Him as well as He now knows us. In fact each of you can begin to get to know Him right now.

J: Aren't you really saying that there is more than one God when you say that Jesus is entitled to the same worship as the God of heaven, the Lord of Sabaoth?

Dr.: No. I am saying that that God has always existed in three distinct personages even though they are morally and intellectually identical. On this earth we will never understand God fully; the closest human analogy I can give you would be genetically identical triplets. Moses in the first chapter of Genesis says, *"Let Us make man in Our image, after Our likeness."* {Genesis 1:26} After the Fall God remarks that Adam had become like *"one of Us."* {Genesis 3:22} In Psalm 110:1, David introduces the ultimate priesthood: *"The Lord said to my Lord"* Psalm 2:12 warns us to *"Kiss the Son, lest He be angry, when His wrath is kindled but a little. Blessed are all they who put their trust in Him."* Isaiah 48:16 says that the Father and the Spirit sent the Messiah. The Angel of the Lord of the Old Testament is the Son of God before He took on human flesh. In Judges 13 that Angel received worship, which an ordinary angel would never do. Hosea 12:3 says that Jacob wrestled with God. Compare this to Genesis 32:24 where Moses says that Jacob wrestled with a Man, not directly named in Genesis. From Hosea we know that the Man who wrestled Jacob was actually God in a form that was indistinguishable from a human. Then consider Isaiah 9:6: *"For unto us a Child is born; unto us a Son is given, and the government shall be upon His shoulder. And His name shall be called Wonderful, Counselor, the Mighty God, the Everlasting Father, the Prince of Peace.* Isaiah 7:14 identifies the virgin-born Son as Emmanuel, meaning "God-with-us". This is not all, but this is enough of a sample to show the solid Old Testament foundation for three identical persons within God starting with Moses and proceeding through the Prophets.

A: You clearly implied that we cannot earn our way to heaven, not by martyrdom or by being good.

Dr.: You understand very well. When Adam and Eve sinned, they died in their spirits and became helpless to save themselves.

J: Then the rabbis who have said that we can enter heaven by good works are all wrong?

Dr.: Yes, because those rabbis failed to believe Psalm 53:1-3

The fool has said in his heart, "There is no God." They are corrupt, and have done abominable iniquity. There is none who does good. God looks down from heaven upon the children of men, to see if there are any who understand, who seek God. Every one of them has turned aside. They have together become corrupt. There is none who does good. No, not one.

We cannot allow any writings -- even my own -- to take the same level as the Holy Scriptures themselves.

A: So how does anyone enter heaven? Has God slammed the door on us completely?

Dr.: No, we can enter heaven through faith in the sacrifice of Jesus Christ, the Son of God, as full and final payment for our sinfulness and our specific sins. We must worship Him as we worship the Father, as John 5 says in the New Testament and as Psalm 2 says in the Old. God has left this one door open through grace and grace alone. Jesus Himself said, "I am the Door." {John 10:7-9} Since He was speaking as the Good Shepherd who lies in front of the door of the sheepfold, it would be legitimate to understand Him as saying that "I am the Gate," as the New International Version translates it. And on one thing He is absolutely clear: there is no other door nor gate to heaven except Himself, but He welcomes people of every background whatsoever without discrimination.

J: Why did the leaders of Israel have Him killed?

Dr.: I cannot be sure that the motives were the same for every one of the participants. So I will try to answer your question broadly while realizing that not every motive would apply to every participant.

(1) Many Pharisees and especially Saducees were so inflexible that they could not accept any changes in the Law delivered by Moses and as elaborated over the centuries by various rabbis. So when Jesus healed a person on the Sabbath, they were enraged to the point of framing Him with false witnesses like Jezebel and Naboth.

(2) Others honestly thought Jesus was a heretic and a false prophet. After all, the Law did prescribe the death penalty for a false prophet. Paul was one of these; he found out his mistake on the road to Damascus.

(3) Pilate could not permit any possible challenge to Caesar, however remote, to exist. So the Sanhedrin played on this fear. But Pilate extracted his price, a pledge that Israel had no king but Caesar, which denied God as King. So many of those who participated in killing Christ had no faith in the God of Israel and so acted for that reason. As for Pilate, he too was guilty of knowingly sending an innocent Man to His death for Pilate's own political purposes.

(4) Jesus exposed sin and by His presence threatened many social and commercial relationships. Twice he cleared the Temple of animal merchants and moneychangers. Instead of the ceremonial, Jesus approved a summary the Law in two commands, both of which are based on love. {Luke 10:27} If there is no love there is no obedience to God from the start. Elsewhere, He stated that the most important points of the Law pertain to justice, mercy and faith. {Matthew 23:23} He denounced greed {Matthew 6:19-24} and even evil thoughts as sufficient to merit hellfire. {Matthew 5:21-23, 27-30} He denounced pride, which is rampant among the powerful in every age. When Jesus talked about humility and prayer, the proud man who kept the outward commands of the law was not justified before God, but the tax collector who asked God for forgiveness was justified. {Luke 18:9-14} This is anathema to most people in power, so many of the powerful turned on Him.

(5) But God meant all this for our good, because without His death there could be no forgiveness of sin, nor any humans in heaven.

A: Isn't it unfair that a good man, or especially a perfect man, had to die? How is that just? We teach that Judas or someone else died on the Cross, not Jesus.

Dr.: In terms of human justice, I agree that Jesus' death was unfair. But Jesus knew what He was facing and agreed with His Father to do it. Peter was one of Jesus' closest disciples, and put it this way {1 Peter 3:18}:

> For Christ also suffered once for sins, the just for the unjust, that He might bring us to God, being put to death in the flesh but made alive by the Spirit.

Out of love Jesus -- not an impostor -- chose to actually bear my sin and the sin of every believer even though it violated His rights as the Son of God. For a temporary time He gave up those rights. As Paul wrote {Philippians 2:5-11}:

> Let this mind be in you which was also in Christ Jesus, who, being in the form of God, did not consider it robbery [or something to be gripped] to be equal with God, but made Himself of no reputation, taking the form of a bondservant, and coming in the likeness of men. And being found in appearance as a man, He humbled Himself and became obedient to the point of death, even the death of the cross. Therefore God also has highly exalted Him and given Him the name which is above every name, that at the name of Jesus every knee should bow, of those in heaven, and of those on earth, and of those under the earth, and that every tongue should confess that Jesus Christ is Lord, to the glory of God the Father.

J: So that means that the Father demands that we worship the Son?
Dr.: Yes, you have understood well.

A: And that there is no other gate -- or door -- to heaven?

Dr.: Yes. You also have understood well.

At this point Asif and Yehudith looked at each other and nodded and both thanked Dr. Thomas for his time. Dr. Thomas gave each of them a pocket Bible small enough to be concealed easily -- Arabic for Asif and Hebrew for Yehudith. While things now seemed quiet in the auditorium which was now empty, Asif offered to escort Yehudith home because of the earlier disturbance, which she gratefully accepted. But Asif said "We should talk together first as to how we are going to do this without exciting suspicion in the neighborhood. I am not known -- what would someone say if they recognized me as an Arab near your home? I wish I could take you home, but I know that my father would not even permit you to come in."

Yehudith replied, "I do want to talk with you and really do want you to help me get home. But you are right about the neighborhood -- and for that matter, my parents. Can we find a cafe for a few minutes where we might have some peace?"

Asif thought for a moment and replied, "Let me think about that and let's exchange cell phone numbers and e-mail addresses that nobody else knows. My father will be checking on me to be home, but I definitely want to talk with you tomorrow. I have never met anyone like you. I will think of a safe place to meet you tomorrow. Also, please use the word 'Ariel' if you suspect that anyone is listening to either of us when we are talking. I will use the word 'Jenin' as a similar signal. I agree with you. I do want to meet but I want to be careful about both of our families. How close to your home can I walk you before my presence would be out of place?"

So Asif and Yehudith walked toward her house as close as they dared given that he was Arab and she Jewish. This dilemma is not new: *Romeo and Juliet* and *West Side Story* have explored the same basic issue in other cultures. But modern Jerusalem with its tension between Jew and Muslim and between the descendents of Isaac and the descendents of Ishmael is probably the most explosive setting possible for a couple reaching across racial and religious lines. Asif and Yehudith did not have an opportunity to talk about Dr. Thomas' sermon or the session afterwards, but both were obviously moved. So they swapped schedules for both their classes and their part-time work.

They did not know this yet, but Asif and Yehudith shared frugality as a trait. Both were good savers. Both still lived with their parents and had had to fend off the inevitable questions about marriage from worried parents. Judith's parents were getting concerned that she was getting somewhat old to be single and wanted her to marry a nice Jewish young man, and Asif's father especially pressed him to go forward with an arranged marriage with a young woman with family ties. Asif had stated in good faith that he wanted to get his studies done first, but nobody in his circle had excited his emotions the way Yehudith had. Yehudith in turn admired Asif's honest and logical approach to Dr. Thomas and also his concern for her safety. She found his quiet lack of pretense attractive. So they set their meeting off both of their campuses at a location where neither would be spotted by inquisitive family members.

When they met the next day, Asif got right to the point as he saw it. He told Yehudith that he was impressed with her and was attracted to her. But he also expressed his concern as to how they could build a united marriage and a united family with their families at enmity with each other. Indeed, how would they function together if they believed different things and even celebrated different holidays? Yehudith replied, "I know that we would need a common faith as a foundation to build a family. What did you make of last night?"

Asif said, "I had never considered the question of the resurrection of Jesus Christ from the dead because I was taught that He did not actually die. So I read from the Gospels last night. But I realize that so many people saw Him die that mistaken identity is humanly impossible. There was no human opportunity to sneak in a substitute. No ordinary human being could have spoken as Jesus spoke while spiked to the Cross. So it was Jesus Who hung there. The *ulama* are wrong about this. Therefore I have to face the issue of His resurrection, given what I already know about His virgin birth and sinlessness. If death is the penalty for sin, and Jesus was sinless, it follows from God's justice that Jesus would not stay dead but would rise from the grave."

Yehudith replied, "I never have had any doubts but that Jesus was crucified. But the resurrection from the dead has always been hard for me to swallow. But I saw where the Sadducees argued with Jesus over the reality of the resurrection. Jesus' answer was devastating. He referred to the passage about Moses and the burning bush and quoted God speaking to Moses, *'I am the God of Abraham, the God of Isaac and the God of Jacob. He is not the God of the dead but of the living.'* So Abraham, Isaac and Jacob were alive when Moses was on the earth even though their bodies were dead. I am told that Job hoped for resurrection also. {Matthew 22:32, Luke 20:38, Job 14:5-22; 19:23-27} David in Psalm 16 apparently believed in resurrection and expected life forever, as he said in Psalm 23:6. So against my initial reaction I must believe in the resurrection from the dead."

"Did Jesus rise from the dead? Taking as truth the fact that Christianity spread so rapidly without military force and despite government efforts to suppress it from the beginning, I must sensibly conclude that the answer is yes. No hoax would have succeeded. It would have been so easy for the authorities to produce the body if it had still been in the tomb. And no Jew in the first century would fool around with a stolen corpse that is stinking and rotting away and make himself unclean during the Feast of Unleavened Bread. And who would dare to challenge a military guard to try to get it? So He did rise from the dead. Peter pointed out the empty tomb less than 60 days after the events without challenge. If we are going to make a family against the opposition we face, this must be our common faith."

At this their eyes locked and they quickly squeezed hands and then let go because they did not want to attract attention. Instead they planned their meeting for the next day just to see each other. Asif and Yehudith had a mountain to climb. In Israel there is no legal provision for people born into two different faiths to marry one another. The old Ottoman laws of each religious community controlling marriage among their own communities still hold sway almost a century after the Ottoman Empire lost control of the Holy Land. Evangelical Christianity is not even a recognized community in Israel, so there is no clearly lawful way for two Christians who are not members of recognized liturgical churches such as those in Bethlehem to marry within Israel with the full protection of the law. This raised still another problem: whether to reveal their new faiths to their parents. If so, how and when? They both understood that they faced troubles that are humanly insoluble. For the moment, they kept their meetings inconspicuous. For example, they would pick out a soccer match not so much for the sport but for the crowd which would give them effective concealment from any prying eyes. They continued attending their usual worship services for now even though their hearts were with Jesus instead of in their familiar religious forms.

After Asif and Yehudith went home after meeting one late afternoon, Yehudith and her father saw the nightly news coverage which featured angry Knesset debate. One of the featured subjects was a speech by a Mapam left-wing member advocating a procedure of secular marriage free of control by any religious body. A deputy from United Torah delivered an angry reply defending the current system of religious control of marriage, and a few members nearly came to blows. Jewish marriage is controlled by Orthodox rabbis; Muslim marriage is controlled by the mosque authorities. In each case religious courts deal with divorce within the community.

Smaller traditional minorities have equivalent systems left over from Ottoman times. Judith's father commented, "I certainly would like to see some Conservative rabbis authorized to marry people rather than have the Orthodox rabbinical monopoly we now have, but religious leaders must maintain control of marriage in order to prevent marriages between faiths or between Arabs and Jews, for example. The current system is better than one would be where immature young people choose their own mates without restraint from religious authority."

Yehudith asked, "Who should perform marriages for people who are neither Jew nor Muslim? We have Druzes in the IDF, and there are Arab Christians in places like Bethlehem and Nazareth."

Her father, not suspecting the personal nature of Judith's question, replied, "I suppose that the Druzes and the Arab Christians have priests that have performed marriages from Ottoman times. They can continue. But in no way can we recognize any new converts to Jesus of Nazareth! Our people for centuries have treated such people as dead and have said *kaddish* for them."

Yehudith ventured a bit further. "You always said that George W. Bush had proved to be a good friend of Israel. He professed Christianity as his faith. President Obama clearly has very different beliefs and you mistrust him because his actions do not show friendship. Are you saying that former President Bush is an enemy of Israel because he is a Christian?"

Her father replied, "Christianity may be OK in America, especially if it helps Israel. But it is not for Israel. This land belongs to the Jews, the descendent of Abraham, Isaac and Jacob. Those evangelicals stick their nose into our religion where it does not belong! I don't trust them! It is true that I don't trust Obama either, but the idea that Jesus was the Messiah makes me angry. He didn't keep us from Roman oppression, did he?"

Yehudith did not dare go further because she was not ready to reveal her own faith in Jesus. Neither was she yet familiar enough with the prophecies of Isaiah, Jeremiah, Daniel and Hosea (among others) to challenge her father's idea that Israel was always entitled to freedom and possession of the land as a birthright regardless of how Israel conducted itself toward God, although her understanding of the *diaspora* would start to come soon. For now, she knew that discussion of her new faith and of her desire to marry Asif was out of the question.

Meanwhile Asif and his father saw the nightly *Al Jazeera* broadcast, which presented the Palestinian demand for East Jerusalem as the capital of a Palestinian state. Israel has resisted such a concept since 1967 at least. Asif's father growled, "There is no reason why Jews should be in any part of Jerusalem! This is *Al-Quds*, the place from where the prophet Muhammed rode the horse to heaven! If the Jews have to live in Haifa and Tel Aviv, I might live with that. But they have to stay away from any part of Jerusalem forever! The heights west of Jerusalem which overlook the city must be Palestinian forever! It is true that we are not yet strong enough to achieve this by force, and so I advocate proceeding little by little rather than risk a bloodbath. But the Jews are inferior to us and always will be."

A: When you say that the Jews are inferior, are you referring to intelligence? I remember that some of the best doctors under the Caliphate were Jewish. And today we have to admit their scientific ability. How are the Jews inferior?

F: Son, you remember that we Palestinians -- and all Arabs -- are descended from Ibrahim's [Abraham's] oldest and first-born son Ishmael. That gives us priority of right over the Jews to the land that the Jews now occupy that was promised to Ibrahim's descendents. You remember how the swindler Jacob drove his bargain with Esau to obtain Esau's birthright and then tricked his father into giving him the blessing that should have gone to Esau. Jacob's descendents, the Jews of today, have functioned similarly ever since. It is true that the Edomites are no longer with us. But ancient Edom is desolate -- only Bedouins pass through there. But because we are descended from the eldest son, we have the right to the land through Ibrahim. For some mysterious reason Allah has not yet made us strong enough to drive them out, but that day will come! I hope that you are a part of it! When you have finished your engineering training, put it to good use!

A: Father, as Sunnis we do not follow strictly the bloodline from the prophet Muhammed as the Shia claim to do. If that is the case, how does descent from Ishmael give us an automatic right to the land since the leadership of the Caliphate did not follow the bloodline at all?

F: Allah did not choose to let the leadership of the faith descend by familial descent. But the concept of the children of Ibrahim is totally a concept of ancestry and physical descent. It is that concept that is tied to the land. We had held the land for over 1300 years and need to take it back, even if it requires a strategy of pinpricks instead of one massive uprising. There may be temporary truces, but there can be no lasting reconciliation with the Jews so long as they claim the Holy Land or any substantial part of it. The Land is ours and ours alone! [While Muslims held the land from about 640 AD until 1917 with the exception of the Latin Kingdom from about 1099 to 1187, much of the time the rulers were not Arabs. Saladin, a Muslim leader who reconquered the land in 1187, was a Kurd. For about 4 centuries until 1917, the rulers were Turks, not Arabs. Then came the British until 1948. So the father's history is considerably more shaky than it sounds with respect to Arab --as distinct from Muslim-- governance of the land.]

A: If we had a Palestinian state, what system of government would you favor?

F: I do not think that the people can be trusted to govern themselves. They are both ignorant and naturally inclined to evil. [Often true as far as it goes, but the rulers are every bit as likely to be wicked as the people. But people are not so ignorant of their own economic interests.] The religious teachers have to pick good men to handle the government. I think that the election system of Iraq, for example, is alien to our people. And look how America is falling apart morally. [Disgracefully true.] We as Muslims should believe in government by the intelligent and by those with Koranic righteousness. [This sounds like Iran, although with Sunnis in charge instead of Shias, or even like Plato.]

A: And so how would marriage be handled in a Palestinian state? Would you keep the system we have inherited from the Turks and which the British and Israelis have allowed to continue?

F: The religious leadership must have control over marriage. It is unfortunate that we have any disagreements among ourselves -- ideally, there should be only one religion. As a temporary compromise, our historical *dhimmi* system which provides an extra tax for non-Muslims in exchange for exemption from military service has been a practical solution to the existence of minorities within Muslim states. Of course, their worship places must be smaller than the smallest mosque. The system we have is satisfactory as to marriage. It prevents mixed marriages and keeps people from making foolish choices for themselves.

At this Asif shelved all ideas of discussing Yehudith or any questions about Christianity. His father had already ruled out reconciliation among peoples, which Asif knew to be part of the heart of Christianity. His father was more realistic than many about the terrible consequences of mass violence, but there was not a hint of personal flexibility. As a secret Christian, Asif was already feeling his way towards the ideas of freedom of religion and of reconciliation of all peoples in Jesus Christ. Asif followed his natural guarded approach, said nothing, and began in his mind to formulate a plan of how he might be able to live and marry without either help or restraint from his father. Asif realized that he could not let his thoughts slip or else his father might restrain him or worse.

Asif and Yehudith were able to meet two nights later. They were concerned that someone would search cell phone records and so did not use text messaging often or for sensitive subjects. When they met, each told the other what their respective fathers had said. Both expressed sadness and estrangement from their families, especially their fathers. Both also had been reading the Scriptures regularly and wanted to practice their faith. Each expected trouble when the truth in their hearts came out in the open. Jesus had had secret disciples even among religious authorities. Asif suggested that they needed to marry and seek some sort of economic base that their parents could not cut in retaliation for leaving the faiths of their fathers for the faith of the Father and His Son Jesus Christ. Both were aware that they had no path of marriage within Israel.

Asif brought up one additional subject with Yehudith. He explained briefly his family background and his experience with polygamy in his father's house. Asif made it clear that he wanted no part of polygamy. "In Creation, God made one man and one woman to join with each other. Since then, he has caused approximately an equal number of males and females to be born in keeping with His original design, with a few extra males to compensate for the higher death rate among male children. I have seen the bickering with polygamy and want no part of it! I pledge to be totally yours and expect that you will equally be totally mine." {1 Corinthians 7 confirms this, although Asif had not read this yet. Neither had Asif read the Song of Solomon, Proverbs or Malachi as yet. But his understanding was Biblical through an awakened spirit and observation.}

Yehudith replied, "I had not even thought that you ever meant to keep the door open to multiple marriages. Nevertheless, it is reassuring to hear you say it without being asked. In Abraham's life, the quarrels between Sarah and Hagar grew so severe that Hagar had to leave. {Genesis 21} Esau married three wives and he was a profane, ungodly man -- not like you!" Asif smiled; Yehudith had a knack of soothing his mind in a tense world. Yehudith continued, "Jacob was tricked into marrying two sisters at once, and they intrigued against each other for Jacob's attention. Especially in the sale of Joseph into slavery, the evil effects of their mothers' intrigue shows in the children's jealousy of Joseph and also their deceiving their father about him. Polygamy prepared the way for family disaster for David and even caused Solomon to slip into idolatry. Evil King Ahab had 70 children, so he too must have had many wives. But Malachi speaks of *"the wife of your youth"* as a sole wife. We know that the New Testament also teaches marriages of one man to one woman. Because we have both agreed that our marriage must be based on the faith of Jesus Christ, we can only preserve ourselves exclusively for each other now as virgins and after we are married as faithful mates."

Asif and Yehudith were already aware that Cyprus was the closest place where Israelis marry where the usual permissions of religious authorities could not be obtained. Assuming that the money could be obtained, Asif thought that they should marry each other in Cyprus. If they could return to Israel, such a marriage could be registered and probably would be recognized as valid because it would be valid in Cyprus, where the marriage took place. There still would be major concerns with both families, however. There was also the issue of earning a living -- who would hire anyone married outside of his or her own perceived identity in Israel? Finally, Asif was concerned that either family would try to kill one or both as a dishonor to the family.

The next problem was getting to Cyprus. Yehudith could presumably go on her Israeli passport. Asif would first go to Jordan to get a temporary passport and then go to Cyprus via an Arab country. Palestinians do this routinely when they want to visit other Muslim countries that refuse Israeli passports. This would make it harder to track Asif from Israel if anyone was interested in doing so. Then they would meet, marry and return to Israel if possible or seek asylum or student visas if not. Asif and Yehudith agreed to secure their necessary papers such as birth certificates, but no definite dates were set as yet.

Both Asif and Yehudith had been reading the pocket Scriptures that Dr. Thomas had given them. As Asif read through Genesis, he was puzzled as to why the descendents of Ishmael had lived in Arabia for over 2500 years (roughly 2000 B.C. until about 640 A.D.) before the army of Mohammed had defeated both the Byzantines and the Persians and had secured military control of the Holy Land. The actual facts could not be denied -- Muhammed had himself grown up and lived in Arabia, not in Palestine. Asif realized that the Biblical account could not be reconciled with his father's claim that God had given Palestine to the Arabs. There was no question that Jews were the majority inhabitants from the the time of Joshua (leaving aside the short interval of the Babylonian Captivity when the land was empty) until 70 A.D. when the Romans massacred the inhabitants of the Holy Land and turned it into a virtual waste. Eventually a motley mixture of various peoples partially repopulated the land over the centuries, according to archeological evidence. At this point Asif's mind went beyond the time of Biblical history to a quick sweep of secular history. Asif also noticed the truth of the promise to Ibrahim/Abraham that Ishmael's descendents would become a great nation, although the people would be wild. How truly this matched Arab history! Even today the Arabs are not one nation but many: Iraq, Bahrain, the United Arab Emirates, Dubai, Yemen, Syria, Lebanon, Jordan, Egypt, Libya, Tunisia, Algeria and Morocco. Many Arabs also live in Sudan. Within Palestine the Arabs are divided between Fatah and Hamas.

Asif could not identify a 400-year period when the Arabs were captive {Genesis 15:13}, a mark of the history of the people that would inhabit what Asif knew as Palestine. But this plainly did happen to Israel according to the Scriptures. Islamic teachers acknowledge the greatness of Moses, thus verifying to a certain extent the Biblical account. So Asif could not see a basis in the Bible itself for the claim of his father that Arabs were placed in permanent control of Palestine so as to exclude Jewish residence there forever. Asif wondered why Jews and Arabs could not live side by side in peace? After all, Yehudith and I are attracted together. Why cannot neighbors at least live together without throwing bombs or shooting bullets? He realized that his father was right about the terrible cost of violence. But most of all, real faith in Jesus Christ would transform both Jew and Arab to make peace with one another. {Asif was not yet familiar with New Testament passages such as Ephesians 2, but his meditations were being drawn in that direction.} He began to dream that his coming marriage and family with Yehudith through Jesus Christ would be an example of the reconciliation that Asif thought would benefit Jew and Arab alike. Asif was a realist -- he realized that most Jews and most Arabs are more adamant about rejecting Jesus as Lord than about any other subject and that it would take at least one miracle for his dream to even make a dent in the conflict.

Yehudith in her readings was looking at another aspect of the same issue -- God's dealings with the nation from which she had come. Yehudith looked at Hosea {see also Deuteronomy 28 and 32} and noticed that long ago Israel had been warned that God would evict them from the Holy Land and scatter them, as indeed has occurred three times:

1) The Northern Kingdom was uprooted by Assyria in about 721 B.C. with most of the people dragged northeastward, never to be established again in the land until the present day. Most of these tribes seem to have been hidden for over 2500 years in various parts of Asia;

2) The Southern Kingdom was exiled to Babylon in three waves from 605 B.C. to 586 B.C. A remnant of these exiles were able to return under Zerubbabel about 535 B.C. and Zerubbabel's Temple was completed about 20 years later. More exiles returned with Ezra and Nehemiah, but the majority of the exiles stayed in Persia or moved in areas of Persian and Greek culture. Most of those who returned would have

been from Judah, Levi, Benjamin and possibly Simeon, with a few from other tribes.

3) The descendents of those who returned to the Holy Land were scattered again in the aftermath of the terrible Jewish War (as the Romans called it) between 66-70 A.D., which Jesus Christ prophesied in Matthew 24, Mark 13 and Luke 21. Another uprising under Bar Kochba was crushed in about 135 A.D. While there was some Jewish population in the Holy Land after 70 A.D., there was no national Jewish government again until 1948.

As a whole, Israel had been unfaithful, had ignored God's warnings and indeed suffered terrible consequences. Both Moses and Hosea had warned specifically about exile. So had Isaiah and Jeremiah. Hosea 3 had summarized Jewish history precisely. Worst of all, Yehudith realized that Israel as a whole had rejected God's government completely when its leadership during the trial of Jesus pledged to Pilate that *"We have no King but Caesar."* {John 19:12-15} This denied not Jesus only but the entire history of covenants that God had made with Abraham, Moses and David. Since this was so badly wrong, Yehudith realized that Jesus truly was King of Israel as Pilate had said. She noticed the genealogies in Matthew 1 and Luke 3 and also David's Psalms mentioning the King, such as Psalms 2, 24, 45, 89 and 110. She now realized that all of these referred to Jesus the Messiah and that the Sanhedrin had rejected both Father and Son. The parable of the vineyard in Matthew 21:33-46 brought this understanding into focus. No wonder that God had given her ancestors over to their own devices!

So just as God was working in Asif's heart and mind to undermine Arab claims of supremacy, God was working in Judith's heart and mind to undermine Jewish claims of supremacy. Even though God is beginning to give the Promised Land back to his original Covenant People, they still have no living, vibrant relationship with God because they reject His Word concerning His Son that He sent to earth. She perceived the truth of what Jesus said, *"He who does not honor the Son does not honor the Father Who sent Him."* {John 5:23} This applies to all peoples of the earth, including her own.

Asif wrestled with practical issues as well as with his new understanding of God and of the Bible. If he were to break from his father, he would have to support himself through God's provision, and Yehudith as well. Asif was considerably more than half-way through his engineering studies. Both spoke and wrote English fluently as well as Arabic and Hebrew. Asif prayed before God and perceived the most likely prospects for work were either translation or use of his engineering and computer skills. Yehudith might be a good teacher -- her warm personality was good with children. But barriers would be high in Israel for them both as soon as they married one another, and reinforced further as soon as they declared their faith. Asif began researching areas over the Internet other than Israel where there were both Arab and Jewish populations in proximity to each other, such as Detroit, Michigan; Toronto, Canada and the San Diego area of California and Tijuana, Mexico where there are Chaldean refugees who speak Arabic. Asif could read plenty of shocking material about America, but he could tell from free Internet material that America is still more friendly to Christianity than the European Union or most of its components. Asif could not imagine being comfortable in any Muslim-governed nation, especially with a racially Jewish wife. Living in either the West Bank or in Gaza was out of the question. As to other nations, Canada, Sweden or Iceland seemed at least thinkable because they have reputations of more generous immigration policies than most. India, Hong Kong or Singapore might at least offer some employment prospects in international trade using language skills. He also looked for high concentrations of "tech" jobs and for ways to complete his engineering and technical education while earning some form of living. Asif did not know anything yet of the missionary world in remote areas where his engineering skill would be at a premium and where Yehudith could have tremendous influence with medical training, especially in pediatrics. Asif also wanted to learn the Scriptures better, but he focused on practical issues of earning a living for himself and his intended wife.

In the meantime, Yehudith was distressed at the possibility leaving Israel, the land promised to her ancestors. But even at this stage she saw heaven as the ultimate Promised Land, so she was comforted in that what she had gained through her faith in the Messiah Jesus was infinitely greater than what she might lose in becoming a refugee from Israel. It is true that Israel is freer than most Islamic regimes, but that does not mean that Christian/Messianic children of Abraham have full equality or freedom in Israel and still less in Palestinian areas. Like the men of faith in Hebrews 11, she sought most of all an enduring city whose Builder and Maker is God. Compared to this, living in Israel was secondary even though the thought of leaving Israel gave her pain. Since God was joining her to Asif, she was under a duty to follow him as He follows the Messiah. As a Messianic Jew, she faced ostracism from her own family. Further, she had no desire to deliberately court either widowhood or even martyrdom in Israel because of probable attempts on Asif's life by some member of his family who would try to kill a convert from Islam. So both were seeking God's way through the dilemma that for the moment there was no tolerable place within the Holy Land for them as a married couple and yet they had as yet no secure place to go. Then again, her ancestress Sarah followed Abraham even though neither of them understood at first where God was taking them.

Neither Asif nor Yehudith saw an apparent solution as they shared their thoughts, so Asif took Yehudith and asked Dr. Thomas for any advice and contacts he may have. Dr. Thomas recognized the two. When Asif told him that they wanted to marry and then wanted advice as to where they might live in peace, Dr. Thomas quoted the Scripture of John 16:33, *"In the world you will have tribulation; but be of good cheer, I have overcome the world.* Since I myself do not have an immediate solution, let us pray together to the Father Who does have one." And so they did. Then Dr. Thomas asked them what funds they had. When they had responded, Dr. Thomas pleaded with God to multiply their funds as His Son had multiplied the loaves and the fish. Both were moved by the old man's simple and vigorous faith. Dr. Thomas knew all too well how Asif and Yehudith were defying all the conventions they knew.

Then Dr. Thomas remembered the wedding ring that his wife had left behind when she died in the hospital the year before. As part of hospital procedure, the ring was removed. Dr. Thomas retained it out of forgetfulness when his wife's body was buried. "You two have much better use for this ring than I do. Take it. If it fits, use it. Otherwise, sell it. Here also is some gold and silver jewelry that she left behind. Arab women use jewelry as a walking savings account against the time of need. Take this and use it as necessary." Dr. Thomas also gave them a list of missionary contacts and signed letters of introduction:

> *These two young people came to second birth when I spoke on reconciliation at the college. They are very young but their faith and courage are strong. Theirs is a marriage that only God can make. Guide them on their way as they walk before our God in faith.*

Both Asif and Yehudith were amazed. Yehudith especially was amazed at the quality of the jewelry and realized that this was the start of God's answers to prayer. The ring fit her perfectly. Both thanked Dr. Thomas profusely. Asif kept the letters among his textbooks. When Yehudith arrived home, she concealed the jewelry to avoid awkward questions from her parents.

With their academic year complete, Asif and Yehudith had more time to see each other, but both felt that their ability to avoid some confrontation with their families was rapidly running out. Asif therefore totaled both his and Judith's resources and proposed that they elope to Cyprus and marry while the way is still open. He had found advertisements for commercial translation work in Mumbai from English to both Arabic and Hebrew for trading companies seeking to sell industrial products in both Arab countries and Israel. Some of the potential trade partners were Chinese or Taiwanese and others were Indian. Possible examples would be Lenovo, Acer, the Tata group and Mahindra. In any case, their language skills would be in demand and at least they could earn their way. Mumbai was also free enough that they could practice their faith openly. So Asif, consulting Yehudith, hammered out a plan to make it difficult for any potential assassins to find them:

1) Leave Israel separately and meet in Nicosia, Cyprus. Asif would start through Jordan to get a Jordanian passport, while Yehudith would go directly to Cyprus;

2) Marry in Cyprus;

3) Notify parents and family from Cyprus;

4) Fly to an American or Canadian city on or near the east coast;

5) Take trains to the Pacific Coast in order to leave a gap for anyone trying to search airline records to track them; and

6) Fly from the West Coast to Mumbai.

This plan also left open the option of trying to remain in the United States or Canada if better opportunities were there. The one major issue was picking a time to head for Cyprus.

Given the heightening tensions within the Palestinian community in the summer and the possibility that Jordan would close the Allenby Bridge and other crossing points, Asif told Yehudith that they had to act now.

Both sets of parents were suspicious of something without knowing what. So both of them gathered their papers before school started on August 15, 2011 and headed their separate ways. Asif made it across the Jordanian border and was able to get a Jordanian passport to permit him to enter other Arab countries. Yehudith caught a flight to Cyprus and waited at a pre-arranged motel in Nicosia. Asif was able to go through Dubai and arrive in Nicosia the next day. Using an English-language website and phone book, they were able to locate a pastor with the legal authority to marry them and get their license. As with marriages among Christians in the early days of the Roman Empire, they married with a minimum of ceremony and a honeymoon with only the bare essentials. Because they did not want anyone in either family to know their whereabouts in the event of a hostile reaction (which Asif anticipated), they found an Internet cafe from which they could notify their families of their new status and new lives. True, the messages might be traced to Cyprus, but they would not be in Cyprus long enough for that to be of any use to anyone chasing them. Asif warned Yehudith not to tell her parents that she was married to an Arab because he did not want to give either family a clue as to the identity of the mate. It would be far easier to track them if a detective or even a hit man had a clue as to the identity of the spouse.

Yehudith took care to have the Israeli consulate reissue her passport in her married name as it showed on her marriage certificate.

The following morning after their marriage night Asif sent a message to his father:

I know that you and I have had growing disagreements for some time. I make no claim to perfection, but I know that part of the strain between us comes from the fact that you have another wife besides my mother. I love you both, but I believe that anyone who has more than one wife or one husband is fundamentally violating the law of nature. God made approximately equal numbers of men and women so that most could pair up. In the original Creation there was one man and one woman. The original marriage was one man to one woman. True, under desert conditions God may have tolerated polygamy in ancient times, just as He permitted Ibrahim to marry his sister Sarah, but neither of these was ever the ideal. We should not practice polygamy today -- you know too well how many quarrels it produces and has produced from ancient times.

We have a disagreement of deeper roots. I have respected your stand against mass violence. In that you are right. But there has been no peace since the foundation of Islam, but war. There is one Man Who is the Prince of Peace, Whom God sent from heaven. His name is Jesus Christ. He is the ultimate Prophet, Priest and King, and also the ultimate Teacher. I am not even a novice yet in His school, but His teaching is the key to everlasting life. He is the complete combination of God and human in one package. The Father in heaven demands that all of us worship His Son Jesus as the combination Son of God and Son of Man. I am obeying that heavenly demand. I worship the Father, the Son and the Holy Spirit as a combination three-in-one unified God. I find joy which I cannot express in this worship. I wish you would too.

You need not concern yourself about trying to arrange a marriage for me. God has already done that. I am a married man and will not marry again as long as my wife lives and remains married to me. Don't worry -- she is a fine and extraordinary woman. I hope and pray that you can meet her some day, but common sense warns me that now is probably not the time.

I do pray for you and mother's health and especially that you both will come some day to know the living God and His Son Jesus Christ. Your son, Asif

Asif's father gave a terse response. He recognized his son's language and had no doubt that the message was genuine. "You are no longer my son. You have dishonored the family and betrayed the faith. I cannot say what other measures may be necessary." Asif understood this to imply that his father would seek a *fatwa* for his murder. At least his father loved him enough to give him a veiled warning rather than to deceive his son about his attitude and lure Asif to his death by deceit. Asif was not surprised and did not reply because he wanted to give his father no further clue as to his whereabouts in the event that someone would be sent to look for him.

Yehudith received an essentially similar reception, although without any hint of possible violence. She also sent her parents a long e-mail witnessing to her faith:

My dear parents, I love you with all my heart, but I cannot find peace in your home. I am getting to an age where I should be on my own, but this runs deeper. There is someone missing in the faith of our ancestors, and now I know what it is. The missing piece is the Messiah that was due about 2000 years ago according to the prophet Daniel. Our forbears failed to recognize Him and in fact our Sanhedrin majority had the Romans crucify Him. That was a terrible injustice, but it was for our good -- the Messiah Jesus was the Passover Lamb for all time to absorb the just wrath of God that is due each of us for our transgressions. You taught me well about the wanderings of our nation. This was predicted by Hosea especially. Our forbears wandered because they were unfaithful to God after Solomon and again in the time of Ananias and Caiaphas the High Priests. The Messiah warned that the generation who heard Him would have to account for the blood of the righteous from A to Z -- from Abel to Zechariah. And so it happened through Vespasian and Titus, as Josephus has written. And it happened again and again in foreign lands, climaxing with the Nazis. All those foreign oppressors were dreadfully wrong and will have to account to God for there actions, but we have to face the prophetic fact (Moses in

Deuteronomy 8 and 32, for example, and also the statements in 2 Kings and 2 Chronicles about the reasons for the first exiles of both Kingdoms) that these awful things came because we have persisted in denying the Messiah, the Son of God. We have also defiled ourselves in deliberate violations of the Law. Consider the sexual crimes and bribes, high and low, that we read daily in the Jerusalem Post. None of that makes the persecutors even remotely right. Obadiah should be a warning to every persecutor of Israel of every age. Joel 3 prophesies destruction to the enemies of Israel. Haman is still another example. Hamas and Hezbollah will be destroyed by God Almighty through the Messiah. We are in the beginning of Isaiah 11:11, where it is prophesied that the blessing will come after God has regathered our nation the second time. The first time was the fragment that returned with Zerubbabel; the second time began with the First Aliyah and is continuing today. Isaiah makes it clear that we will not be fully dispossessed again. But we have to repent on our part for calling God a liar concerning His Messiah Whom He sent to the earth for us, and Whom we reject to this day.

The Messiah once said to two of His followers, *O slow of heart to believe all that the prophets have spoken!* I can't identify all of the prophecies concerning the Messiah, but I will try to list quickly for you some of the main ones: Psalms 2, 22-24, 45, 69 and 110 and many other references; Isaiah 2,6,7,9,11,40, 42, 53, and 61 among others; Zechariah 9-14; and Micah 5 are just a start. There are even references in Genesis 1-3. But now that I can see the outlines of the prophecies that point to the coming Messiah as Jesus of Nazareth, I cannot go back.

This is more than an intellectual issue. We need individual transformation from the inside out, as shown in the New Covenant prophesied in Jeremiah 30-33 and Ezekiel 36. Jesus the Messiah has done this in me and in countless others of every background imaginable. We need that once-for-all sacrifice for the blessedness of David in Psalm 32 which

He finished for all time. The last prophecies of both Isaiah and Zechariah point to ultimate blessing of Israel, but why wait for that tumultuous time? This wonderful peace and everlasting forgiveness is available now to any who will ask the Messiah Jesus to reveal Himself and change them. O please, worship Him now as the Father has commanded!

You should also know that I am married to a wonderful young man who has the same essential faith that God has given to me. I want to introduce him to you some day, but I can't right now. But don't worry about me. He now bears the responsibility and through God he should be able to meet it. I do not know when I shall see you again, but I do love you and especially love your souls. Your loving daughter, Yehudith

Judith's father was thrown into turmoil and from his own bitter anguish wrote that:

"We have scheduled your funeral and will say the prayers as for the dead. You are now dead to us and no longer part of our family." Yehudith was able to send a quick e-mail just before they left for the airport. "You are right that the old Yehudith is dead. A new and better Yehudith has been born. I am indeed "dead to sin and alive to God through the Messiah Jesus my Lord." Love, Yehudith

Both Asif and Yehudith were careful not to give any clue as to the identity, appearance or background of their spouse. An Arab man and Jewish woman traveling together would be an important clue for anyone trying to follow them -- a clue that Asif especially did not want to leave. So far as he was concerned, he either had a price on his head or was about to have one placed because he now professed Christianity. It was important that his father not know that his wife is a Jewess, which would compound the incentive to find and kill him and also make him easier to track.

With the marriage complete and both sets of parents notified, it was time for Asif and Yehudith to leave Cyprus. Asif then had a new idea, a variation of his previous concept of going across the United States on land to avoid leaving a paper trail. He and Yehudith flew to Sofia, Bulgaria in order to get Europasses and use the European rail system to travel north and west in a combination of inexpensive honeymoon and escape from any pursuit that either family might raise in an effort to undo their marriage, or worse. In fact nothing was then afoot, but Asif was taking no chances. Asif did not expect any European country to present economic opportunities, but he decided to go all the way to London on the rail system, perhaps using a ferry from Belgium to save some money instead of using the tunnel under the English Channel. Since both he and Yehudith spoke English, he thought that they would be better off in England or conceivably Ireland than anywhere else in the European Union while they figured out the details of their crossing to North America or conceivably a direct flight to Mumbai from London, saving thousands of miles. On the way, they could see famous European cities such as Vienna and Paris along the rail routes and stay in relatively inexpensive hostels or hotels. In the meantime Asif and Yehudith maintained their Internet search for job opportunities in places they considered reasonably safe. So far as they could tell, the international trade sector in Mumbai seemed best.

The pain of exile and loss of family ties was pushed to the background by their honeymoon with each other and their new love for their Savior Jesus the Messiah. Nevertheless, both Asif and Yehudith knew that they were isolated from the Holy Land and from their families. They would have to settle in an alien land and earn their bread. They briefly thought of children and their nationality, but this too was a concern down the road rather than an immediate issue. They had no settled place of worship. For the moment Asif and Yehudith were happy in their newfound love for each other and for the Lord Jesus despite their exile from home and family.

When Asif and Yehudith reached London, they decided to review sites connected with the Christian faith. They visited St. Paul's Cathedral, the Tower of London when Anne Askew was executed and the place where Oswald Chambers ministered before he went to Egypt for his final ministry. Oswald Chambers' writings would prove to be a great encouragement, but their visit to the successors of the congregation where Spurgeon once preached in Southwark proved to be most important. After the service they were welcomed by Geoffrey, one of the elders who took the time to find out what was so unusual about this couple. This man was "addicted to hospitality" and invited the strangers to his own home to eat and talk. In the providence of God, he and his wife had a wide knowledge of international affairs and history, so they were able to grasp immediately the dangers that Asif and Yehudith thought they were fleeing. Asif and Yehudith trusted Geoffrey and told them of their background, conversions, marriage and their parents' responses to their witness.

Geoffrey agreed with their desire to work, but he wanted them grounded in the faith even more than employed immediately. There had been so much change in their lives so quickly that both Geoffrey and his wife thought that Asif and Yehudith needed a breathing space before they tackled a new home and new jobs. Geoffrey and his wife had them stay for a few days and also some modest financial help. Asif and Yehudith still had a considerable portion of their savings; Judith had not sold any of the jewelry yet. The pressure to find a job was not immediate. Geoffrey and his wife therefore made several recommendations for the next month or so:

1) That they both see one of the sites of the persecution of the Jewish people such as Dachau, Sachsenhausen, Mauthausen, Ravensbruck or Auschwitz to fix in their minds that the *shoah* was a real series of events and not just a falsehood to justify the creation of Israel;

2) That they, if possible, at least contact L'Abri in Switzerland to get additional materials for a basic grasp of the intellectual basis of the Christian faith. A short stay would be even better for basic discipleship and a brief rest;

3) That they try to contact a solid Christian church in advance of their settling down and working so that they would have a place to grow as a family and receive regular instruction.

In the meantime Geoffrey would try to find suitable fellowship in Mumbai if indeed that is where God is calling them to go. For the moment, Geoffrey did find for them reprints of Spurgeon's sermons and devotionals to help Asif and Yehudith with their Bible studies both separate and together.

Asif and Yehudith decided to go to Germany first before contacting L'Abri, on the principle of doing the hardest thing first. Asif especially found the exhibits upsetting to the point where he wanted to weep but thought it unmanly to do so. He was certainly aware of Palestinian living conditions and the economic disruption caused by periodic flare-ups of the conflicts among the West Bank Palestinians, the Hamas leaders based in the Gaza Strip and the Israeli government. But his Palestinian-based schooling had omitted all mention of the slaughter of the Jews under the Nazis and omitted further the connection between those slaughters and the recognition of Israel as a nation in 1948. Asif's father was not bloodthirsty like the Mufti of Jerusalem who supported Hitler, but even so Asif had been raised on a steady diet of hatred toward Jews racially as well as toward Christians. Al-Jaazera is not the most objective of networks. So Asif was in intellectual and emotional shock as he saw the exhibits.

Yehudith had a better idea of what to expect. She appreciated the hardships that her forbears had escaped to live in Israel again by seeing the exhibits at the German concentration camps. She understood why the IDF vows that "Masada shall not fall again!" Yet Yehudith also reflected that Christians have a limited place in Israeli national life, especially if they are Jews by descent. The fact that she and Asif were not free to marry in Israel was a personal illustration. Christians indeed have much more freedom in Israel than in most Arab states such as Saudi Arabia, but Christians in Israel do not have the same freedoms as Yehudith had read of on the Internet concerning the United States. For example, there are no prominent counterparts in Israel to openly Christian political figures such as Mike Huckabee or Sarah Palin.

Yedudith thought long and hard about the story of Corrie ten Boom as she saw the camp exhibits. She had learned something of forgiveness in marry Asif, but Yehudith had not suffered personally at the hands of Arabs. Yet Corrie ten Boom forgave Germans and taught reconciliation between former foes. She was tested sorely when a person Corrie recognized as a former prison guard at Ravensbruck came to seek reconciliation with her. Ravensbruck was where Corrie's beloved sister was mistreated and had died. At other locations Corrie had lost her father and other male members of her family. Corrie struggled but did forgive the guard. Yehudith inwardly shuddered at the thought of having to forgive someone like that under the circumstances, but did reflect that her Lord Jesus did pray to His Father to forgive the soldiers that nailed Him to the Cross. God had answered that prayer specifically -- the execution squad gave testimony that *"Truly this Man was the Son of God."* Matthew 27:54, Mark 15:39. So Yehudith made progress down the road of forgiveness -- for her family, for other unbelievers and for Arabs.

After a few days of seeing these grim sights, Asif and Yehudith were ready to go to L'Abri for a brief rest. As they talked, Asif told Yehudith that he believed that God had a special mission for them as a married couple as a paired witness to the power of Jesus Christ to reconcile sinful people to Himself and to reconcile apparently irreconcilable people to each other. Here are the verses that planted this concept in his heart:

> *Now all things are of God, who has reconciled us to Himself through Jesus Christ, and has given us the ministry of reconciliation; that is, that God was in Christ reconciling the world to Himself, not imputing their trespasses to them, and has committed to us the word of reconciliation. Now then, we are ambassadors for Christ, as though*

God were pleading through us: we implore you on Christ's behalf,
be reconciled to God. For He made Him who knew no sin to be sin
for us, that we might become the righteousness of God in Him. 2
Corinthians 5:18-21.

Asif perceived a unique opportunity for an Arab-Jewish couple to exemplify publicly this reconciliation. He also warned Yehudith that in time that they would have to stop hiding and enter a phase of public ministry. However, Asif did visualize that they would have to use some Internet security precautions in order to conceal their exact location because he expected a hit squad to be sent after him. Like Paul in Damascus, Asif was taking precautions not to present an easy target. In fact Asif's suspicions were somewhat premature but well-founded. The L'Abri counselors prayed with Asif and Yehudith and sent them with further materials both on Christianity and on belief systems in the Middle East.

As planned, Asif and Yehudith returned to Geoffrey's home in London by train. Geoffrey did find contacts in Mumbai, and now Asif and Yehudith faced a decision to either proceed to America first or to go directly from London to Mumbai, because Asif was confident that he would find employment there with less complication than obtaining an American immigrant visa. Going for a short period as a tourist would be easy enough, but obtaining a proper visa for employment in the United States would be another matter. As to Canada, they did not have enough assets to enter as landed immigrants and Asif did not view employment prospects as favorably as he did in Mumbai. So they all prayed and decided that Asif and Yehudith would travel directly from London to Mumbai non-stop to create no unnecessary visa records. Geoffrey provided one-way tickets for each on separate flights.

While Asif and Yehudith were having their unusual honeymoon, both of their families were trying independently to figure out the location of each missing child. Asif's father was angry and talked to fellow imams about the possibility of a *fatwa* commanding Asif's killing or at least his abduction to face his father and answer questions. Asif's mother bore her grief stoicly. The imams were hesitant for several reasons. First, some were less than sure that the e-mail from Cyprus was in fact genuine and was sent by Asif. Although Asif seemed to have vanished, there was no other evidence that he had even gone to Cyprus, nor any motive for Asif to have gone there. Nobody even dreamed that Asif might want to marry an Israeli. Had Asif been snatched by some rival group or intelligence service which had sent the e-mail in Asif's name as part of a deception plan? Or might the e-mail be spurious or even have been misdelivered by an Internet Service Provider? Asif's father was convinced that Asif had in fact sent the e-mail, but the imams thought it premature to issue an assassination decree on the grounds of either departure from the Islamic faith or of dishonoring the family. They did ask the Palestinian authorities to see if Asif was located in Palestinian-administered territory and whether Asif had in fact used his passport, but this research took time and responses were slow. In the meantime Asif's father continued with his religious duties at the mosque, stewed and grieved. Even after a few weeks when it appeared that Asif was not in PLO-administered territory, there remained the possibility that Asif had sneaked into the Gaza Strip. Hamas would not cooperate with the PLO. When at length it appeared that Asif had exchanged his passport for a temporary Jordanian passport, that opened up possibilities of travel to other Arab countries but of itself provided no other clue as to where Asif actually was. By this time, Asif and Yehudith were actually in Mumbai and Asif and Yehudith were translating documents for pay into Arabic and Hebrew. Asif was also writing some computer code, so Asif and Yehudith were earning a modest living.

Yehudith's family was appalled at her absence and then at her e-mail from Cyprus. They were shocked that she would leave Israel even temporarily without talking about it with them first. The location of Cyprus was a hint that Yehudith had left to marry someone whom she could not marry in Israel, as the e-mail said. But it did not dawn on them that she might marry an Arab, especially one of Muslim background. Certainly her profession of belief in Jesus as Messiah was no hint that she had an Arab husband. When she did not return home, her family assumed that she had come back to Israel but did not disclose her location. It was terribly painful that she was absent, but the family viewed Yehudith as a rebel who had abandoned the family and its faith as well as excluding her family from her apparent marriage. They chose to wait and hope that the nightmare would somehow end. Asking the government to help trace Yehudith would simply publicize the tragedy, which they all wished to avoid. So the family had its funeral for Yehudith, grieved privately and let matters go at that.

So the total upshot was that Asif and Yehudith were able to enter Mumbai undetected and earn enough to live modestly and quietly in Mumbai. They did find an English-speaking place of worship but were very careful about giving details as to their personal lives. This did limit their fellowship to a considerable extent. Innocent questions such as "Where are you from?" or "How did you meet as a couple?" had hidden risks for them that could not be explained readily. Asif and Yehudith did study the Bible and participate in worship of Jesus Christ with the fellowship but gave little information about their background. They did keep Geoffrey informed in a general way that they were growing in the faith and staying afloat economically. They also shared what they were learning as they studied the Scriptures and prayed.

After several months Asif and Yehudith decided that the time had arrived for them to witness in public as a Christian couple. They did take precautions that their Internet postings would not allow them to be readily traced to Mumbai. So they together hammered out and composed and released *A MANIFESTO ON RECONCILIATION.*

God has reconciled each of us individually to Himself even though *our iniquities have separated us from our God.* Isaiah 59:2. This is humanly impossible, but through the sacrifice of the Messiah Jesus of Nazareth God has accomplished the seemingly impossible. Matthew 19:26, Mark 10:27. As an illustration of the reconciliation of sinful humanity with the awesome, holy God, God has united the two of us, one Arab male and one Jewish female by human descent, into one joyful marriage. In the days of the early Christian church God created of Jew and Gentile one body, His Church and Bride. *There is one body and one Spirit, just as you were called in one hope of your calling; one Lord, one faith, one baptism; one God and Father of all, who is above all, and through all, and in you all.* Ephesians 4:4-6. *There is neither Jew nor Greek, there is neither slave nor free, there is neither male nor female; for you are all one in Christ Jesus. And if you are Christ's, then you are Abraham's seed, and heirs according to the promise.* Galatians 3:28-29.

So the fact that we both are descended from Abraham is theologically incidental. If we are to be Abraham's true and spiritual sons and daughters, we must believe in the Messiah -- Jesus of Nazareth -- Whom God promised to Abraham. We become true sons and daughters of Abraham by faith, not by human descent. All of Romans 4 and of Galatians 3 are devoted to this central pillar of truth. *Abraham believed God, and it was accounted to him for righteousness.* Genesis 15:6. Abraham was not delivered by his works but through his faith in the Almighty God. *But we are all like an unclean thing, and all our righteousnesses are like filthy rags. We all fade as a leaf, and our iniquities, like the wind, have taken us away.* Isaiah 64:6.

Why do Abraham's children quarrel over the Holy Land? The fundamental cause is that neither group of Abraham's children will worship and obey Jesus the Messiah. The tension between Hagar and Sarah and between Ishmael and Isaac has persisted through the millenia because only a few of their descendents are reconciled to God through His Son Jesus the Messiah.

It is clear that the Holy Land belongs to God and that He has the right to give it to whom He chooses. The Bible teaches that this particular land was in the end promised to those descended from Abraham, Isaac and Jacob. That nation, now called Israel after Jacob's spiritual name, at least twice has forfeited its right to possession of the Land by aggravated sin. The first time came during the times of the prophets and was accomplished by Assyria and Babylon. The second time came when Israel rejected Jesus the Messiah and His Father as King over Israel and chose the Roman Caesar instead. John 19:12-15. The process of Israel's return from its second and final exile (Isaiah 11:11) has begun. However, God did instruct Israel that the foreigner living within Israel should have the same legal privileges as the native-born citizen (at least if the foreigner will live peaceably). Exodus 12:49, Numbers 15:15-16.

Abraham's prayer for Ishmael was also heard. God promised to make a great nation from Ishmael and He has done so. The Arab peoples dwell from Morocco to Iraq. They have taken the former dwellings of Ham in Egypt and of the other children of Abraham to the southeast of the Holy Land. The lands that once belonged to Edom and to the children of Lot now belong to Arabs. While God did not grant Ishmael primary control over the Holy Land, God has granted the people of Ishmael much space and many resources, especially oil.

But it is so easy to receive earthly blessing from God and be ungrateful. One can make *aliyah* to the Holy Land and yet completely miss the most essential *aliyah* of all -- from earth to heaven. There have been many who have had the blessing of living in the Holy Land and yet have died under eternal condemnation, facing everlasting judgment from the Almighty.

The earthly Jerusalem, as beautiful as it is, is only a symbol and a shadow of the heavenly Jerusalem that will be home to people of every description who are saved through faith in Jesus the Messiah. The most important pilgrimage is not to Mecca, nor to Jerusalem or to any other human site, but is to heaven which is home to the Messiah Jesus and to His Father. This is a pilgrimage of the heart and mind and only a pilgrimage of the body when it has been transformed into a glorious body like the one that Jesus the Messiah has now.

Each human being (Jesus the Messiah excepted) has a particular pattern of sins that he or she relishes, and other to which that person would succumb under temptation. Some people may be prone to lie, cheat and steal; others may be wasteful. Some may seek sexual pleasure outside of marriage; others may be hateful and angry. Some may be callous and uncaring; others may be quick-tempered and thoughtless. The precise patterns are individual, like fingerprints. Some of these sins consist of doing things that we are commanded not to do, such as direct violations of the Ten Commandments. Others consist of failing to do things that we are commanded to do, such as showing sacrificial love for others. Jesus summarized the Law into two Commandments of love: (1) Love the Lord your God with all your heart, soul, mind and strength (Matthew 22:37-39; Mark 12:29-31); and (2) Love your neighbor as yourself. So an understanding of love is essential to understanding the Torah and of any portion of the Hebrew Scriptures. Love is an essential ingredient in God's character, which is why He willingly seeks intimate fellowship with human beings such as Abraham even though they are sinful. At the same time, that fellowship has a purifying component that begins to purge away our human sinfulness and which will eventually climax in the complete elimination of human sin in the believer. (Hebrews 8:10-13; 9:14-15; 10:14)

We stress Jesus the Messiah because of the abundant testimony that the God of Heaven has given of His Son. Three times God spoke from heaven in approval of His Son -- once at His baptism, the second time at His Transfiguration and the third time less than a week before His death. Matthew 3:17; Luke 9:35, John 12:27-28. Jesus raised Lazarus from the dead in the sight of most of the people of Bethany, about 3 miles from Jerusalem. In modern terms, it would be as if He walked the earth and raised a resident of Bethlehem from the dead in the sight of the whole town!

Jesus the Messiah demonstrated His power from heaven in so many ways. He fed 5000 men plus their families (Matthew 14:21) and then 4000 men and their families (Matthew 15:38) with almost no food to start. He turned water into wine instantly. (John 2:1-11) The two elements of bread and wine became the Communion elements, and were the same that Melchizedek gave Abram in Genesis 14. Jesus of Nazareth healed uncounted people in public, where there was no denying the miracle. Two of his closest disciples, Peter and John, healed someone who have never walked, and not even their enemies denied the facts. Acts 3-4. Peter and John made it clear that it was in Jesus' name that they were able to heal and not by their own power. Jesus fulfilled prophecies concerning the place of His birth (Micah 5:2), concerning His emergence from Egypt (Hosea 11:1), concerning His preaching of freedom to those spiritually in prison (Isaiah 42:7, 61:1), concerning the manner of His death (Psalm 22), concerning the enmity of the people at the time of His death (Isaiah 53:4, Psalm 22:16-17) concerning the wealth of the owner of the tomb where He was buried (Isaiah 53:9) and concerning His rising from the dead (Psalm 16). He came and ministered at the time pinpointed by Daniel (9:24-27).

Jesus Himself proclaimed that He is God and equal with His Father. He claimed to be the Bread (or Manna) that came from heaven -- not from earth even though He was indeed born to a Virgin on earth. John 6:32-41, 7:28-29, 8:22-23. He claimed to have lived before Abraham and to take precedence over Abraham. John 8:52-59. Jesus claimed to be the Door (or Gate -- John 10:9) and the Good Shepherd Who was prepared to lay down His life for the sheep (John 10:10-18) and in fact did so shortly after He spoke those words. He also claimed to have power to take up His own life after His death (John 10:18) and in fact proved His claim on Resurrection Morning. If either one of us or anyone else were to make such a claim, we would be rightly disbelieved as deluded and insane. Since Jesus Christ, we cannot point to a single person who has both risen from the dead and appeared on earth in an immortal body, although both Peter and Paul through the power of the risen Jesus the Messiah did each raise a person back to a pre-existing mortal body (Acts 9:40-41, 20:9-12). Only Moses and Elijah made a fleeting joint appearance at the Transfiguration of Jesus (Matthew 17) before His death. By comparison, Jesus made multiple appearances in His resurrection body (Luke 24, 1 Corinthians 15:3-8).

In the face of this evidence and of many other fulfilled prophecies that we have not mentioned, we treat God as a liar when He proclaims Jesus as both Lord and Messiah. Acts 2:36. Instead of seeking God's mercy on our unbelief, we obfuscate, prevaricate and blaspheme. In simpler language we try to justify our unbelief by covering up the evidence, lying and blaspheming the name of Jesus Christ. People today are tried, convicted and executed for blaspheming the name of Muhammed, which is a legal and logical impossibility. Like other human beings, Muhammed was a man created by God but was not himself a god. By his own account he endorsed the kissing of the Black Stone. We also know from his own words that he married a 6-year-old girl and consummated the marriage when she was 9 years old. Blasphemy must be directed against God -- it is impossible to blaspheme any sinful man or woman, because the best of us fall so short of God's glory as to intrinsically deserve everlasting punishment.

Even John the Baptist as a prophet knew that He was not even worthy to untie Jesus' shoe. (John 1:27) Isaiah knew that he was not worthy to see heaven. Isaiah 6:1-8. One can try to curse or slander a man or a woman, but one can blaspheme only God the Father, or Jesus the Messiah or the Holy Spirit.

It is the Heavenly Father Himself Who demands that we worship His Son as well as Himself. His Son echoed His Father's command:

> *For the Father judges no one, but has committed all judgment to the Son, that all should honor the Son just as they honor the Father. He who does not honor the Son does not honor the Father who sent Him. Most assuredly, I say to you, he who hears My word and believes in Him who sent Me has everlasting life, and shall not come into judgment, but has passed from death into life. John 5:22-24*

To believe in the Father, one must believe what He has said about His Son. We are not permitted to claim that we believe in the Father and at the same time accuse Him of falsehood concerning His Son. The Father Himself will not judge -- it is His Son Who will judge at the Last Judgment. So if we persist in accusing His Son Jesus of Nazareth of falsehood concerns His claims of equality with His Father, we can expect no mercy from either. However, He has promised mercy to whomever will call upon His Name for salvation. *Whoever shall call upon the name of the Lord shall be saved.* Acts 2:21. *Jesus said to her [Martha], "I am the resurrection and the life. He who believes in Me, though he may die, he shall live. And whoever lives and believes in Me shall never die.* John 11:25-26. So we must believe what the Father says about His Son Jesus the Messiah and we must also believe what Jesus said about Himself. Although we were both taught against it, the Holy Spirit has brought us to the point where we do believe and must build our life and our eternities on this foundation.

Asif and Yehudith set up a website in English, Arabic, Hebrew and Spanish (with the help of sympathetic Latin-American translators) and circulated this manifesto among their former friends through cyberspace. They did their best to attract attention to the whole world and from their savings paid for advertisements that would link to the manifesto. They took care to conceal their actual location because they expected many among both sets of friends to disapprove strongly of what they said. They were right.

Yehudith's relatives had already exhausted their dismay in saying a funeral for her, so they did not at first recognize her as an author of the manifesto. Young members of the mosque of Asif's father brought the manifesto to his attention. He read it with disgust and said so briefly, without sharing his suspicion that his son Asif was an author. At this point he went back to his colleagues with the manifesto and told them of his belief that his son had written it. Upon this, they all agreed that Asif was apostate and issued a *fatwa* for his death upon sight. Their difficulty was that Asif's location was still unknown. One of them came up with a brilliant expedient. He scanned photographs of Asif into the computer and circulated the photographs to Muslim networks the world over with the following message: *Have you seen this man? Please let us know if you recognize him because we have to deliver an important message to him from home.* The reader would be left with the impression that they would be doing a service to Asif to reply to the e-mail. Sure enough, a Muslim co-worker who knew Asif and had no idea of the intended "message" recognized Asif in Mumbai and replied truthfully to the e-mail. This gave the issuers of the *fatwa* the clue they needed to plan an assassination to carry out the *fatwa*. Professionals were contacted and dispatched to Mumbai.

The hit squad did not have Asif's home address and at this point knew nothing about Yehudith. They did not wish to kill on the Muslim worship day of Friday and did not know anything about Asif's schedule on weekends. So they had to seize Asif either entering or leaving work and then stake out a location to kill him. They planned to take video of the execution as a recruiting tool for new assassins and as a deterrent to any future conversions to Christianity. While each member of the squad carried a firearm, several also carried hand-held high-definition cameras. Given these purposes, the squad did not want to get caught, but neither did it want to conceal the killing itself. So they did obtain false visas and had a "safe house" for use before and after the killing. Because it would be necessary to transport Asif before killing him, they also considered traffic patterns to avoid getting caught in a jam. They confirmed Asif's usual workplace and schedule and decided to strike on a Wednesday afternoon. For cover, they obtained a van that looked like a police van and bought clothes that resembled those of the Mumbai police. Because Mumbai is so crowded, they could not find a killing site as isolated as they would have liked within the city, so they opted for a cleared area a few kilometers outside that was owned by a Muslim who would not interfere, although he would not participate either. The owner did not know exactly what was planned, but he was intimidated by the militants into making himself scarce.

At first the plot went smoothly. Asif left work without anybody else and was seized, cuffed, gagged, blindfolded and bundled into the fake police van. The leader loosened the gag enough to permit Asif to talk quietly and removed the blindfold. The leader told him that Asif was marked for death because he was a Christian. Asif looked the leader in the eye and averred that indeed he is a Christian. Since Jesus the Messiah had died for him, he would not complain if he had to die for Jesus. He turned to his captors and told them that he would forgive them any sin against him but that they would have to ask Jesus to forgive them for their sin against Him, because His forgiveness is not something that Asif could grant. At this the leader blasphemed the name of Jesus. Asif replied, "Your own faith tells you that Jesus will return with Mohammed, and yet you curse Him? Aren't you behaving like a fool? In fact you are cursing your future Judge, and He has heard it and will remember it if you do not ask His forgiveness."

Everyone became quiet as the van reached the killing field. The blindfold was replaced as Asif was dragged to the middle of the field. Three of the group formed a security perimeter. The leader and the photographers accompanied Asif and the rest of the squad. The photographers were in position to film the act while the leader read the *fatwa* and started his execution routine with the sacrificial knife. But Asif was not cowed; he started singing hymns to Jesus Christ. The leader was afraid that the singing would attract attention and therefore cut short his usual ritual and slashed Asif accross the throat, silencing his hymns.

As a precaution, the leader ordered everyone in his group to bare their weapons in case the police came immediately and to hurry away from Asif's corpse so that they could leave the scene. It was part of their mission to escape Mumbai successfully and thereafter head for a country which would view their killing as a holy act and therefore would not extradite if indeed they were identified. In the hasty departure one of the photographers in switching from photographer to armed guard dropped the camera and did not realize it. Indeed the haste was warranted because a Muslim neighbor in fact called the police on a cell phone, who responded with surprising swiftness within 15 minutes. The van had left about 5 minutes earlier. The alert patrolman found the warm corpse and the camera. When he played the camera, he was nearly sick to his stomach. But he realized that the camera was vital evidence despite his nausea and called for back-up. In the meantime he took the neighbor's statement and got a good description of the van, which was heading for the safe house. The camera images and sounds gave a clear description of the leader and a name identification. It also identified generally those who had decreed Asif's death.

While police evidence experts were taking shoeprints, soil samples, fingerprints from the camera and were checking rental companies for a van described by the neighbor, others were seeking information about Asif himself. His identification had also been left on the corpse in the hasty departure along with a picture of his wife. Because money was still in his wallet, robbery was not the motive. So the police began searching for Asif's wife in order to inform her of her husband's death. In the meantime, she called a police station because her husband was overdue. An inspector put the pieces together and knew he had found her from the photograph. By 8:00 PM, the main pieces of the puzzle were in place, and Yehudith sought out their pastor. She was shown the abbreviated videotape of her husband's death. With the same spirit shown by Christian women through history, she released a statement concerning her husband's death.

God gave me a wonderful husband for a short time, and now in His wisdom and love He has permitted murderers to send Asif to heaven with Him ahead of me. The killers of my husband may hope to intimidate believers in Jesus as Messiah everywhere. Courage, Christians! Jesus Himself said it perfectly, *"And I say to you, My friends, do not be afraid of those who kill the body, and after that have no more that they can do. But I will show you whom you should fear: Fear Him who, after He has killed, has power to cast into hell; yes, I say to you, fear Him!"* Luke 12:4-5. I grieve, but with a difference -- I have a sure hope that Asif is already present with God with special honor for dying for the true faith. Through the mercy of God I will follow at the time appointed for me. *The Lord gives, and the Lord has taken away. Blessed be the name of the Lord.* Job 1:21.

Yehudith's televised defiance enraged the assassins and especially their leader, driving them beyond the point of cool reason. Her defiance was making the killing of Asif backfire. On their own, they decided to go beyond the *fatwa* and to kill Yehudith also without considering fully the added risks they would be taking. The most natural way to get at her would be to find out the funeral arrangements for Asif. The Mumbai Christian community indicated that they would gather at Asif's church for a public funeral and burial the following Sunday afternoon after usual morning services. For this purpose the hit squad obtained long-range old British Enfield rifles so as to shoot Yehudith at the funeral from a distance and then flee in the confusion. But the planning was cursory rather than professional.

The assassins now knew Yehudith's appearance from the television broadcasts and staked out the church for her. When she turned up the walk, she was hit from several directions and died instantly so far as her body was concerned. Others were wounded with stray bullets. However, the assassins did not count on beefed-up police protection in the vicinity, augmented by other government security forces. These reacted quickly after the initial shots and the assassins were unable to reach their meeting point to flee. One by one they all were caught and arrested. Investigators located the safe house and gathered the remaining evidence. In short order the entire conspiracy was rolled up from start to finish. The assassins made no attempt to hide their acts, both because it was hopeless and because they were at this point proud of what they had done. Quickly the local prosecutors drew up two murder charges and a kidnaping charge for seizing Asif and transporting him to the killing ground. Then they added three conspiracy counts, one each for the two murders and for the kidnapping of Asif just before his death.

The identity of the defendants became quickly known, and various press organs quickly reached out to Asif's and Yehudith's parents. Asif's father fended away the press from his wives and spoke for himself. "My son betrayed the faith laid down by the prophet Muhammed, and to top it off married a Jewish woman. I feel pain that my son has died after all this, but I do not blame those who killed him. This is what the Prophet commanded."

Yehudith's father expressed sorrow over her death, but he too believed that his daughter had strayed from parental authority and protection.

"Her disobedience to us set in train consequences that led to her death. As Solomon said, 'The eye that mocks his father, and scorns obedience to his mother, The ravens of the valley will pick it out, and the young eagles will eat it.' Yehudith disobeyed us in becoming a follower of Christ and giving us no voice in her marriage." When one reporter asked him whether a daughter of a Christian family should obey her parents concerning matters of marriage, he answered, "I have nothing to say to Christian families. Their belief in Jesus as Messiah runs counter to our most fundamental beliefs as Jews."

Of course neither Asif nor Yehudith were able to reply, but the pastor of her congregation did say in response to press inquiry, "We Christians grieve with Asif's and Yehudith's parents, but it has been the tragedy of most of the children of Israel and of the children of Ishmael that they have been blind to a central message of the Old Testament. At the time prophesied by Daniel the Messiah would come from God, as indeed He did. I would plead with all Israel and with all Islam alike to stop battering your heads against a stone wall in denying the reality that Jesus is the Messiah. This is the spiritual equivalent of denying the law of gravity. The only reconciliation of the enmities within the human race will be the mutual worship of and submission to Jesus as Lord and Messiah. He is the Prince of Peace."

The investigators took the customary step of interrogating each participant in the killings in isolation from the others. One of them, Murad Ali, appeared less strident than the others, so investigators focused on him and made sure that his co-Defendants could not communicate with him. He was one of the photographers of the execution of Asif. Having recovered one camera at the scene of the killing and others in the search of the safe house, the detectives could check the statements of the various defendants against the camera film as well as against each other. Since the statements of Murad Ali were verified by the film, the authorities sought to divide the defendants and to persuade Murad Ali to testify in exchange for a more lenient sentence. Since he was a photographer and had not necessarily used a weapon himself in either killing, there was some additional "cover" for prosecutors to make a deal in exchange for his cooperation against the more violent defendants. The others maintained a more or less united front of defiance.

To fill his idle time, Murad Ali asked for both Koran and a Bible, which the jail authorities supplied. One would guess that Murad saw something unusual about Asif or Yehudith or both that piqued his curiosity. Murad Ali began reading both books and comparing the two. In the meantime his conscience was bothered about his participation in the deaths of two people, one a woman. He puzzled about Jesus' emphasis on sacrificial love compared to Mohammed's emphasis on combat. Mohammed led a military conquest while Jesus suffered instead of fighting. Jesus had claimed the ability to summons 12 legions of angels and yet made no effort to do so even under horrible pain. If Jesus was sinless and died voluntarily, there must have been a reason. As Murad Ali read the New Testament, he could grasp the primary reason for Jesus' voluntary death when He was sinless -- to pay for the sins of His people and save them. Mohammed would never have done that. Mohammed's system of thought has one earn salvation by deeds of valor or by dying in military operations on behalf of Islam. Under Jesus' teaching, one does not earn salvation at all. One receives salvation as a free gift if and when one asks for it with an honest heart.

The Islamic faith which Murad Ali had learned had no true counterpart to Jesus the Messiah as the perfect and complete combination of God and man. Murad had been taught that God is unknowable in an intimate sense. Humanity can know something about God but cannot truly know Him. But then how did Abraham pray to God for Sodom and Gomorrah? How did Abraham know that God was commanding him to sacrifice his son? There must be something to true faith more than knowledge about

God -- even a wicked professor can study. Moses, too, prayed intimately with God.

Finally, Murad Ali in his soul recoiled from the idea of killing a non-combatant because of his faith. A parent cannot have an unqualified right to determine the faith of his children -- there comes a time when each person must decide for himself or herself. Although Murad could not at this time cite the Scriptures, he was wrestling his way to the truth of Jeremiah 31:29-30 and of Ezekiel 18. Then Murad had to face the central issue that motivated his own part in the conspiracy: was Jesus a mere man and inferior to Mohammed as he had always believed, or is he the Son of God, far above all men and women?

Murad's first approach was to consider the Crucifixion. He had been taught that someone resembling Jesus -- not Jesus Himself, but perhaps Judas -- was crucified and that Jesus escaped this gruesome death: Certainly Jesus did not deserve to be crucified. But <u>someone</u> was on the Cross. Murad considered the seven things that the Man on the Cross said -- who could have said them? Judas the greedy traitor and thief? Hardly. If Judas or someone like him were on the Cross, he would have been cursing like bloody murder, just as the two other robbers cursed and mocked the latecomer at first. The pain of scourging and crucifixion would be ample to strip the veneer from someone's conduct, so the words must reflect the speaker's true character. There were seven sentences from the Cross:

A) "Father, forgive them, for they do not know what they do."

B) "Mother, behold your son. Son, behold your mother."

C) "Assuredly, today you shall be with Me in Paradise."

D) "My God, my God, why have You forsaken me?"

E) "I thirst."

F) "It is finished."

G   "Father, into Your hands I commit my spirit."

Murad noticed that the first three sayings were early in the crucifixion process. The fourth introduced the darkest three hours when the suffering was greatest. The last three were all at the end when death was imminent. As at the beginning, the Man on the Cross was able to address God as Father instead of formally as "God." If a holy man (as Muslims including Murad confess Jesus to be) is able even under excruciating pain to address God as Father, their fellowship must have been intimate indeed, even closer than Ibrahim. Only during the three darkest hours was the intimacy broken. The Man on the Cross showed forgiveness and care for family. He also claimed to be able to take one of the other dying men to Paradise as well as assurance of where He Himself was going as He was about to die. He had the presence of mind to deliberately fulfill prophecy (Psalm 69:21) by saying, "I thirst." Murad could not help concluding that the Man on the Cross was actually Jesus and not someone else. The only reason this could have been done was that Jesus was paying other people's price to Paradise, because He had committed no sin worthy of death personally. So if He was paying the price for others' sins, then the Christians are right. He is the Lamb of God -- His conduct on the Cross stamps Him as the Son of God, just as the soldiers at the crucifixion scene who nailed Him to the Cross and watched Him die had said. It was only logical that the Son of God would not stay dead but would and did rise from the dead, just as Peter proclaimed less than 2 months after the event. Peter would have been laughed off as ridiculous or even killed out of hand unless there was evidence in Jerusalem that the resurrection was true. So Murad had crossed a bridge in his thinking, and thereafter there was no going back.

The next problem Murad faced was severing his defense from the other conspirators. He knew that the other defendants might try to kill him if they were aware of his new convictions. He therefore sent word to the inspectors that he wanted to speak to them again and also was concerned about the character and willingness of his appointed legal counsel to carry out his decision to tell the whole truth without glorifying his actions. Murad believed that he deserved to die. If he were to die, it should be only after telling the entire truth about the planning for the murders and the intended methods of escape. So Murad had a reason to live, at least for now.

Murad approached his attorney cautiously. He sought clues as to his attorney's attitude by asking about his rights and legal alternatives, without disclosing his own beliefs. When he found that the attorney responded professionally rather than with *jihadist* rhetoric, he went one step further and asked the attorney to speak of his own family and background. Murad was concerned whether the attorney would be prejudiced against him by the nature of the charges. Murad's attorney spoke of his legal studies in India and explained that he was of the Hindu professional caste from which many Indian lawyers came. He detailed his legal training. At this point Murad decided that he was dealing with a professional lawyer who would keep his secrets and then told his lawyer that he was seriously considering some form of guilty plea both because of the obvious evidence and because of his moral guilt for his part in two deaths. Murad warned his counsel not to reveal this to anyone connected with the other defendants. His attorney agreed. Murad did not disclose his own religious convictions, but focused on the issue of his initial plea to the murder charges. With that came the possibility of his testimony in the others' cases. Counsel warned Murad that any hint of a guilty plea at this stage would enrage the other defendants and cautioned Murad not to talk to any of the other prisoners about the case, whether they were connected to his case or not. Counsel would speak to the prosecutors. At length they hammered out a deal: Murad would plead guilty to his part in Asif's premeditated kidnapping and murder in exchange for a dismissal of the charges against Murad with respect to the death of Yehudith. But this was kept secret for the time being.

Each defendant had his own legal counsel from the very start, even though it was at first anticipated that they would all hang together in their defenses. The trial judge, supported by the prosecution, insisted on this because each defendant might have individualized legal defenses to the murder charges such as coercion or compulsion by other defendants. Some might argue that they are not responsible at least for murder because they were not armed, especially in Yehudith's case. Some who were armed did not fire at her but were posted in a vain attempt to block pursuit. Someone might seek a reduction in sentence by testifying against other defendants. The trial judge took a strict approach to potential conflicts of interest and refused to allow any defendant to waive these potential conflicts in order to permit joint representation of any combination of defendants by one counsel. This made it impossible for extremist sympathizers of the defendants to control their representation by hiring a single counsel to coordinate the defense and to try to keep the defendants' testimony and positions uniform.

The trial evidence was of course overwhelming with the weapons and film taken by defendants themselves admitted into evidence. In fact the defendants except Murad maintained their united front, alternately challenging the evidence and claiming justification because of Asif's defection from Islam to Christianity. The defense considered Yehudith a devil's instrument in Asif's downfall and tried to excuse her murder for that reason. None of it washed in the Mumbai courtroom, as indeed the defendants realized would happen. They were looking forward to their Islamic martyrdom after the trial.

The main surprise at the trial was Murad's testimony, so totally out of step with the other defendants. As a surprise prosecution witness, he started by detailing the methods by which the conspirators entered India, armed themselves and then traveled to Mumbai in response to the lead provided by the Internet message saying that Asif needed to receive an important message from home. He described the exit plans which were never carried out. When the conspirators knew their target, Murad described how Asif was traced, seized and transported to the death scene. Murad identified the camera tapes. Then Murad explained that the decision to kill Yehudith was taken by the conspirators on the spot after her television broadcast. That was not part of the original *fatwa*. The conspirators were concerned that she would press the issue of her husband's death to compel a vigorous and thorough investigation, which in turn would lead back to Palestinian territory with damaging diplomatic consequences. They hurried to try to complete her killing in order to carry out their original exit strategy if possible. That failed.

The evidence of Murad was more damaging that the feared consequences of Yehudith's pressure. Many observers who had had no particular sympathy for Christianity were shocked at the cold-blooded shooting of a woman in mourning by those who had killed her husband. Taken off guard, various legal counsel representing the other defendants tried to discredit Murad as a traitor who was lying to save his own skin. The following exchange with the lead counsel for the ringleader summarizes the lengthy cross-examination of Murad:

Q   It's true, is it not, that you left the territory of the Palestinian Authority doing your part to kill Asif?

A   Yes.

Q   And were you one of the people in the van that took Asif from downtown Mumbai outside the city?

A   Yes

Q   And you wanted to see Asif die?

A   Yes

Q   You knew that Asif had betrayed the Islamic faith?

A   I have been told that. This was the basis of the *fatwa*. I believed that. But I personally never knew Asif.

Q   And is that not sufficient justification for Asif's kiling?

A   No!

Q   Did not Muhammed command the killing of apostates?

A   Yes he did.

Q   So is not any Muslim justified in obeying Mohammed's command?

A   No!

Q   By what authority do you refuse to submit to Mohammed's command?

A   The authority of the Almighty God Himself!

Q   But that's impossible for a Muslim to think that, since Mohammed is the greatest and last prophet of God!

A   God Himself spoke the Ten Commandments from the heavens. The Sixth Commandment forbids murder, which is one of the things I have done. Cain was banished for killing Abel; the death penalty for murder was instituted in the time of Noah by God Himself, when there were only eight human survivors of the Flood. No prophet of God can set aside such a fundamental law instituted for all humanity by God Himself.

At this point, the defendants would have seized and strangled Murad themselves if courtroom security had not been so heavy, because of Murad's indirect though respectful attack on the authority of Mohammed. The judge with difficulty gaveled the defendants to order and invited their counsel to make any objections known to human law on the record. But since no defense counsel had objected to the question before Murad's answer, no objection was possible on these terms. So the cross-examination continued in the heavy, tense atmosphere:

Q You cited the Sixth Commandment. Are you a filthy Jew? [The prosecutor let the slur go because he thought that it served his case for capital punishment or at a minimum for life imprisonment to let the defendants spew out their prejudice and lack of remorse.]

A No.

Q Then how can you say that any authority supersedes the authority of Mohammed?

A Because the authority of the virgin-born Son of God from heaven supersedes all human authority just as the authority of His Father in heaven supersedes all human authority.

Q Are you claiming that Jesus of Nazareth is the virgin-born Son of God?

A You have spoken the truth. Mohammed acknowledged the Virgin Birth also and expected Jesus to accompany him when Mohammed expected to return to earth. Yes, Jesus of Nazareth was, still is and always will be the Son of God, born of the Virgin Mary through the overshadowing of the Holy Spirit. Luke the doctor affirmed this also.

Q So are you a Christian?

A Now, yes. When I committed my acts of conspiracy, kidnaping and murder with all of the defendants, no. I was a fanatic Muslim and Christianity was the farthest thing from my mind.

Q Traitor! Apostate!

A I adhere to the truth. Jesus of Nazareth, the Messiah or Christ, was steadfast in insisting that His followers speak the truth. So is Psalm 15.

That is why I am telling the truth to the court even though it means that I myself am subject to death sentences.

Q Are you not expecting a lenient sentence in exchange for your testimony?

A I have made no deal that frees me from the risk of the death penalty. I have not been charged in connection with Yehudith's death, but I am admitting guilt before the law for conspiracy, kidnapping and murder with respect to Asif. The murder plea exposes me to the death penalty. I do not claim that I deserve less than death because I am telling the truth. What the court will do I do not know. That is in the control of God alone. (*The king's heart is in the hand of the Lord, like the rivers of water; He turns it wherever He wishes.* Proverbs 21:1)

This exchange "went viral" on the Internet. Murad certainly would have had no safety in any place where there was a substantial presence of militant Muslims of any variety if he were to be released eventually. He could never go back to Palestinian Authority jurisdiction but would have to seek asylum in a society friendly to immigration such as Canada, the Netherlands or Sweden. Elsewhere, the vehemence of the attack on Murad added to the wariness toward Muslims by others. Even those Muslims who were horrified by the killings felt a chill from others despite their vigorous disapproval. Murad became a hero to born-again Christians worldwide just as he became a traitor to militant Muslims. This exchange also magnified the eventual long-term effect of Asif and Yehudith upon the investigators, attorneys, judges and others who learned of their story. The final verdicts of the court and the sentences still lay in the future.

The funeral organizers had had to postpone Asif's funeral to permit the police to do their work. The Wednesday following Yehudith's death, Christians in the Mumbai area mourned Asif and Yehudith as a couple, as they had been in life. However, the joint funeral proclaimed publicly the joy that Asif and Yehudith were now experiencing in heaven and the sure hope of the Christians that they would one day join them in the presence of Jesus Christ. Members of the Christian community in Mumbai pledged to maintain their witness for reconciliation between God and humanity and among human beings, with Jesus the Messiah as the crossroads (or the one and only Mediator – 1 Timothy 2:5) through which all true and lasting reconciliation would pass. Their work outlived their human bodies and in fact will follow them to heaven. Asif and Yehudith, being dead as to their human bodies, yet speak. (Hebrews 11:4) *Then I heard a voice from heaven saying to me, "Write: 'Blessed are the dead who die in the Lord from now on.' " "Yes," says the Spirit, "that they may rest from their labors, and their works follow them."* Revelation 14:13.

AFTERWORD

One may point out any number of gaps in this short story. I am
certainly short on details in my settings. I have also avoided exploration of
the potentially complex relationships between Asif's father and his wives or
between Yehudith's father and mother. I have not dealt in detail with the
relationships between children and parents or among potential siblings.
Neither have I gone into romantic detail as to just how Asif and Yehudith
were attracted to each other nor into the private details of their marriage.
From a literary point of view such criticisms would be justified. But my
purpose is not to write a prize-winning novel but to use fiction as a vehicle
to portray and focus on spiritual truth.

I have made no attempt to create an alternative universe similar to C.S.
Lewis or J.R.R. Tolkien. So far as I am aware, the conditions I describe
in modern Israel are real as of the time that I am writing (late 2010). The
issues of marriage within Israel can be followed in the *Jerusalem Post* or
Wikipedia online and first became known to me through James Michener's
The Source when I was a teenager. I make no claim that I am an expert on
Israeli politics or law.

I suspect that some Jews and some Muslims would feel aggrieved at
some of my characters. While any fiction writer has literary license, I have
consciously tried to avoid caricature. I am sure that some Muslims may

complain that I portray them as more violent than the Jews. I have barely touched the distinctions and skirmishes between Sunni, Shia and Sufi. My answer is that in this current era there is more organized violence intended to kill civilians among militant Muslims than among Jews. The violence of September 11, 2001 has little parallel anywhere. Then this was followed by explosions in Madrid and London and attempts elsewhere. Neither should we forget the tragedies in Russia from Muslim terrorists. In Iraq there have been attacks by Muslim upon other Muslims. The history of Saddam Hussein acting as a life insurer for homicide bombers has no historical parallel known to me. This was ended only by the force of the United States government in overthrowing Saddam Hussein and thereby cutting off the insurance money. It should also be said that the Muslim successors to Saddam Hussein gave him a far fairer trial than he would have given to any of his foes and then did mete out to Saddam Hussein his just sentence. That regime has also kept the peace with its international neighbors, as have Muslim governments of Egypt, Jordan and others since the 1970s to the time that I write. Many, but not all, Indonesian Muslims tolerate those of other religious beliefs.

It is not fair to paint all Muslims as militant or violent, and I have avoided this. In my short story, Asif's father opposes mass violence. Another Muslim calls the police as Asif is being slaughtered. The difficulty is that militant Islam has portions of the Koran on which they base an ideology of world conquest and enforced Islamization. Militarist Islam is far from the whole of Islam, but these spiritual seeds in the Koran reproduce a militarist conquering ideology that echoes what I heard as a child when Nikita Khrushchev boasted that "We will bury you" and that "Your grand-children will live under Communism." I have taken pains to avoid tarring Muslims as a whole with this brush, but I cannot ignore the existence of the ideology of militant conquest within segments of Islam. Neither can I ignore the teaching within portions of Islam that sanctions the assassination of a convert from Islam to another faith and also condones killing of evangelists. In terms of human justice, it is unfair to peaceable Muslims that they suffer from the consequences of the violence of the Taliban, of Al Qaeda, of Hezbollah and many others just as it was unfair that even anti-Nazi Germans suffered from the actions of the the Nazis. But we cannot ignore militants with an ideology of world conquest of any label.

It is true that I do not have a violent Jew in the short story. That comports with the main flow of modern history. I recognize that the Stern Gang and perhaps portions of Irgun before the United Nations resolution of 1948 did commit acts that we would call terrorism, but these were repudiated by Israel as a whole. There was the explosion at the old King David Hotel. I also recognize that Mossad has engaged in occasional assassinations of terrorist criminals whom they were unable to bring to trial. But there have been no Israeli bombs in shopping areas of Damascus, Baghdad or Mecca. One reads of bombs among rival Muslim groups as one or another are going to religious processions. If there were a comparable Israeli act, it would be a bomb set off among the massed pilgrims making the Hajj or an Israeli-approved bomb among Muslim worshipers at the Dome of the Rock. Such an atrocity has not happened as I write.

If we go back to the ancient world in the times of Jesus the Messiah and the generation immediately after Him, this picture is different. Islam did not yet exist. Among the Jewish people, there were *sicarii*, violent men would sought to assassinate Romans by use of swords hidden under their cloaks. Paul suffered violence on several occasions at the hands of his fellow Jews. Stephen was stoned by a mob encouraged by the Temple leadership and assisted by the man who later became the Apostle Paul. James, the half-brother of the Lord Jesus, was thrown down from the top of the Temple. If I were writing of the times of Jesus the Messiah up to the destruction of the Temple in 70 A.D., it would be historically legitimate to include a character who was a terrorist Jew. But Jewish terrorists today are extremely rare and are not remotely representative of any portion of Jewish culture or belief. Therefore there is no such character in this short story.

I brush very lightly over the issue of the Law of Return and the settlement of Jews in their ancient homeland. This is of tremendous importance as a major part of the prophets' predictions for the times near the return to earth of Jesus the Messiah. There can be no question but that the prophets predict first the scattering and then the regathering of the Jewish people to the land promised to Abraham, Isaac and Jacob. Moses in turn instructed the Jewish people to use the same laws for foreigners living in the land as for themselves. Painting with a broad brush, it is fair that the Bible makes clear that the Promised Land will be returned to the descendents of Jacob and that the *diaspora* will one day end. There is little doubt that all of the West Bank is within the boundaries of the land originally promised to Abraham, Isaac and Jacob. The Jewish people so far have made great efforts to accommodate those Arabs who chose to remain after 1948. Most of the West Bank Arabs whose control shifted in 1967 want to live in a majority Arab state, which is in the long run impossible where they are because of God's ancient decree and because there are so many more Jews who some day will return to Israel. I am reasonably sure that the return of the Jews is less than 50% complete; my own guess would be that 15-25% of the eventual total have returned. There are several tribes with almost no representation at present. But this question of the Law of Return, so important to prophecy and Middle East politics, is nevertheless secondary to the question of individual salvation of each human being.

It is quite possible to follow God's will unconsciously without having any intent to obey God. Consider Ezekiel 21 as one such case. The King of Babylon was deciding between an attack on Ammon and on Jerusalem. His method was abhorrent to God: the use of divination by methods of the occult. Yet God directed this heathen King on His chosen path to accomplish His judgment against Judah in that day. In an analogous manner it is quite possible for a Jew to make *aliyah* to Israel today with no clue as to the spiritual meaning of his return. Even scavenger birds will obey God's call to Armageddon. (Revelation 19:17-21; compare Matthew 24:27-28) Significant numbers of returning Jews today even deny God's existence. If these die in unbelief, they will be condemned eternally as all other unbelievers from any ethnic background will likewise be condemned. It is tragic for anyone to leave this life in defiance of God and of Jesus Christ, His Son and the future judge of all mankind. It may be important for the descendant of Israel to return to the ancient homeland, but it is truly an eternal life-and-death issue for that person and for anyone to go from earth to heaven (to enter the Promised Land as did Abraham by faith, and to make *aliyah* from perishable earth to imperishable heaven, and to make true submission to God) through faith in the mercy of the Lord Jesus, the Son of God.

I do portray both faiths as vehemently hostile to Jesus the Messiah because this is fact. I realize that there are efforts at interfaith cooperation in certain respects, but what happens when a Christian calls for either Jews or Muslims to worship Jesus Christ as the Son of God from heaven? I should add that aggressive secularism is also hostile to Christian evangelism and there are instances of violence against Christians by adherents of other faiths also. In this sense Christians have always been and until the Rapture probably will always be a minority, unappreciated by the world as a whole even though the world (Satan's kingdom) is divided into mutually antagonistic camps. (Matthew 12:25-26) Yet the Christian church, sustained by the Spirit, will endure to the Rapture.

The situation will change radically when the prophecies of Zechariah 12-14 are fulfilled. At that time all Israel will finally see Jesus as Messiah and give Him and His Father the honor that Jesus' own generation as a whole denied Him. The characters that I portray now will be hopelessly outdated then. I believe that the same will be true of at least many of the Arab nations as well, based on the last portion of Isaiah 19. I believe that this portion of Isaiah 19 is a direct consequence of the tremendous changes in Israel recorded in Zechariah 12-14. My Islamic characters will likewise be hopelessly out of date. With the highway portrayed, there is obviously lasting peace in the Middle East for those prophecies to come true.

The central point of this entire story is that all people -- Jew, Arab or anyone else in whatever national origin or combination -- need to repent of their sins and worship God as Father and Jesus as His Son and Messiah. They need the Spirit to enter within and create spiritual life inside them. In this respect there is utterly no difference among peoples. All descendants of Adam (Jesus the Messiah excepted, who had no human father but was fathered by the Holy Spirit -- Luke 1:35) have sinned and constantly fall short of God's requirements and God's glory. The only reconciliation between God and humanity is on the basis of the sacrificial blood of Jesus the Messiah, God's Son and risen King. That reconciliation will then bring about reconciliation among peoples.